ELITE HOCKEY DEFENSE

Skills and Strategies for the Modern Game

DAVE CAMERON

Library of Congress Cataloging-in-Publication Data

Names: Cameron, Dave, 1980- author
Title: Elite hockey defense : skills and strategies for the modern game / Dave Cameron.
Description: Champaign, IL : Human Kinetics, 2026.
Identifiers: LCCN 2025029918 (print) | LCCN 2025029919 (ebook) | ISBN 9781718232730 paperback | ISBN 9781718232747 epub | ISBN 9781718232754 pdf
Subjects: LCSH: Hockey—Defense | BISAC: SPORTS & RECREATION / Winter Sports / Hockey | SPORTS & RECREATION / Coaching / General
Classification: LCC GV848.75 . C36 2026 (print) | LCC GV848.75 (ebook)
LC record available at https://lccn.loc.gov/2025029918
LC ebook record available at https://lccn.loc.gov/2025029919

ISBN: 978-1-7182-3273-0 (print)

The web addresses cited in this text were current as of June 2025, unless otherwise noted.

Acquisitions Editor: Diana Vincer; **Developmental Editor:** Anne Hall; **Managing Editor:** Kim Kaufman; **Copyeditor:** Bob Replinger; **Senior Graphic Designer:** Joe Buck; **Layout:** MPS Limited; **Cover Designer:** Keri Evans; **Cover Design Specialist:** Susan Rothermel Allen; **Photograph (cover):** Darcy Finley/NHLI via Getty Images; **Photographs (interior):** Jonathan Kozub/Point Shot Photography/© Human Kinetics; **Photo Production Specialist:** Amy M. Rose; **Photo Production Manager:** Jason Allen; **Senior Art Manager:** Kelly Hendren; **Illustrations:** © Human Kinetics; **Printer:** Versa Press

We thank the hockey for all centre in Winnipeg, Manitoba, for assistance in providing the location for the photo shoot for this book.

Human Kinetics books are available at special discounts for bulk purchase. Special editions or book excerpts can also be created to specification. For details, contact the Special Sales Manager at Human Kinetics.

Printed in the United States of America

10 9 8 7 6 5 4 3 2 1

The paper in this book is certified under a sustainable forestry program.

Human Kinetics
1607 N. Market Street
Champaign, IL 61820
USA

United States and International
Website: **US.HumanKinetics.com**
Email: info@hkusa.com
Phone: 1-800-747-4457

Human Kinetics' authorized representative for product safety in the EU is Mare Nostrum Group B.V., Mauritskade 21D, 1091 GC Amsterdam, The Netherlands.
Email: gpsr@mare-nostrum.co.uk

E9664

CONTENTS

Drill Finder iv
Acknowledgments vii
Introduction ix
Key to Diagrams xiv

CHAPTER 1 Skating 1

CHAPTER 2 Puck Skills 45

CHAPTER 3 Shooting From the Point. 73

CHAPTER 4 Stick Position 103

CHAPTER 5 Puck Retrievals 115

CHAPTER 6 Joining the Rush. 135

CHAPTER 7 Accepting the Rush. 149

CHAPTER 8 Communication and Scanning 173

CHAPTER 9 Defensive-Zone Coverage 185

CHAPTER 10 Strategies in the Offensive Zone 201

CHAPTER 11 Neutral-Zone Play 217

CHAPTER 12 Applying Concepts to Practice 239

About the Author 249

DRILL FINDER

Drill title	Difficulty rating	Players	Primary skill emphasis	Secondary skill emphasis	Page number
CHAPTER 1					
Five-Tire Warm-Up	Moderate	Small group	Skating	Edges	34
Transition Skating Paper Clip	Easy	Small group	Skating	Transition	35
Forward and Backward—Single-Leg Pushes	Easy	Small group	Skating	Stride	36
Edge Work Lines Down Ice (One Foot)	Easy	Small group	Skating	Edges	38
D Shuffle Down Ice	Moderate	Small group	Skating	Backward movement	40
Edge Development—Two-Foot Edges	Easy	Small group	Skating	Two-foot edges	42
V Transition Skating	Easy	Small group	Skating	Passing	44
CHAPTER 2					
3-4-5 Puck Warm-Up	Moderate	Small group	Stickhandling	Eyes up	60
D Spin	Moderate	Small group	Passing	Skating	62
Neutral-Zone Transitions	Easy	Small group	Stickhandling	Skating	64
Around in a Circle	Easy	Small group	Stickhandling	Skating	66
Puck Control With Pivots	Easy	Small group	Stickhandling	Passing	67
Defensive-Zone Passing—Six Players	Moderate	Small group	Passing	Awareness	68
Simple Passing Sequence	Easy	Small group	Passing	Receiving passes	69
Defender-to-Defender Introductory Work	Easy	Small group	Passing	Skating	70
Stickhandling Warm-Up Lines	Easy	Small group	Stickhandling	Passing	72
CHAPTER 3					
Stationary Shooting	Easy	Small group	Shooting	Balance	93
Use the Lane You Create	Easy	Small group	Shooting	Eyes up	94
Shooting Partner Work	Moderate	Small group	Shooting	Passing	95
Shooting From the Offensive-Zone Blue Line With Activation	Moderate	Small group	Shooting	Skating	96
Diving With Puck Movement	Hard	Small group	Shooting	Passing	97
Backdoor Activation	Moderate	Small group	Shooting	Short one-timer	98
Shooting With a Purpose	Moderate	Small group	Shooting	Deflection	99
Shooting With Control	Moderate	Small group	Shooting	Balance	100
D Three Shot	Moderate	Small group	Shooting	Passing	101
Shooting for Sticks—Decision Making	Hard	Small group	Shooting	Deflection	102

Drill title	Difficulty rating	Players	Primary skill emphasis	Secondary skill emphasis	Page number
CHAPTER 4					
Stationary Poke Checks	Easy	Small group	Stick check	Balance	109
Neutral-Zone Stick Work	Easy	Small group	Stick check	Skating	110
Stick Position Around the Circle	Easy	Small group	Stick check	Balance	111
Defensive Stick Work to Puck	Moderate	Small group	Stick check	Checking	112
Defensive Blue Line Stick Work	Easy	Small group	Stick check	Hand-eye coordination	113
Knock It Down	Moderate	Small group	Hand-eye coordination	Balance	114
CHAPTER 5					
Neutral-Zone Shoulder Check	Easy	Small group	Shoulder check	Skating	126
Solo Puck Retrievals	Easy	Small group	Retrieval	Skating	128
Big Circle	Easy	Small group	Retrieval	Passing	129
Shoulder-Check Retrievals	Easy	Small group	Retrieval	Shoulder check	130
D Retrievals	Hard	Small group	Retrieval	Passing	131
Up Up Wheel—One D	Hard	Team	Awareness	Communication	132
Continuous Reverse	Easy	Small group	Retrieval	Skating	133
CHAPTER 6					
Receiving Passes in the Rush	Easy	Small group	Pass reception	Timing	142
Yale Connection	Moderate	Team	Passing	Communication	143
Up Up Wheel—Two D	Hard	Team	Awareness	Communication	144
Defender-to-Defender Neutral Zone (High Level)	Hard	Team	Timing	Passing	145
Skyreach Shooting	Moderate	Team	Passing	Communication	146
CHAPTER 7					
1 vs 1 Neutral-Zone Circle	Easy	Team	Skating	Gap control	162
2 vs 2 Half Ice	Moderate	Team	Gap control	Communication	164
2 vs 2 × 2	Moderate	Team	Gap control	Skating	166
3 vs 2 Around the Pile	Hard	Team	Checking	Gap control	168
Diamond 2 vs 1	Moderate	Team	Passing	Awareness	169
1 on 1 × 2 Same Side	Easy	Team	Gap control	Stick check	170

Drill title	Difficulty rating	Players	Primary skill emphasis	Secondary skill emphasis	Page number
CHAPTER 8					
Stickhandling Communication	Easy	Small group	Eyes up	Communication	179
Listen to Your Partner	Easy	Small group	Communication	Decision making	180
Call Out What You See	Easy	Small group	Puck placement	Eyes up	182
Blue-Line Rule	Easy	Small group	Skating	Awareness	183
CHAPTER 9					
Defensive-Zone (DZ) Box-Out Drill	Easy	Team	Box out	Awareness	195
1 on 1 × 2	Easy	Team	Gap control	Awareness	196
1 on 2	Easy	Team	Decision making	Read support	197
Read Pressure	Easy	Team	Awareness	Skating	198
5 vs 5 Off Faceoff	Easy	Team	Faceoff alignment	Communication	200
CHAPTER 10					
Dot-Line Attacks	Easy	Small group	Shooting	Timing	210
Backside Dot Off Pass	Moderate	Small group	Pass reception	Shooting	211
Resetting Pucks	Easy	Small group	Rim	Awareness	212
Pinching Down the Wall	Easy	Small group	Timing	Awareness	213
Diving and Sliding	Hard	Small group	Activating into zone	Timing	214
Puck in Corner	Moderate	Small group	Rim pickup	Skating	215
Double Up	Hard	Small group	Passing	Awareness	216
CHAPTER 11					
Neutral-Zone Retrieval	Moderate	Team	Shoulder check	Passing	226
Shallow and Deep	Easy	Team	Passing	Communication	227
Neutral-Zone Regroup × 2	Hard	Team	Timing	Passing	228
Rocket Regroup	Moderate	Team	Passing	Support	230
Neutral-Zone Retrieval for Deflection	Moderate	Team	Passing	Shooting	232
Neutral-Zone Figure Eight	Moderate	Team	Passing	Communication	234
Neutral-Zone Tracking	Hard	Team	Skating	Passing	236

ACKNOWLEDGMENTS

The topics in this book are my areas of focus on a daily basis with players and more specifically defensemen. These are answers to a lot of questions from players and parents about what we should focus on in practice to continue to develop.

In Winnipeg, the Jets Hockey Development Program runs programs for developing defense as well as private (or small group) sessions for players who want to understand a topic better or work on something specifically. It is in these sessions that the ideas from the book are brought forward and placed in front of players to work on.

When we see a defenseman who is having trouble, we start to break down areas to get better. It is through attention to detail and work that the player will see improvements. They can listen and understand the ideas, but if they do not get a chance to work through them their improvement or development will be small. Working through repetition under the guidance of a coach enables players to develop and improve their skills. This is something that I think about each time I step on the ice for a session with either a team or a player.

Thank you to Human Kinetics for their support to put my thoughts to paper to create this piece you are about to read.

Thank you to my wife and daughter for being the support in my life that I need and for challenging me to do more and keep pushing.

I am fortunate to be able to be on the ice a lot with players and work to push them to get better and understand concepts within the game. Thank you to the parents of players who trust me to work with your child and thank you to all the players who are coming to see me with an open perspective to allow for development.

I will continue to work to put together topics and sessions to allow players to continue along the path of their own development!

INTRODUCTION

The idea of developing defense is a topic that I enjoy focusing on because coaches in hockey often overlook it. Coaches work with a team, and the team plays games. When coaches develop the players on their team, their team can play at a higher level. With this book, I hope to help coaches gain a clearer understanding of the position of defense so that they can help their players continue to develop. If you are a player reading this book, I hope you can identify specific areas of your game to work on to continue your development.

When I was 18 years old, I played junior hockey in Prince Albert, Saskatchewan, for the Raiders. That season, I was traded to Saskatoon and met up with then-coach Brad McCrimmon. He played a major role in developing my mindset and skill development plans for a player looking at playing defense. Although I played center for him, I was a responsible player and played defense on the power play. Brad and I spent a lot of time talking about the game, and I absorbed as much information from him as I could. Brad played 1,222 games during 17 years in the NHL and was regarded as a tough defenseman who could play the game. He hammered home the importance of puck movement and receiving passes. He talked about moving to support the puck, looking off other players, and creating deception by looking one way and passing the other. He drew an X on his stick because that was where he wanted the puck. If you did not hit him there, you would hear about it either quietly in your ear or loud enough for everyone to hear that he liked his passes on the tape. I became close to Brad over the time I was in Saskatoon, and he taught me many lessons that a defenseman must learn and the skills that they must be able to execute. I am grateful for the lessons he taught me—lessons that I now to pass on to the next generation of players.

The position of defense has been constantly evolving. In recent years, we have seen a change in the position to allow offensive, mobile defensemen to be more involved in the offensive game. A position that used to be big and mean is now more mobile and more involved in puck movement. A position that defended the team's net is now included in the offensive scheme through the neutral zone and into the offensive zone. With that, we are seeing defensive players who are well rounded in their skill sets. They can skate extremely well, they can handle the puck with all kinds of confidence, they can pass the puck and receive passes in stride, and they can shoot the puck from the blue line as well as off the rush.

As I continue to work with defensive players all over the country, they inevitably ask, "When will we shoot a puck?" My answer is always something like this: "If we can't get out of our own end and through the neutral zone, you will not get any shots. Why don't we work on those areas first?" If I am running an eight-week spring development program for defense, I build the curriculum to have skating development, puck-skill development, passing work, retrieval work, and partner work—all before shooting. I do this to help players learn that there is a lot more to defense than just shooting from the point. One of the things I often see (when I am watching practices) in that teams split with forwards and defense (which I love), but the defense goes right into shooting. They miss the development opportunity to work on skating or transitions or backward acceleration or passing and receiving passes. They completely overlook the importance of retrieving a puck when it gets dumped past them and they have to go back and get it out of their own corner. How do they do that? Where are their eyes looking? What options do they have when pressure is coming from behind them? What options do they have when pressure is coming from in front of them? What options do they have when an opponent is right beside them in their hip pocket? These situations come up frequently in games, and coaches must help their players learn to recognize the situation and then make the correct decision.

IMPORTANCE OF DRILL PRACTICE

Improving a player's ability to play at a high level in games starts in practice. Few players understand this unless it is clearly outlined for them at the start of the season. Coaches should be able to put together a plan that allows everyone to work on specific areas of their game. Each player should be able to identify something in each drill that helps them to develop. When players look at the components of a drill rather than the drill as a whole, they see quicker development. Take a warm-up shooting drill, for example. Players and coaches can look at the drill as a whole: It is players skating around, making passes, and finishing with a shot.

The other way to look at it is to focus on the details of the drill. By dissecting the drill into skating, timing, spacing, passing angles, passing, receiving passes, managing the puck, attack angles, and shooting (perhaps with different release points), coaches can better help players continue to develop. That way, whether a player is a forward or a defenseman, they have specific things they can focus on for their development. Each player should be able to identify what they need to work on and then be able to do that in practice. It is through the explanation of drills that players can learn how the drill relates to the game. How does this drill allow options for the players to pick from and then develop in them enough confidence to execute the play in a game?

Giving players specific areas to work on in the drill also enables the coach to add something to it or progress it in upcoming practices.

COACH'S FEEDBACK

Coaches should be able to rotate through drills and come back to something if players need more time in practice to continue to develop. Players may struggle at first, but through constant attention and consistent feedback they may be able to break through. Feedback can come in practice or in games. I always tell players,

> If I give you information or a game situation comes up and you make the wrong decision, you must learn what the correct decision looks like. If you continually make the wrong decision in a situation, we need to sort out why that is happening. Either (a) I have not been clear enough in my explanation, so we need to spend more time on it; (b) the pace of the game is faster than your decision making, so we'll need to work to speed up your decision making; or (c) you are not listening to what I am saying, and you are trying to do things on your own.

As a coach, I can live with (a) and (b), but I have an issue if someone is not willing to listen (c).

I tell players, "As each player contributes more to the game, the team gets better." The contribution may not be scoring a goal, but it could be something like stopping a 1 vs 1 or 2 vs 1, initiating a breakout, finishing a check in the corner and creating a loose puck, joining the rush to create a scoring chance, activating into the offensive zone to create more time in the offensive zone, getting a shot through from the line (instead of getting it blocked), or maybe scoring a goal as a result of a play that the player worked on in practice.

One thing you may notice as you read through the book is that two specific areas of team focus, the power play and the penalty kill, are not covered in this book. These game scenarios were left out intentionally for two reasons:

1. They revolve around a team-based structure that very heavily relies on what your coaches would like to see. As a result, you will need to learn about each system from your coaches.
2. If you are able to work on all the specific topics in the book, you should be prepared to play in either scenario.

COACH'S ROLE IN PRACTICE

I believe that it is the coach's job to help players prepare for games. They do this by planning practices and working on areas specific to the player's game that allows each one to develop. Often in practice, I see defensive players make a soft pass, float up to the blue line where they receive a pass, look at the puck, and take a shot without knowing what is happening in front of them. The coach must challenge players to move their feet, pass pucks hard so that the forward gets the puck quickly, hurry up the ice so that they can be involved in the play, take ice, and move back to the blue line where they receive a pass, get their eyes up to the net, and shoot with a purpose. When players practice properly or with a purpose, they will develop. Each year in spring we run a developing defense program through Jets Hockey Development in Winnipeg. The program is roughly 10 weeks long (depending on tournaments and holidays) and covers a variety of topics. During the first half of the program, players do not shoot a puck. We work on retrievals, breakout options, passing and receiving passes, angling, and neutral-zone situations all before we get to shooting. After we work on moving the puck up the ice, then we can get into offensive-zone work with shots. A coach's goal through the season should be to help players develop in a way that enables them to play at a higher level. That improvement could come during the season, or it could come the following season when the player makes a team that is a step up.

PRACTICE PLANNING

When Brad McCrimmon was my coach he told me, "You are either getting better or getting worse—you don't stay the same." I understand what he meant by this, and I try to use it with my practice planning. Players need areas to work on. They need topics that are relevant to them and skills that they can practice to get better. We focus on incremental improvements, meaning that we are working to help players get a little bit better each day. If we take all those small daily improvements and add them up over the course of a season, players can come a long way.

COMMUNICATION WITH PLAYERS

Communication allows players to trust their coaches. With trust, players will be receptive to information that will help them make changes. The more a coach talks to a player and gives them information, the better that player can become. This can happen in practice when other coaches are leading the session. It can happen after practice in meetings with players. It can happen on road trips on buses, in the airport, or at the hotel. If the coach can show players what they are doing and give them information that helps them develop, they will become better players. For me as a coach, the communication piece is by far my most powerful tool. Not always is the information positive with players, and hard conversations sometimes occur. Positive information can be delivered before the negative information comes, but at times players need to hear that some of their decisions are not the best decisions to make in a game. When a player trusts their coach, the coach can more easily and effectively share information that will help the player improve.

DRILLS FOR DEVELOPMENT

In this book, I discuss many topics that will help players develop. I try to identify specific areas for practice that players can work on and develop. Areas that can be improved through either repetition or understanding of specific situations happen often in games. We look at both skills to work on and zones where plays come up (defensive zone, neutral zone, offensive zone), and I give players information on things they can do to improve.

Drills are presented for each chapter. These are the drills that I use with defensemen to help in their development. Drills can be modified depending on age to be either easier or harder. They can be made harder by adding passes, adding movements (like pivots or transitions), or adding pressure. The goal for the drills is to allow repetition for the defense to further their development. Some drills are slow and individual in which players work on their own development. Some drills are team based and have more players moving. These drills can be used in a team practice to help with development of the bigger picture. As you read through the book, try to reflect on some of the details and skill work and think about how that relates to your practices. The more that you can add for your defense, the better you and your team will become.

As I wrote this book and traveled around through the hockey season, one thing came to me. It didn't matter if I was in Calgary with Hockey Canada or in Texas with the Manitoba Moose, the players I was working with would have an opportunity to develop. My goal in writing this book is to help more players develop and get better. They can get better through improving both their individual skill set and their understanding of the game. Giving players reps is great, but giving players reps with coaching and ideas that help them improve will take their game to another level.

KEY TO DIAGRAMS

X O	Player
X |	Player with stick extended
X.	Player with puck
C	Coach
D	Defensive player
O	Offensive player
▲	Cone or tire
- - - - - - - - -➤	Pass
———————→	Player skating
ᴗ^ᴗ^ᴗ^ᴗ^ᴗ^ᴗ	Backward skate
{	Net
∴∵∴	Pucks
⇒	Shoot
—	Stop
⌒	Leg push (1)
^	Leg push (2)
⎍	Leg push (3)
F	Forward
OD	Offensive/defensive player
/\	Shoulder check
↳	Fake
∩∪	Forward C cut (right and left foot)
⌝ ⌞	Backward C cut (right and left foot)
/	Crossover (outside)
Ø	Crossover (inside)
●	Puck

CHAPTER 1

Skating

I get asked this question all the time: If I were to develop a defenseman, where would I start? My answer is always skating. A player's ice time and game development come from their ability to move around the ice. The goal is to conserve energy and move around during a shift in a way that seems effortless. A player who saves their energy is able to use it when they need to take their game to another level. Being able to jump in a play or defend while keeping defensive-side positioning is a task that comes harder for some than others. A defensive player should work toward having the ability to skate backward as fast as the opposing team skates forward. Players who can do this minimize chances against their team and limit the times that the other team has a clear look to the net. If the opposing team is consistently having to work through a defensive player, that is a good thing for their team. Players need to develop straight-line skating and speed both forward and backward, edge development on one edge as well as two, lateral movement to cover ice and move quickly, the ability to stop and start quickly, and many more areas.

This chapter is aimed at building an effective skater for the position of defense. The whole position is based on a player's skating, and all topics are tied to the player having the ability to move around the ice effectively. The drills in this chapter are aimed at building the fundamentals of skating. Many more things can be done with skating, but this chapter is an introduction to the necessary topics for each defenseman.

FORWARD SKATING

When I start with players' skating, I typically work on forward skating first. This approach allows me to see generally how players are moving. Working on forward skating first also allows me to see the players glide. Many high-level players lack the ability to glide between strides. A reporter asked me one time, "What do you think the difference is between the players in the NHL and the players in the AHL when it comes to skating?" My response was, "The NHL players glide better. They can make the game look easier through their movements, whereas some AHL guys have to work almost twice as hard to cover the same ice."

Players should be able to glide straight on one foot without their gliding foot shaking. They should be able to glide straight on two skates on the flat part of their blade, meaning that both the inside edge and outside edge are on the ice, allowing them to go straight. Players should be able to go from two skates to one skate, switching back and forth with balance and control. Everything for me with skating comes back to players being balanced. The starting point for balance is being able to glide straight and feel comfortable moving forward.

When I look at what players need to work on with the forward stride, I teach in the following categories:

- Body position
- Stride extension
- Stride recovery
- Stride location
- Upper-body movement

Other areas that coaches talk about generally fall into one of those categories. I think that players need to work on all of these to be able to continue to improve. The one thing about skating is that players can continually work on their skating to stay ahead of the competition.

Body Position

The easiest way to explain what this looks like is to think about the position that players will take when they are squatting off the ice. With the weight on their back, they can drop down with a knee bend and a neutral spine. Their shoulders are back, and the weight is over their feet. If they were to remove the weight at the bottom of their squat and simply grab a stick, that position is close to the position they can work to get into while skating (see figure 1.1). Coaches can help players get lower to the ice through their knee bend and not through their upper body. A common error is leaning the shoulders out in front of the feet and then trying to get the head up, which is harder. In this forward body-lean position, the head is often the first point of contact against other players. I try to get players to think about keeping their shoulders back, so that the upper body is more relaxed and the neck can rotate to see the play. With the shoulders back, the head is protected, and the shoulders are the first point of contact rather than the head. The head can stay up, and the eyes can see the ice as the player is skating.

The knee bend can also help to increase stride length, which ultimately allows players to go faster. Players can work to try to get the bottom part of the thigh close to parallel to the ice. This knee bend allows players to extend fully and work to recover back under the body.

Figure 1.1 Forward skating body position.

Players should try to imagine that a line runs from their skates up through their legs, through their hips, and connecting the shoulders. When players are working on skating, I like to see this imaginary line nice and straight. That is, the knees do not drop in toward each other and touch, the shoulders do not rotate, and the edges do not drop to either the inside or outside edge. Players can imagine they have an object about the size of a glove between their knees, which will help prevent the blade from dropping to the inside edge.

Players should be able to glide down the ice in this position with their knees bent and shoulders back to allow them to start to work on striding.

Stride Extension

When I work with players on the extension portion of their stride, my goal is to have players keep their blade in contact with the ice as long as possible from when they start to push until they finish their stride and lift their leg to start the recovery. Players can extend this contact by using plantarflexion of their ankle to keep contact rather than lifting their blade up all at one time. The goal for the extension portion of the stride is for players to push until their leg is straight (see figure 1.2). I work to get players to understand how far they can push to maximize their power. After they get the hang of a full extension, it can be shortened as needed.

Figure 1.2 Forward skating stride extension *(a)* on ice; *(b)* off ice.

As players are learning to push, they should also focus on their gliding leg underneath their body. With a solid gliding leg, they should feel as if they have a strong base to push from. The leg under their body can make a big difference in the amount of power that players are able to generate. If players do not have a solid leg underneath them, they can feel as if they are not generating enough power when they push. When they are working to make corrections to a player's gliding and striding, coaches can watch for a knee that falls to the inside or a skate that is on the inside edge

This is where the body position will increase the length of the stride and the ability to generate power from the extension. If players have their legs straight, they can extend only to a certain point. When players bend their knees, they can extend their leg farther and generate more power. I start with this position to show players what it looks like. It generally hits home pretty quickly when I show players how far I can push with straight legs compared with how far I can push with my knees bent.

When players start to understand what their extension can look like, they will start to go faster. This comprehension leads into the next portion of their skating, which is the recovery aspect of the stride.

Stride Recovery

Stride recovery is one of the areas that many players can continue to work on to increase the efficiency of their stride. I tell players all the time that I should hear their extension (that is, when the blade pushes off the ice and grips) but not their recovery. A couple of the common errors in players is that they either stomp their foot down into the ice on the recovery or drag their toes back in. If they stomp their foot down, they are pushing energy down into the ice, making it harder to glide. If they are dragging their toes, they are increased resistance to their skating, slowing them down rather than speeding them up.

When working on stride recovery, I try to get players to pull their full leg back underneath their body. They should lift the skate off the ice and place it back underneath them, gliding on the ice (see figure 1.3). I see many players who have trouble with their recovery because they always have their toe pointed out. When the toes are pointed out, gliding is difficult because the player must always be working through strides. A smooth and effective recovery allows the skate to be brought back under the body with the toe pointed forward. How long that toe stays pointed forward depends on the skating and game situation, but this action enhances the ability to glide and conserve energy.

When I work on stride recovery with players, I have them work to glide the top of their skate back in on the ice. I am careful in the wording that I use with this skating drill because many players have a tendency to drag their toes in. When I say "glide" their toe on the ice, I mean recover as they would normally but by keeping the top of their skate touching the ice. This technique encourages them to keep their heels low, which increases the speed of the recovery.

When I was young, I worked on my skating with a skating coach named Dave Roy. Dave was great for me and went on to be the skating coach for the Philadelphia Flyers. When we worked on recovery, Dave had us work to recover our skate and touch the supporting heel on the way back in. This routine reminded me to work to pull the leg back underneath. Dave always told me to recover the leg "across the center of gravity," which I can still hear him saying as I coach players

COMMON ERROR

Players need time to develop their skating. I am frequently asked about how to improve a player's skating. Parents will say, "They have lost their stride." My answer is to ask, "Have they grown lately or have they put on weight?" When a player's body changes, they must adjust to the new height or new weight. This adjustment takes time, both in the gym and on the ice. When I work with players on their skating, I start slow and make sure that players have a good understanding of how their body can move and what they need to do to move more efficiently. The goal is to move using less energy but go equally as fast.

Figure 1.3 Forward skating stride recovery *(a)* on ice; *(b)* off ice.

today. Now, I am trying to get players to work to pull their leg back underneath their body quicker to allow their next stride to start.

After getting through the stride recovery portion of the players' skating, coaches can add in stride rate and work to get players to recover faster and thus be able to push out faster. I often see players cut their recovery short and work to push more with shorter strides. I try to get players to understand that to go faster, they need to increase two things:

1. The power by which they can push
2. The speed at which they can recover

One of the areas I try to make sure that players focus on when they are working out off the ice is to strengthen their abductors (recovery of stride) and adductors (stride extension) equally. If players focus on only one of those, the risk of injury increases when they play a game. If players can build up both muscles in the gym, they can start to push harder and recover faster, leading to more speed on the ice.

Stride Location

Stride location is a topic I work on with players to get them to think about their extension with power. I want them to keep their full blade on the ice for longer to allow them to generate more power. This result comes from a wider push and the use of plantarflexion from the ankle at the end of their stride to grip the ice.

One common mistake that players make as they are learning is pushing too far back behind their body. When the stride is back behind their body, the player will often not get to push off their full blade for long. The heel will lift off the ice, and the player will push off only the front part of their blade. A stride location back behind the player's body will often limit the amount of power that can be generated in the stride.

The change that I have players make is to push wider. Making this change is tough to think about if players are moving down the ice, so I typically start with players standing still on one of the neutral-zone lines. When they start, I tell them to bring their toes up to the front of the line and when they push one leg, to extend to the back of the line (see figure 1.4). This is generally a little wider than they push after they add forward movement, but for the purpose of stationary strides, this method gets them to think about pushing wider. They do this for 8 to 10 pushes on one leg and then switch to the other leg to push from the other side.

As players start to add forward momentum, they can create a more powerful stride through extension and location than they can from only quickness. If players can add quickness to the extension and recovery with good location, they can become excellent skaters. Often when I see players who push quickly, they do not recover and leave their feet very wide. This lack of recovery makes their stride shorter and does not allow them to generate much power. When coaches can teach players how to push from underneath their body, through full extension to a good spot and with full recovery, they start to see their players' stride really develop.

Figure 1.4 Forward skating stride location *(a)* on ice; *(b)* off ice.

Upper-Body Movement

This topic for me is the most debated issue in forward skating. I have heard skating coaches teach players to do many different things with their upper-body and arm movement. Players often become confused when they work with coaches who have significantly different opinions. When I work with players on forward skating, I try to get them to think about two things that happen from their upper body—keeping balance and using both hands.

Keeping Balance

By having good body position and their weight back over their skates, players should feel balanced. For me, everything with skating comes back to being balanced. The upper body doesn't need to fall forward down toward the knees or twist and rotate away from where the player needs to go. Players should be loose with the arms and solid with the core. Their shoulders can remain level, and upper-body movement comes from the arms.

When I start working with players on upper-body control and balance, I have them hold their stick with their hands shoulder-width apart and their palms on the stick facing forward. The stick is underneath their nose so that their eyes can look over top of their stick. With this position, players can push right leg only (or left leg only) down the ice. The intention of this exercise is for players to keep the stick balanced and thereby learn what their upper body should look like (see figure 1.5 *a-b*). If coaches see players moving their stick so that it falls forward, rotating their stick, or tilting their stick to one side of the other, then their upper body is not balanced. When players can keep their core solid as they are skating, they can then add in arm swing and movement of the arms.

Each player who works on this will be different, so coaches should not expect every player to have the same arm swing. I give players guidelines to follow and then allow them to explore what works for them. I make corrections to errors that I see, but I don't correct every movement. Players should use movements that work for them.

Maintaining Option of Using Both Hands

Wherever players are skating, they should have the option to go to two hands on their stick. They might do this to receive a pass, to handle a puck, to shoot a puck if they are joining the rush, to slash someone (just kidding), or possibly just to check someone with good body position. If the hands get too far away from the stick, reacting to get to two hands on the stick takes longer (see figure 1.5 *c-d*). I work with players to be loose with their arms, and the movement does not have to go past the midline of the body. The stick hand creates a straight line between the arm and the stick, and the free hand (hand off the stick) moves in a similar motion. I tell players to bend and extend their arms to create an upper-body movement that is smooth and controlled with the legs driving.

Figure 1.5 Forward skating upper-body movement *(a)* correct single-handed; *(b)* correct both hands; *(c, d)* incorrect side-to-side arm swings.

BACKWARD SKATING

When I work with defensemen on their backward skating, I try to explain to them that they must be among the best skaters on their team. They must be good forward skaters but even better backward skaters to ensure they do not lose defensive-side positioning against attacking forwards. Backward skating is an area that I think needs to be worked on more in practice, not only by defensive players but by every player on the ice. Typically, when a coach does a drill that involves backward skating, they can quickly pick out the forwards because they are not as comfortable skating backward. I work with players to help them understand that the goal of skating backward is ultimately to match the speed of the opposing forward so that they do not get beat back to their net. Based on game situations and positioning, at times players must turn to challenge opposing players skating forward or angle them to get closer and check them. When I teach backward skating to players, I look at the following skills and have players work through all of them:

1. Straight-line backward skating
2. Backward crossovers
3. Backward shuffle

Developing these skills takes time. The start of practice is often a good time for players to work on their backward skating by building stride length and speed.

Straight-Line Backward Skating

The goal here is to be able to match the speed of attacking forwards, accomplished through good stride mechanics, good balance, good hip control, good stride length, and good recovery. When players can push one leg at a time while the other leg glides them backward, they can build efficiency and cover a lot of ice. As I work through the backward skating stride, I again break it down for players. The following categories are included:

1. Body position
2. Stride extension
3. Stride recovery
4. Stride location
5. Upper-body control

As players work through these five areas, they are challenged to slow themselves down before they go faster. They will need to work on gliding and balancing on their supporting leg because this leg becomes vital to helping them go faster.

Body Position

The body position used when skating backward is similar to that used when skating forward. The player gets lower to the ice through the knee bend while keeping the shoulders back. This position helps them keep their head up, which allows them to scan the ice and see the play develop (see figure 1.6). The body lean does not have to be as far forward as the body lean when skating forward, but keeping the shoulders back is a big part of remaining balanced. I often get players to squat with their stick across their shoulders (like a front squat in the gym) to get a sense of what it feels like to have their knees bent with their weight over their skates. A common mistake that I see when players are having trouble is that they lean too far forward, with their feet outside their shoulders. This body position puts them in an awkward stance for gaining power. Their body weight is in front of their feet,

Figure 1.6 Backward skating body position *(a)* on ice; *(b)* off ice.

their head is down, and their strides are very short. To correct this position, I have players work to keep their shoulders back, head up, and feet under their hips. When their feet are under their hips (or roughly shoulder-width apart) they should feel balanced. They should feel that they are able to generate power from this position because their ankles, knees, hips, and shoulders are all lined up. Their shoulders can remain square, and they can generate power from the lower part of their body.

Stride Extension

Problems with stride extension often result from a body position that makes it more difficult to extend the leg. A good stride extension comes from good body position (see figure 1.7). Players should have the ability to push from their hip and use the strength of their full leg to help them generate power. A common error that I see is players pushing from the knee down and not using their full leg to get power. Such players do not feel comfortable extending their stride. With the shorter stride, they may feel as if they can move their feet faster, and they often turn their skates together. When players do this, they have trouble getting faster and feel that they are getting beat in games.

When I have players start work on their extension, I have them start with good body position and work on pushing just their right leg. As they are pushing their right leg only, I watch their left leg to see if that skate can glide easily. If I notice the left leg (or gliding leg) shaking, I can tell they are working to hold it there. When players get smoother and understand weight distribution, that leg will glide with no effort or thinking on the player's part. Coaches can work on the right leg a couple of times down and back on the ice to get them to think about their extension, and then they can do the same thing on the left leg.

Figure 1.7 Backward skating stride extension.

The goal in the extension is to learn what a full extension feels like. They may not need a full extension in games each stride, but if they practice only with the shorter stride, that will be all they know. I get players to extend as long as they can, and then they can shorten the stride based on the game situation. Here is where the shuffle comes in whereby players shorten their strides to after their path and shut down lanes around them.

Stride Recovery

The stride recovery for backward skating is a little different from the stride recovery for forward skating. Players are still looking to recover the stride quickly, but looking to do so without lifting the skate off the ice. They can do this by simply adjusting the weight to the supporting leg as soon as they finish the stride and working to pull the leg back in underneath them. The timing of the stride recovery allows the pushing leg to recover back underneath the body. The leg that was gliding will then be able to drive the next stride out.

When looking at the shape of the recovery, the player's path on the ice looks more like a question mark (?) than a half circle (C). The reason for this is hip control. When players "cut C's," they end up turning their hips because keeping the gliding leg straight is difficult. When players are moving in a straight line, the leg pushes up in front of them just a little bit. From there, they can turn the skate and recover the stride without lifting the foot off the ice. This technique promotes balance through the stride and recovery.

A common error that has already been mentioned is that a forward lean that places the shoulders out in front of the skates makes it challenging to recover the strides back underneath the body. The shorter recovery leads to a shorter stride and often means that players are left working harder to cover space. The other common error is that the recovery occurs back behind the hips as the player works to turn their skate back in. I ask players to imagine that there is a line through their hips and that their goal is to keep their stride and recovery in front of the line. Nothing should go behind the imaginary line through their hips.

When players can maximize the extension in their strides and work on pulling back in quickly, a smoother skater will start to emerge.

Stride Location

The stride location when pushing straight backward is a little bit ahead of the body to ensure that the player can move in a straight line (see figure 1.8*a-b*). The goal should be to expand the range of motion and work on extension with good location.

The common error with backward skating is that players push out to the side (as they do with forward skating). The recovery is then back behind their body, forcing their hips to turn and consistently putting them off balance against an attacking forward (see figure 1.8*c*). When players are skating backward, they are working to keep their hips square to the attacking forward. To do this, they push from their hips to gain speed through their extension and recovery while keeping their stride location in a good spot.

The easiest way to work on stride location is to work from a stationary start and push backward away from either the red line or the blue line. Players can start with their skates on the line and try to move backward in a straight line. They can think about taking one stride first and gliding and then add another stride off the other leg. This exercise helps them understand the body control needed for their skating.

Figure 1.8 Backward skating stride location *(a)* start; *(b)* finish; *(c)* incorrect finish.

Upper-Body Control

The upper body in backward skating is different in the sense that moving the arms does not help drive the skater forward as it does with forward skating. Players need more balance to skate backward, and the upper body can play a big part in that. With the shoulders back and the weight over the skates, the upper body doesn't need to do much (see figure 1.9). The work comes from the lower body. The legs are driving and recovering, while the upper body creates stability and good stick position for checking.

A common error when it comes to the arm swing is simply doing too much movement. The constant movement of the arms makes it tough to balance or starts to throw the hips from side to side. Too much arm movement by the defenseman makes it easier for an opponent to beat them in a 1 vs 1 scenario because players can read or anticipate where the defenseman's body weight will be. Players who throw their arms forward and back as well as side to side across their body are working very hard to go faster. When I show them that the ability to go faster comes from their legs with a relaxed upper body, they instantly start to smile because they can feel the difference. Players who develop the ability to skate backward have a relaxed core with limited upper-body movement, which allows them to push from the waist down.

To practice this, players can hold their stick across their shoulders with their palms facing forward. I tell them to keep their stick level. With young players I ask them, "What is your favorite cereal?" I tell them to imagine they have a bowl of that cereal on the end of the stick. With their stick level, they can push one

Figure 1.9 Backward skating upper-body control for balance.

leg only or alternate legs with their skating, but now they do not get to use their upper body. They must hold their balance with their stick and simply focus on what their legs are doing.

The upper body being solid allows players to feel more balanced as they are skating faster. By being balanced, players can stop quickly, change directions laterally, or turn and skate forward as needed. The skating mechanics for backward skating can be simplified to allow players to defend against the rush. They want to accept the rush with a tight gap between the attacking forwards and themselves.

Backward Crossovers

Players frequently use the backward crossover, but many use it incorrectly or too often. Working backward, the backward crossover is used to move laterally. The proper mechanics allow the feet to work together, and when the player finishes the crossover, they should be in a different lane from where they started. Used effectively, the backward crossover can help players cover a lot of ice. But when used incorrectly, the crossover moves a player straight backward. A change in skating in the game over the last number of years is that players are using crossovers much less than they did before. Often, players are crossing over too much because they think that moving their feet quickly will be a benefit to their skating. This happens frequently when players are starting backward and take three or four crossovers rather than one good crossover.

When players take too many crossovers, the results are generally that they did not move too far and their hips remained turned. Their steps are short and not powerful, although they can be quick. My suggestion to players it to take one full crossover with full extension off their outside edge and see the difference. Their hips will become square faster, and their body will be facing the skater coming down on them. When I work with players, I try to get them to understand that using the proper footwork will make the game easier for them. They will stay out of trouble and out of situations they do not want to be in. If a player is coming down the ice in a straight line, the easiest way to counter them is to skate in a straight line. If a player must rely on crossovers to gain speed backward, they risk pushing away from the opposition, allowing them more space. Or a player might move over closer to the opposition, allowing them space to get back to the inside position.

Ultimately, coaches want players to minimize the amount of time they have their feet crossed over in a game. The goal is to make the game easier, not harder. When I talk about this with players, I tell them we are working to help them move more efficiently to cover ice quicker using fewer steps. When players constantly rely on crossovers to move, they are either giving up ice or allowing opponents to read off the feet. If an opposing player can change their attack angle and get the defender to cross their feet over, they can create more open ice. If the defender can keep their feet underneath them and not commit to one side, they have a better chance to react to the opposing player.

Figure 1.10 Backward crossover *(a)* start; *(b)* finish.

When I add crossovers to skating, I tell players to eliminate things they do not need. Rather than taking three or four quick steps with crossovers, players should take one good one with good width between their feet. The width between their feet allows players to create balance and use the feet to work together through the edges. The first foot can push, and now the recovery is in front of the other foot. As the foot that pushes first is coming in front of the other leg, the second leg is pushing off the outside edge and then stepping out to get the hips square again (see figure 1.10).

When adding crossovers to backward skating, I start by having them work around a circle and reach to grab ice with their inside foot. As they pull the ice with their inside leg, they can start to add speed to their step laterally. From this, players move down a line and imagine they have a line to cross. With each crossover, players must move laterally across the line and cover ice. When players can move laterally, they can pick between straight backward skating and crossovers.

Backward Shuffle

The backward shuffle is a step that players use to cover space laterally without using the crossover (see figure 1.11). This step allows multiple pushes off the same leg to happen quickly so that players can turn their gliding leg and move laterally. The backward shuffle is useful when a defensive player is working from the dot line to the wall to help close down that lane to the net. The goal of this step is to be able to make a quick lateral move either to eliminate a player with a check or get to a loose puck quickly.

Figure 1.11 Backward skating stride extension: *(a)* shuffle, stationary; *(b)* working.

The way I work on this step with players is to get them to think about crossing an imaginary line as they are moving backward. This imagery helps them think about turning their gliding leg to be able to glide and move on an angle backward. By using what I call a stride and a half, players can push off the same leg more than once. By starting with a stride and half and moving over an imaginary line, they can work on one side and then the other. The next step would be to cover more space like the dot line to the boards, a space more representative of the space they need to cover in a game.

Players can work to keep their hips and shoulders square up the ice and just work on turning their gliding leg. As players get the hang of moving with backward stride (no crossovers), backward crossovers, and backward shuffles, they are developing the ability to move around the ice for their shift almost effortlessly.

EDGE DEVELOPMENT

Skates are made with two edges that help players in their movement—an inside edge on the inside of their skate and an outside edge on the outside of their skate. Players can also work with both edges on the ice, which allows them to glide and cover ice in a straight line.

Edge development is a key component of skating in today's game. Players need to develop both their inside edge and their outside edge and then work to put the two together. They need to develop their edges at a young age so that they feel comfortable not only on their edges but also when using their edges to accelerate. The goal in edge development is to help players feel comfortable moving off a straight line and to have the ability to react quickly without thinking about what their feet are doing. When players have good edge development, they will feel comfortable using either or both of their edges to escape pressure.

Players need to have a good, solid forward stride so that they can push and recover smoothly. I work with players to recognize situations that come up in games, such as moving off a straight line and reacting to something different, such as chasing a puck, beating a defender, reacting to a pass, moving off the wall, skating around the net, or other game situations. In those situations, players need to be able to use their edges to move and react.

One-Foot Edges

Players often use one-foot edges in games, and they need to be able to identify when to use both the inside and outside edges. For example, one-foot edge work happens frequently when players are using crossovers (see figure 1.12). As they are learning, some players are more comfortable with two feet on the ice because they feel more balanced. Other players may find it easier to execute crossovers on the inside edge but more challenging on the outside edge. As players learn to move around the ice, their use of crossovers to move freely will become more automatic. The range of motion from the hips and ankles is important in helping players use their edges effectively. Players who have a good range of motion in their hips and ankles can quickly develop a powerful push off their edges.

Figure 1.12 Edge development: one-foot edge work *(a)* start; *(b)* finish.

Inside Edge

One of the problems that comes up when players are using crossovers is that they lift their inside edge off the ice and rely only on their outside edge to push. The problem is that they are benefiting from only half of their potential power. If they learn to push with first their inside edge and then their outside edge, they can start to go faster. If they can add a full range of motion from the outside-edge leg, they can really start to add acceleration off their edges.

To work on this, players can start with a simple inside-edge glide. To do this, they push off one leg and glide on the other. This action is beneficial because it allows players to hold their balance when moving off a straight line and pulling their pushing leg back close to the gliding leg (stride recovery). They can think about stick position and upper-body control as they are moving to allow other areas to be stressed as they work on their edges. Their knee bend should be low to the ice, and their pushes should be full to produce full strides.

Outside Edge

Players can do the same with outside-edge work after they work on both skates on the inside edge. The first outside-edge drill that players should do is to focus on just stepping over the other foot. Their hips will stay straight down the ice while they step over the other leg. They can work on pushing off their outside edge to build momentum as they are moving forward down the ice. I tell players, "Don't start skating first and use the momentum—I want you to build momentum as you go." Players should do this off both legs to identify whether they have any deficiency in skating or outside-edge development. After players get the hang of trusting their outside edge, they can start to include moving their hips a little more with more movement off the straight line. With this step over the other leg, players should keep their skates low to the ice and avoid having a high kick between strides. Again, players need to do this off both legs before moving on.

Range of Motion

The next step to one-foot edge development is for players to work in drills that require them to take their ankle through a full range of motion from inside edge to outside edge. It may take some time to work on strengthening the weaker leg for players who do not use this leg as much as the dominant leg. I had an NHL player who was not able to pivot on his left leg because he simply never did so in games. He got very good at hiding the fact that he never used his left leg for edges or pivoting. It took some time and some simplified work on his edges to build confidence back into his skating and his edge development. They could do something as simple as moving on one leg and working to trust their edges as they move down the ice. As players work on their edges, they can start to push off both their inside edge and their outside edge. Learning to trust their edges is a big part of each player's development. When they trust their edges, they will start to push a little harder off each edge individually. Players will be able to push forward a little easier at the start off their inside edge and glide through their outside edge, but as they improve, they will be able to push off their outside edge as well. Players must work on both the left and right legs in this drill so that their coach will learn where they need additional work. Generally, players are stronger on one side than the other. Coaches should work with players on each leg to balance out their body. One simple drill is to have players working around two pucks in a figure-8 pattern. At each puck, players must trust that their outside edge will take them around the puck. The goal is to glide all the way around the figure 8 and push to the next puck for the other foot. The push can be done with or without a crossover depending on what techniques the coach wants to develop.

Two-Foot Edges

The term *two-foot edges* refers to times in a shift when both feet are on the ice. These circumstances could be the process of using shuffle strides (with the puck and not striding), gliding and turning, tight turning, opening the feet and going inside to the edges on both skates (turning the toes out), transition skating (pivoting forward to backward or backward to forward), and other instances. As players continue to develop, they will feel comfortable in having two skates on the ice. Players who are at an elite level have no issue transitioning between one-foot edges (crossovers) and two-foot edges in a game or practice. The idea of having both skates on the ice should allow players to feel balanced and stable as they move. This is a common theme when coaches talk about players protecting the puck and being able to play under pressure from the other team. Their feet should be about shoulder-width apart, and they should be able to react either way with balance.

Edge Work for Strides

When working on two-foot edges, players can start by gliding with one foot straight and pushing the other leg out. Players should push down through the heel of their skate and cut into the ice. This can be done as an edge drill or a stride drill; the difference is where the stride finishes and in the recovery. With an edge drill, the player finishes down to the heel of the skate and allows the skate to come back (see figure 1.13*a*). With a stride drill, the player finishes off the toe of the blade and lifts the skate back in (see figure 1.13*b*). Players should do this multiple times off each leg to get them to think about extending their leg and using the edges properly. After players have this motion down, they can work to take their movement through a full range of motion by pulling their leg back in behind their other foot and adding in the outside edge. Players should be able to keep their edge on the ice through the full range of motion. They should work on this movement on each leg to identify weaknesses.

Figure 1.13 Edge development: *(a)* edge drill; *(b)* stride drill.

Edge Work for Unpredictable Paths

After players are comfortable using both of their edges together, they can start to work on creating unpredictable paths by adding some deception to their skating using their feet. They can do this with toe turns or 10-and-2 turns (referring to the 10 and 2 positions on a clock, which allows players to move with their toes open) when moving in tight spaces. Players can use 10-and-2 turns to move around an opponent or slip into new space away from a check. To do this, players turn their toes out and get on both inside edges. They should be able to glide in this position, as well as rock the weight between skates (shifting weight) to produce some power and push. Players like Sidney Crosby are very good at this, and some coaches even call these Crosby turns. Players who can create unpredictable paths have a skating skill that makes them harder to check. Players who are predictable are easier to check because opponents know where they are going. Those who can add puck skills and fakes to the ability to move on the ice become extremely hard to check.

Another way to create unpredictable paths is by using toe turns. The player turns the toes one way to make a checker or defender think they are going one way and then reacts and gets out the other side. Selling the turn one way makes the defender move their stick or get their skates facing the way that the offensive player wants them to go. After the defensive player has committed to that direction, the offensive player simply cuts back the other way quickly using a tight turn to get to the available space.

Edge Work in Turns

When players are turning, one of the things I ask them is to think about turning their outside foot around their inside foot. This will not happen, but it helps them remember to keep their inside foot back underneath their body so that they stay lower through the turn. Their inside leg holds their knee bend and allows them to drive out of the turn off the outside edge of their inside skate (see figure 1.14). If a player is turning from left to right, their left foot is on the inside edge and their right foot is on the outside edge. As they go through the turn, they should be thinking "get out of that turn quickly," so they push off their left foot (inside edge) and then their right foot (outside edge), crossing over to drive out of the turn. One common error I see with players is that they extend their inside leg into the turn and almost have to stop and then restart coming out of a turn. A player can keep more speed and glide through the turn if their feet work together. They should be able to again use both edges and drive off their outside edge after they push off their inside edge coming out of a turn. Players should feel comfortable turning both ways and should work to get out of turns quickly.

Players can improve their ability to use both edges on the ice in many ways. When players are working on stickhandling, they are most likely in a shuffle stride. When they are working on shooting, they are most likely on two feet with either a weight transfer happening or a change to one foot to shoot the puck. When players understand how often two feet are required in a game and then develop the ability to transfer weight and feel weight distribution in their skates, they can start to elevate their game.

Figure 1.14 Edge development: turning technique *(a)* right; *(b)* left.

TRANSITION SKATING

This section refers to the ability to have players change directions from forward to backward and backward to forward. The ability to do this smoothly allows players to put themselves in a good spot to play against either the rush or immediately check the opposing players with good gap control. When pivoting from forward skating to backward skating, players can typically use one of two ways, a heels-first pivot or a toes-first pivot.

Heels-First Pivot

Performing a heels-first pivot simply means that the heels go first. The heels lead the way when changing direction from forward to backward. When players pivot heels first, the first thing I tell them is that they need to manage their ice. When I say this, I am referring to the space required to move through the pivot. A couple of common errors when pivoting are taking too much ice and crossing the feet over too much. Taking too much ice means that players are moving in a big circle to change direction. They should work to move in a more confined space rather than a bigger area. If players cross their feet too much, they will not get their hips squared around quickly enough to the play. Players need to control their hips to get them pointed back up the ice quickly so that the hips are square to the player coming down on them. Before a player pivots, their hips are pointed up the ice; after a player pivots, they should be pointed in the same direction but now the player is moving in the opposite way. To do that, players need to think about three things:

1. Body position
2. Footwork
3. Width between feet

Body Position

Body position allows the player to move through the transition with balance and control. The transition between forward and backward skating is done with more efficiency when players assume the correct body position. The first part of the transition means having the knees bent so that the lower part of their leg is parallel to the ice through the movement. The knee bend lowers the center of gravity and allows players to maximize each push (see figure 1.15). A common result for players who do not bend their knees is that they fall over as they try to move quickly or they change their knee bend through the movement. Players should keep their head on the same level both coming into the transition and leaving the transition so that they can get right back into their skating.

The second part of the correct body position is keeping the shoulders level and back. By having the shoulders back, players can keep their weight over

Figure 1.15 Transition skating: body placement during pivots.

their skates and not in front of their toes. If players allow their shoulders to fall forward, they are off balance and their eyes are no longer on the play. Players often fall forward with the quick change of direction. Having the shoulders back allows the head to stay up, enabling the player to scan the ice. When players are having trouble learning to pivot, the coach can watch their shoulders and make sure that they can see the logo on the front of their jersey.

Footwork

Having simplified footwork enables transitions to happen quicker and smoother. Using simplified footwork means performing one crossover and transitioning into backward skating. This idea comes from watching players struggle to control their hips and taking three or four small steps or crossovers. As with teaching proper crossover technique, I tell players, "Eliminate things you do not need." I typically follow that instruction by asking, "Why take three or four steps when you can get more out of one good one?" By using their feet properly, players can be more efficient with their movement to generate power and speed coming out of the transition. When players take too many steps, their hips do not get straight and they can get beat to the inside or end up chasing the play. When players can take one good crossover, they can remain in position through their transition (see figure 1.16). Players can push their outside leg, slide it back under, and pull the ice from their inside leg. This crossover should allow them to glide moving backward with their hips straight and feet underneath them. Players can say this

Figure 1.16 Transition skating: foot position during crossovers.

in their head as they are working: Push, cross over, move backward. Even if players begin by standing still to get the footwork down, they can ultimately change their skating in their transitions. Simplifying their footwork allows them to get back into a position of backward skating faster after their transition.

Width Between Feet

By increasing the width between their feet, players can be more balanced and keep more momentum through the transition. One common heels-first error is trying to make a pivot with the feet very close together and almost trying to stop before starting again. When working on pivoting with players, I try to get them to stretch their outside leg out and push it forward off the front part of that skate (see figure 1.17). The reason that players push off the front part of the blade is to make sure they do not catch the heel of the skate that is pushing. If they extend the leg and push but they push off a flat blade, they will catch the heel and most likely go down. When players can extend the outside leg off the front part of the blade, they can move more freely through the transition. With this good first push, the player's feet are farther apart, creating more balance. After their leg is extended (which will not be for a long time), they can pull their foot back in front of their supporting foot.

One thing that players can do when they are working on creating width is to imagine a line through their hips separating front from back as they turn to pivot. Their outside skate should not go behind this imaginary line. Players should

Figure 1.17 Transition skating: heels-first pivot *(a)* right leg; *(b)* left leg.

extend their leg to the line and not let their pushing leg get behind their hips. When the leg gets behind their hips, players must lift their foot back to get it in front or move it in an awkward manner to recover it. When the leg is extended out and stays in a good position, they can recover the leg easier and get right back into backward skating. Imagine that a player is pivoting, moving from left to right. The right leg pushes as they turn their hips facing to the left. The right leg should push straight out (not behind their hips) and off the front part of the blade. The left leg supports their body weight with lots of knee bend as they now pull the right leg back underneath them, crossing the right foot in front of the left foot. The left foot pulls ice and drives them backward with their hips facing forward again.

Players should practice pivoting or transitioning on both right and left sides so that they work on extending each of their legs. Coaches should remind players that everything they do on one side of their body they should be able to do on the other side as well. The extension on the right leg should match the extension on the left leg.

Toes-First Pivot

Toes-first pivots means that as players change direction from forward to backward, they are leading with the toes of their skates. The toes-first pivot is a movement that allows players to move and not have to worry about crossing over. Players can use this movement to read available ice and move with a good gap or continue to skate forward, surf through the neutral zone, and establish a good angle. Going toes first allows players to keep their stick in front of them and their shoulders facing up ice. With this movement, they can keep momentum and move with their feet roughly shoulder-width apart to maintain better balance. As they move, leading with their toes first, their eyes can remain up the ice and on the play that is happening. As they pivot from forward to backward, they should be able to turn their hips and not cross over as they get into backward skating. With regard to how to move in a toes-first manner, it really depends on the game situation. If players have to be faster, they need more knee bend. If they can move slower based on space or puck position, they can be more upright. Ideally, players move with balance having their shoulders back, knees bent, and control of the stick. If they are moving in a way that requires them to check an opponent, they can lead with the stick to the puck to take away time and space. Players can think of the same three things as in the heels-first transition.

Body Position

As players move, they move with balance. The knees are bent, and they are moving to take away space or recover into space. The shoulders are back so that they can scan the ice and see everything happening around them.

Footwork

The footwork for a toes-first pivot is essentially a tight turn. Players move with their feet parallel and with one foot on each edge until they flip their hips around and start to move backward.

Width Between Feet

As players are moving, they do not need to allow their feet to touch. Getting lower to the ice when the feet are together is difficult. Players should try to keep their feet about shoulder-width apart to be able to move with balance and control (see figure 1.18).

A common mistake I see is that after players pivot toes first, they start skating backward and then cross over. Ideally, when players pivot toes first, they do not need to cross over. They should be able to skate forward, start to turn with their stick in front of them, flip their hips to skate backward, and then skate backward without crossing over. When players pivot toes first, they can also skate and open up to skate forward again without crossing over.

Figure 1.18 Transition skating: toes-first pivot *(a)* right foot; *(b)* left foot.

BACKWARD TO FORWARD TRANSITIONS

Backward to forward transitions can happen in different ways for players, largely depending on the available time and space. Players use some common footwork when performing a crossover, which comes up a lot for defensive players. When I talk with players about the options, I always remind them of two things.

1. *Body position is important as they move.* Having good body position (with knees bent and shoulders back) allows players to keep a lower center of gravity and good balance. Their balance allows them to be reactive and to explode and get into forward strides without taking many extra steps.
2. *Whichever movement they are using, they should try to keep their hips and shoulder square coming backward and moving forward.* The problem of turning their hips coming out of their transition will require them to add more steps. As players move from backward to forward, their hips and shoulders should point in the direction they want to go. The hips and shoulders are aligned and move together facing the same direction. When players do this effectively, they should be able to use footwork that enables them to skate straight out forward or work to get up the ice forward. The only time that players may need to turn their hips coming out of a transition is when they have the puck and are under pressure. This pressure requires the player to put the puck in a spot where it is protected, but they can continue to drive their feet.

The options for backward to forward transitions are essentially based on the space available to the player. If a player is under pressure, less space is available. If no one is near the player, more space is available. Whichever movement they are using, players need to be aware of how they are moving and what space is available to move into. The defensive player can work on all three of these movements to make sure they are prepared for whatever situation comes up in a game.

1. Backward to forward—hold an edge
2. Backward to forward—crossover
3. Backward to forward—escape spin

Hold an Edge

With the holding of an edge, the player's space is a little tighter. Imagine a defensive player in the neutral zone moving backward, getting a puck, and wanting to get it moving forward as quickly as possible. This movement should not require the player to cross over and then push forward. The goal of this movement is to get the puck heading back the other way quickly.

A common error when working on holding an edge is that players do not hold it long enough and transfer their weight too soon. When this happens, their hips turn and they add unnecessary crossovers. Players can imagine a line at the bottom of their transition; they have to hold their inside edge beyond the line and then transfer their weight to the other skate to start their skating. Coaches can add a line to help players in their transitions in practice so that they can see what it feels like to move beyond the line. Players need to feel comfortable on their edges before working on this transition. Coaches need to give players time to work on both their left foot and right foot with their transitions.

If players are doing this motion with a puck, they should be trying to keep the puck loaded as much as possible on their forehand. With this move, at times players will need to move the puck from their forehand to their backhand to protect it. They can then pass it or move it on their backhand. Players move the puck to their backhand simply because they are under pressure on their forehand side. If there is no pressure, players can keep the puck on their forehand as long as possible. If players feel pressure, they should have the option to slide the puck away from pressure to their backhand side where they can protect it again.

Crossover

With the crossover transition, players are thinking of using one crossover to allow them to move laterally. This means they have time and space to move and are looking to cover ice. Imagine a player moving backward and receiving a pass close to the boards. To increase their options with the puck, they push and cross over to get to the middle of the ice to create more passing lanes for options with the puck. As players are coming backward, they can think about using their outside foot like a brake in their car. They do not hammer on the brake and come to a stop; they apply the brake simply to slow down. When they are at a comfortable speed, they can push and take the weight off that foot and slide it in front of the

COMMON ERROR

Players can think, "Push, cross over, move forward" to help them get the footwork correct and move with greater efficiency.

Players can add a puck to this movement and work to keep the same footwork without adding a bunch of stickhandling. Players can work to pull the puck from backhand to forehand (moving to the right for right-handed players and to the left for wrong-handed, or left-handed, players), and they can work to keep the puck loaded on their forehand as often as possible moving the opposite way.

other leg. When they step out of their crossover, their hips should allow them to skate forward. When working on this move, players should take ice before their transition and move their whole body a little wider. This wider movement allows them more space to move into as they move forward. Players often think they can move with their feet close together and they don't use their outside foot to slow them down. As players improve at this skill, they can move with their feet wider and won't need to slow down as much to cover ice laterally.

Escape Spin

Players use this movement when they are under pressure or a puck gets behind their hips and they have to turn and work to get away from pressure or readjust puck position. Imagine that a player receives a pass and bobbles it a little bit so that it ends up behind their hips. Rather than skate backward and try to find the puck, they simply spin on their edges, locate the puck, and get it loaded again. If a player is under pressure from an attacking player, they can spin tight or spin into space. Spinning into space allows them to move on their edges and cross over to get away from pressure. Developing this skill builds players' confidence with their edges so that they feel comfortable changing directions. Again, players use the spin to get into position to move the puck faster up the ice. Players should be able to spin and use two-foot edges (one foot on the inside edge and one foot on the outside edge) at the same time. This movement allows them to spin tight, or they can choose to add crossovers and start to really drive their feet to escape pressure.

Players need to be able to spin on both sides of their body so that they can move effectively and react properly in games. Players can work on their escapes in practice to ensure that they are comfortable turning both ways in games.

As players get better with their escapes, they can start to create unpredictable paths with their feet. That is, they can create deception with their feet. Earlier, toe turns were mentioned to help get away from pressure. The goal is to get checkers going one way and then cut back the other way to avoid pressure. The intention is to work against pressure and get the forechecker to think that the player is going somewhere they are not going. As soon as the forechecker commits their stick to a new space, the defensive player with the puck comes back to the other side. Players can fake with their feet, their hands (and stick), and their eyes. Using one of those three often works to move a stick or create space.

LINEAR TRANSITIONS

The idea of a linear transition is essentially moving in a straight line backward and having to open up and move in a straight line forward. For example, a player may be trying to beat the defensive player wide and the defender may feel they have lost shoulder position. If that happens, the defensive player might have to turn, work to keep an angle on the attacker, and push them to the outside.

When working on linear transitions, players should start slowly, literally standing still and working on turning one foot underneath them and pushing off the other leg. The goal is to have players understand what the turn will feel like as they start to move faster.

Players can work on turning their skate in with no weight on the leg that turns underneath and then right away pushing off the other skate. As they turn their skate in, they should think about pointing their toe in the direction they want to end up going. Players often have trouble with this, and one of the reasons is that they cross their feet over. Typically, players cross their feet for two reasons:

1. They do not point their toe to the new direction and leave their leg pointed forward. When this happens, if they want to go back on an angle, they need to cross over to get there.
2. They have their weight on the wrong leg. If a player is turning to the right, they should turn their right skate underneath them. To do this properly, their weight should be on the left leg. When players have trouble with weight distribution, they shift their weight to the wrong leg. Now, when they need to push off their left leg, their weight is not there so they must cross over to reload.

COMMON ERRORS

With linear transitions, players make other common mistakes.

1. *They turn and go straight backward.* If they are beat, this can be OK, but ideally, players are working to push opponents away from the net. The goal is to push the opponent to the corner so that when turning, the defender can get closer to the opponent, pushing on an angle.
2. *Players turn with their feet too far apart.* To correct this problem, players can think about turning their leg and bringing their skates almost heel to heel. This movement allows players to feel that they are balanced, with their feet underneath their body. As they work to pull their skates back in, they can start to turn quicker and get out of the turn quicker. They can now start skating forward without missing any strides.
3. *Players start to lean forward either through the turn or coming out of the turn.* This error commonly occurs as players are rushing to get to the new ice. Players should keep their shoulders back and head up as they turn and start to accelerate again forward. This technique leads to more control with the stick and being in a better position if they need to get physical.

(Continued)

Common Errors *(Continued)*

4. *Players constantly cross their feet over as they are turning.* I have had players throw sticks in frustration when working on this because they don't believe they can get it. Players need time to get the proper footwork and weight distribution to move efficiently. They should turn their skate in and point their toe to the direction they want to go. Players should sit on their back leg and work to minimize the time it takes to go from backward skating to forward skating. Ultimately, the goal is to be able to turn and drive their skates so that they do not miss any strides. An opposing player coming down on them will be going full speed, so players need to work to match that speed on the transition.
5. *Stick position is crucial when turning to allow players to take away space quickly.* Players sometimes turn with their stick behind them, or they have to "helicopter" their stick back over their head, that is, swing their stick over their head to get it back in front of them and on the ice. Players can work to turn with their stick leading the way and extended to take away more space. Coaches should encourage players to work on maintaining good stick position in practice. They turn their lower body, their upper body also turns, and their stick leads the way. When players can skate with their stick in front of them, aim for stick to puck, and keep their feet moving, they become better defenders. Stick position is an important part of this movement because it can make the player appear bigger and take away time and space from the opponent.

This linear transition movement is also an important one when the puck gets dumped past the defender and they need to go and get it from the corner. The defenseman will be under pressure from the opposing team, so they must work on turning and getting back to the puck quickly. The faster they can get back to the puck, the more time they will have to make a decision that leads to a positive breakout for their team. Shoulder checks and scanning the ice before they turn and before they touch the puck are important factors to be combined with skating. This can be done by the outside defenseman or possibly by the inside defenseman, which will be addressed in the following chapters.

BACKWARD START

One last area that can be worked on in skating development is the backward start. This start is a little different from a forward start because players need to work on getting their hips square to players in games. As they are starting to push backward, they can think of this move as more of a push and less of a cut. This way they can push themselves straight back backward as opposed to on a curve moving backward. Ideally, they are taking one crossover and getting their hips square to the play. When they are starting, they can turn and face one way and work to load their front leg. This powerful push will help to drive them backward. After they push, they can turn their heel and bring it back in front of the other foot for the crossover and then work to step out.

Where players have trouble with this push, they are usually taking too many crossovers to try to get going and failing to accomplish much. The solution falls into the category of "eliminating things you do not need." When a player can accomplish what they need to do with one crossover, why would they take four or five? The feet can start a little wider outside the shoulders, and with the first push and pull underneath, players will notice that they can get moving pretty quickly. This type of footwork comes in as defensive players are pushing off the blue line to move backward into the neutral zone.

Skating is the key development factor for all defensemen. Skating skills should be emphasized in practice, especially at the start of the season so that players can work on specific movements. Drills can be planned around topics worked on so that players can see how they will use those topics in games. The key to helping players work on skating is feedback. Coaches can ask players how they are feeling with their movements and whether they can pick up differences in their balance, extension, power, and more. Coaches should encourage players to continue trying to become more balanced with their skating. If they are fighting balance, skills like puckhandling and shooting become much more difficult. As coaches work on skating with their players, they can progress topics based on what is needed. The following progressions are useful:

1. Stationary
2. Add movement
3. Add speed
4. Add pressure
5. Add game-simulated drills

Progressions can be worked on with skating drills when coaches challenge players to work on something specific. Coaches can progress the idea according to the players' age and the way that the topic relates to the game. They can add pucks and challenge players to do drills with a puck or add speed and challenge players to do the drill faster. Coaches can add other players and challenge them to work around others before getting into game situations. Every team will have different skill levels. By choosing appropriate progressions, coaches can help their players continue to develop.

FIVE-TIRE WARM-UP

Level of Difficulty

Moderate

Players

Stationed at one of five circles with multiple players on each circle

Objectives

To isolate edge development

Setup

Pucks, cones, or tires can be placed in five spots—one at the bottom of the circle, one at the top of the circle, one on each edge of the circle, and one in the middle of the circle.

Procedure

Players start on their inside edges and go toward the middle tire. After that, they head to the hashmarks and make a circle around it. They head back to the middle and then up to the top and around the tire. After they go around the top, they come back to the middle and then to the last tire before heading back to the middle and out. Players can hold their inside edge around the tire and then switch feet at the outside tire before switching again around the middle.

Coaching Tips

- Balance and edge control are key in this drill.
- Players should think about stick position and keep working to have their stick in front of them.

Variations

- Start with inside edges.
- Work on outside edges.
- Work with two feet on the ice (no crossovers).
- Work with two feet on the ice with crossovers out of turns.
- Add a puck to work on puck control.

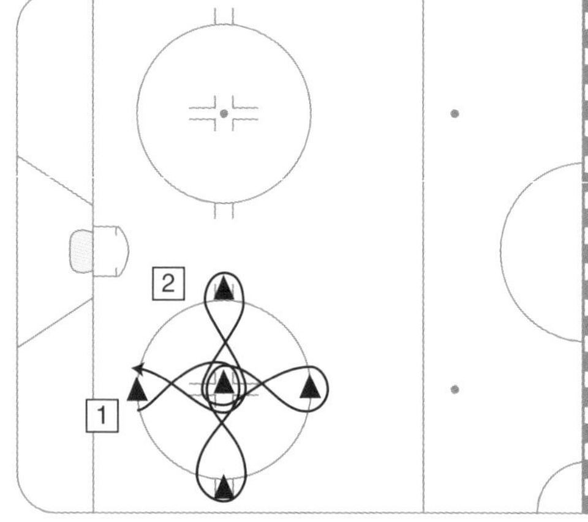

TRANSITION SKATING PAPER CLIP

Level of Difficulty

Easy

Players

Players in groups of equal numbers

Objectives

To work on transition skating (heels-first pivots, toes-first pivots, stops and starts)

Setup

Players need three pucks spaced out around a circle—one on the bottom of the circle, one in the middle of the circle, and one on the top of the circle.

Procedure

To start the drill, players start up one side, pivot heels first around the short puck, come back to the bottom one, and go around again. This time they go to the top puck and come back around to the bottom one again. Players can work on using one crossover at the top two pucks to pivot from forward to backward and none at the bottom to pivot from backward to forward. They should go the other way as well.

Coaching Tips

- Players can think about controlling their hips in their movement and pushing up to start their pivot from forward to backward.
- Players can work to hold their edge on the bottom past an imaginary line at the bottom of the pucks to move from backward to forward.

Variations

- Players can add a stop at the bottom facing the puck and then accelerate forward to the puck to pivot backward.
- Players can do the pivot toes first so that they use no crossovers in their movement through the drill. They can go two or three times around the whole sequence.

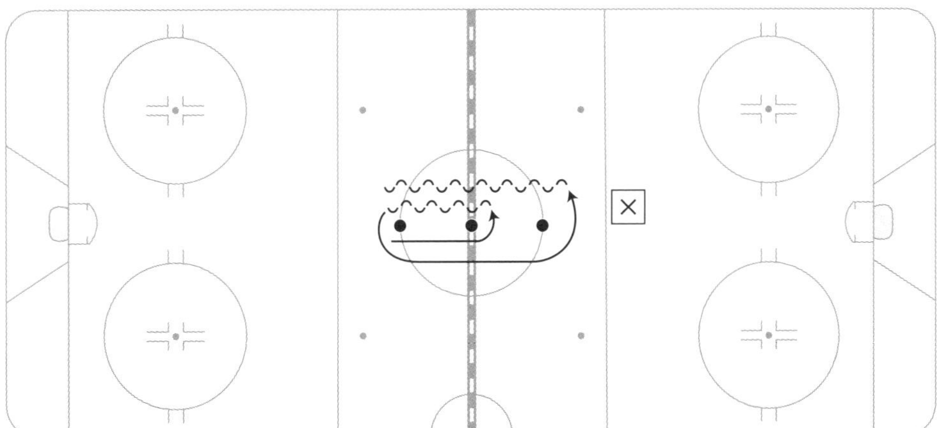

FORWARD AND BACKWARD—SINGLE-LEG PUSHES

Level of Difficulty

Easy

Players

Any number of players

Objectives

To work on lengthening the stride and making the recovery full

Setup

Players work in a line down the ice. A full team can be split into four or five lines. A small group can work down one side of the ice.

Procedure

Players move forward first, pushing their right leg only (see line 1 in diagram). They should try to extend their stride fully and recover all the way back underneath their body. Their left leg should be gliding straight, while their right leg pushes and recovers. After they have done their right leg, they can work to push their left leg while their right leg glides (see line 2 in diagram). Players should think about width when they are pushing rather than pushing back behind their body.

Coaching Tips

- Coaches should encourage players to think about keeping as much of their blade in contact with the ice as long as possible.
- Players should finish by pushing down to their toe (plantarflexion) and work to grip the ice.
- Players should think about having their leg fully extended at the end of the stride and working to pull the leg back in quickly.

Variation

- Players can do the similar stride and recovery work while working on backward skating (see lines 3 and 4 in diagram). The only differences are that with backward skating, players do not lift their leg on the recovery after they push in front of their body. The goal in the stride is not to lose the leg behind their hips. Everything should happen in front of their hips with the stride, and the recovery is pulled back in under the body. After players push with the right leg and glide with the left, they can switch feet and push with the left foot and glide with the right.

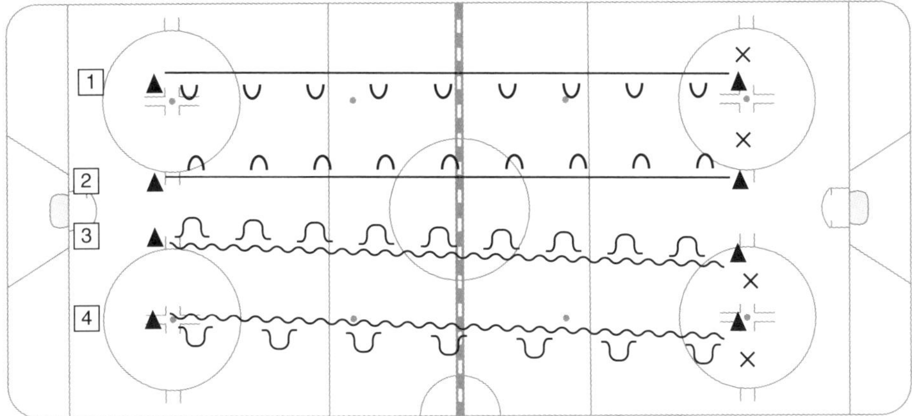

EDGE WORK LINES DOWN ICE (ONE FOOT)

Level of Difficulty

Easy

Players

Any number of players in groups of three or four

Objectives

To introduce edge work and challenge players to glide and balance

Setup

The setup is simple for this drill that has players move down the ice in a line. Tires or cones can be placed across the ice from each other to give players something to aim for.

Procedure

The drill starts with players using inside edges to move down the ice (see line 1 in diagram). Players work to the other end of the ice pushing on one foot and gliding on the other. When they get back to the middle, they push and switch feet to glide on the other foot. They use the time during which they are gliding to move in a small half circle. In this drill, players should glide through their half circle rather than cut into the ice. They can do the same thing on the way back with another area of focus (stick position, gliding-leg knee bend, shoulder position, head up, etc.).

Coaching Tips

- Players should focus on keeping a full blade on the ice for the full rep of the drill.
- To start, they will have one foot on the ice, so balance could be tough. Players should work on holding their balance and pushing hard to keep momentum.
- This drill works with beginners or more advanced players.

Variations

- Outside edge development—tight (see line 2 in diagram). This option has players keeping their hips facing forward and simply stepping in front of the other foot and pushing off their outside edge.
- Outside edge development—bigger (see line 4 in diagram). This option allows players to let their hips go and becomes bigger. Players can step over their other foot and drive off their outside edge to allow their hips to turn.
- Inside outside combo. Players start on their outside edge and then rotate forward to their inside edge. When they switch feet, they can push to the outside edge on the other foot before rotating forward to their inside edge. The key to this is that players can always rotate forward with their eyes looking down the ice. If they are looking back where they came from, they will rotate the wrong way.
- One foot inside and outside edge (see line 3 in diagram). Players push only on one foot, switching between inside and outside edges. This movement is more difficult as players develop their outside edge. To start, players can push through their inside edge and glide through their outside edge until they are able to push off their outside edge as well.
- If players are young and having trouble on their edges, they can do this drill across the ice instead of down the ice.

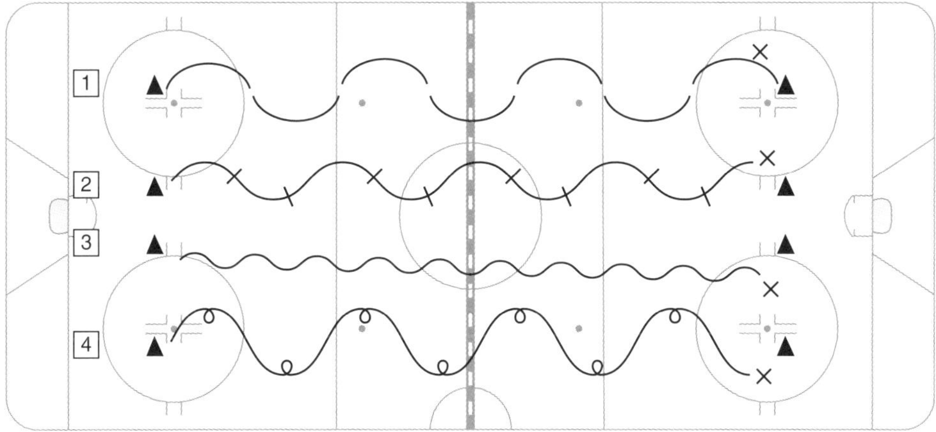

D SHUFFLE DOWN ICE

Level of Difficulty

Moderate

Players

Any number of players

Objectives

To work on moving over from the dot line to the wall quickly

Setup

Players line up in line with the dot behind the goal line and start skating backward toward the dot. Little setup is required for this drill.

Procedure

Players move backward from the goal line to the dot and then push over to the wall to the top of the circle. As they are pushing, they can turn their gliding leg to move them over to the wall. They should think about moving on an angle backward as compared with moving on a 90-degree turn. After they get to the wall, they move forward across the top of the circle to the dot line, pivot backward moving backward to the blue line, and then push over to the wall at the red line. Players move up the red line to the dot line, backward to the blue line again, and then over to the top of the circle. After they finish, they can move behind the net into the other line and come back the other way with the same pattern.

Coaching Tips

- Players should be pushing their one foot multiple times to help them move over. Their gliding leg is important to turn just a little bit to help them move over.
- Players should be able to move with their stick in front of them as they move over.

Variations

- Players can work on linear transitions to move from backward skating to forward skating. To do so, players can turn their outside foot in heel to heel and then push with their inside foot. The goal is to do this without crossing over and without missing any strides. As players turn their foot underneath them, they should be driving off the other foot to get into forward skating. As their lower body turns, their upper body should be turning as well, and players should lead with their stick in the direction they are going. Having their stick in front of them will help take away space and make them appear bigger. Players should think to push back on an angle to meet up with the player trying to get around them. Ultimately, the goal for the defensive player is to shut down the space from the dot line to the wall quickly.
- This drill can also be used as a stick-position drill. Players turn with their stick leading the way and go stick to puck against a coach moving down the wall.

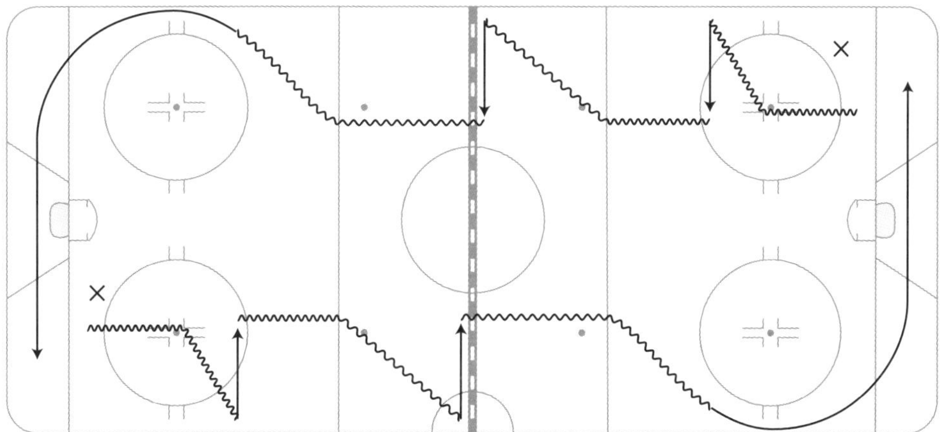

EDGE DEVELOPMENT—TWO-FOOT EDGES

Level of Difficulty

Easy

Players

Any number of players

Objectives

To work on moving using both edges on the ice

Setup

Players work down the ice in a line, so the setup depends on the number of players on the ice. Cones or tires can be placed at each end to have players work in a line.

Procedure

Players start moving down the ice, always keeping both feet on the ice.

Coaching Tip

- This simple progression drill has players start to work on developing confidence in their edges working together.

Variations

- Players start by pushing both feet out and making a circle with their feet (see line 1 in diagram). The goal is for players to push themselves forward.
- Next, they push the right leg only in a simple cut with a full extension (see line 2 in diagram). The skate pushes them forward and then recovers, all staying on the ice. The left foot glides forward.
- Players do the same action on the left foot.
- This time players let their edges work together (see line 3 in diagram). One foot falls to the outside edge, while the other falls to the inside edge. The goal in this variation is to avoid letting the inside foot get way in front of the outside foot. Players try to keep the skates parallel as they move. The width for balance is created by the space between the feet (roughly shoulder-width apart), not by splitting the feet forward and back.
- Players use the same idea as in the previous variation, only this time they can push multiple times off the same leg to help them move around a corner without crossing their feet over (see line 4 in diagram).

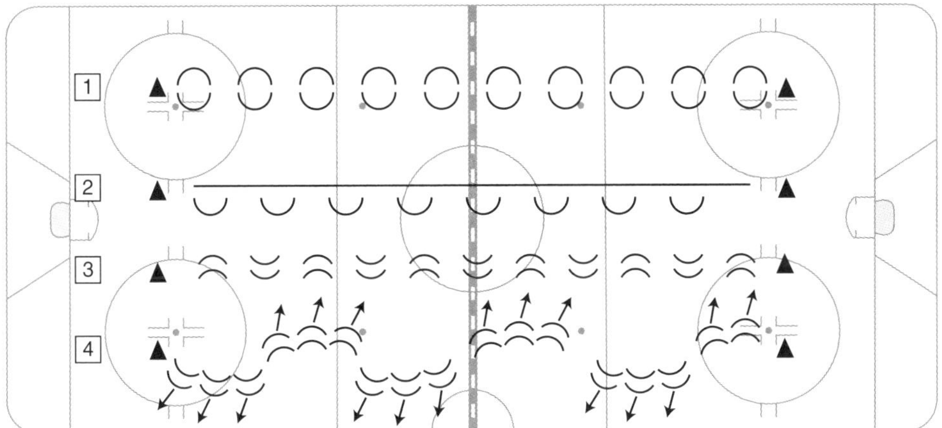

V TRANSITION SKATING

Level of Difficulty
Easy

Players
Any number of players

Objectives
To work on transition skating with more movement and a set pattern to follow

Setup
Three tires (or cones or pucks) are placed in a V. Two tires are placed at the top.

Procedure
Players move backward toward the single tire at the bottom of the setup and move around it. They then head up the outside toward one of the pucks and pivot backward into the middle. As they move backward again, they skate toward the tire at the bottom and move around it. As they come up the other side of the setup, they come to the outside of the puck and pivot around it. One repetition is four times around, with two pivots on each side.

Coaching Tips

- Players should think about width between their feet when they pivot because this positioning enables them to pull ice underneath them and keep their motion.
- Players can work to think about taking only one crossover as they are moving and pivoting.

Variations

- Players can pivot heels first to start and then as they get the hang of the drill, they can pivot toes first.
- Passes can be added to the drill to include puck skills. Players receive a pass moving backward and give it back moving forward.
- Escape turns can be added to the drill at the bottom with the puck to escape pressure and to work on the edges.

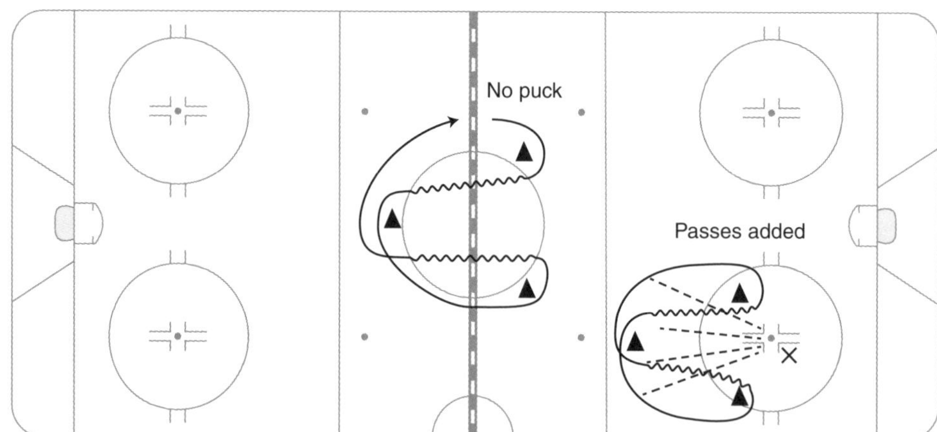

CHAPTER 2

Puck Skills

The core concept behind strengthening puck skills involves developing confidence with the puck. Puck skills include the ability to handle to puck, of course, but also comprise giving and receiving passes, protecting the puck, faking with the puck, and any other action related to having a puck on the stick. For me, the best part about puck skills is that they can all be worked on and improved.

STICKHANDLING

Before players learn to handle the puck, they must first be holding their stick correctly. The top hand controls the rotation of their stick, while the bottom hand adjusts width by sliding up and down. The top hand grips on top of the stick, and the bottom hand is placed on the stick with the thin part of the stick facing out into the half circle between the thumb and finger. The bottom hand never turns the stick in the hand (or top hand) but instead tightens and loosens depending on the situation in the game.

The ability to stickhandle starts with simply having a stick of the correct length. I see young players have trouble handling the puck simply because of the length of their stick. If the stick is too long, the player has the puck farther from their feet, which causes them to have to work harder. The length of stick is often personal preference. A slightly longer stick allows players to shoot the puck harder, whereas a shorter stick enables better puck control. I like to have my stick length at about the level of my lips when I'm off the ice. With my skates on, my stick comes in just below my chin. That length allows me to control the puck and get shots off my stick quickly. When a coach watches players who are using a stick that is too long, they can either recommend that players cut it or try a shorter stick to see what they think. My advice to players who are cutting a stick is to cut a little bit at a time rather than the whole amount. That way they can feel the difference in the length of the stick when working with the puck and make further adjustments in length if necessary.

Coaches may want to think back to when they first grabbed a stick and puck and started stickhandling; their puckhandling was surely not as smooth as it is today. To feel what a player goes through when beginning to learn to stickhandle, coaches can grab a stick with the opposite hand to what they normally use and see how it goes.

One thing to note is that players will not feel as comfortable on their backhand side. They may feel that their feet cannot go straight or that they cannot turn far enough to get to their backhand side. Players should feel comfortable getting the puck all the way over to their backhand side so that the puck can travel forward and backward while their feet are pointed forward. I have worked with NHL players who were not able to get to that spot on their backhand and only go essentially a little off their toes. This position would not allow them to protect the puck, causing a number of turnovers per game. When this was showed to them, the reaction I got was, "How come no one told me that before?" The game becomes easier for players who develop confidence in their backhand.

After players get comfortable with the puck between their toes, on their forehand side, and on their backhand side, they can create width in their stickhandling. The width positions on their forehand side and backhand side are the positions outside their toes (see figures 2.1 and 2.2). Players can work on sliding their bottom hand to bring it closer to their top hand to create more reach. Players

Figure 2.1 Stick handling: adding width on ice *(a)* forehand side; *(b)* backhand side.

Figure 2.2 Stick handling: adding width off ice *(a)* forehand side; *(b)* backhand side.

must feel comfortable on both sides of their body (forehand and backhand) to be able to react in games. The one situation that comes up on the backhand side is that sometimes players drop their bottom hand off their stick (see figure 2.2*b*). Going to one hand on the backhand side allows players to create more reach against pressure. Players need to decide whether they need to be stronger on the puck or have more reach. If they are going around someone and really need to protect the puck, they can go to one hand and work to keep their feet moving. If they are going to need to make a play, either passing or shooting, they must keep two hands on their stick.

To practice width development, players go to their forehand side, bring the puck back to the middle of the toe, execute one stickhandle, and then move the puck to the backhand side. By working on this pattern, players can create different levels of width to get comfortable around the body. Combining this with the three spots the players started with, players can start to expand the range in which they feel comfortable handling the puck.

PUCK-CONTROL BASICS

Players of any age can work on the basics of puck control. I encourage young players to handle a puck in practice to get more confident with it. They can do this when stationary or in drills and when moving, but to build confidence with the puck, they need to handle the puck often.

Some simple things that defensive players can think about when working on puckhandling are the following:

How far apart are the hands?

Players should have their hands roughly shoulder-width apart to allow smooth puckhandling (see figure 2.3). The hands need to be able to adjust based on where the puck is in relation to the body. The top hand rotates and turns the blade, while the bottom hand slides to create width.

Where should the puck hit the blade of their stick—on the toe, on the heel, or in the middle?

Players should think about the middle of their blade hitting the ice and the puck hitting the middle of their blade (see figure 2.4). The puck can then be moved up and down the blade when it is being handled and there is also room for error.

Figure 2.3 Puck handling: hand placement.

How do you get the puck to stay flat?

Players must focus on this important concept so that they can move the puck

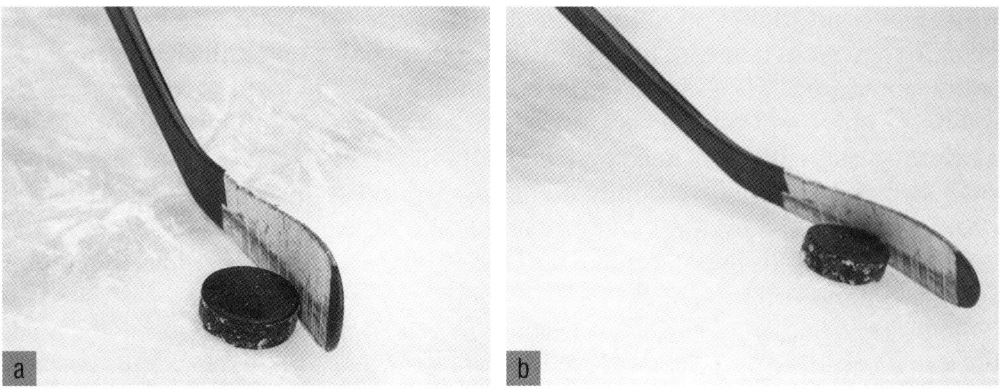

Figure 2.4 Puck placement: *(a)* on toe; *(b)* in middle.

quickly or load it to shoot. They can focus on turning their top hand to allow their blade to turn (see figure 2.5). If the player hits the puck with the bottom of the blade, the puck will likely sit up or flip up. As the puck moves outside their toes, the blade needs to rotate a little more so that the top edge of the puck is more in contact with the blade. The blade can then pull the puck flat on the ice. As players get the hang of the wrist rotation, they can start to move the puck faster.

To become adept at puckhandling, players must be able to handle the puck in front of their body, on their forehand side, and on their backhand side. They need to be able to see the puck on their blade and then work to bring their eyes up as they start to move. The following progression is useful in teaching puckhandling:

1. *Stationary.* Players stand still to work on the basics of controlling the puck.
2. *Add motion.* Players now move, gliding down the ice. Topics like scanning, speed, and width can be added to this stage.
3. *Add speed.* Players now move faster. They do drills with other players and must handle the puck while skating faster.

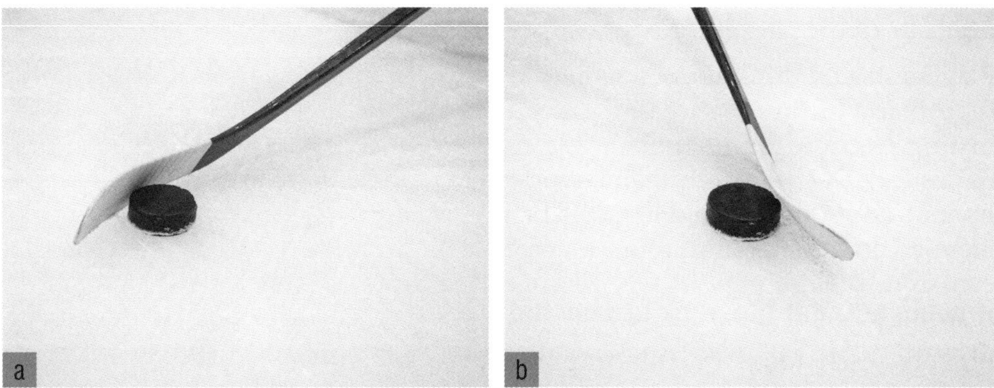

Figure 2.5 Hand turn to rotate blade *(a)* forehand; *(b)* backhand.

4. *Add pressure.* Pressure can come in different forms. One way is for a coach to force players to make a decision. Another can be in the form of other players working against them. The goal is to have an opponent that the player with the puck must work around.
5. *Add game-simulated drills.* Drills in practice can replicate game situations that involve decision making with the puck.

With this progression, players can build on what they worked on previously and progress the areas that they work on. Each stage in this progression can be modified to match the players' understanding of the topic and ability to execute the skill.

FAKES

The idea of adding fakes with the puck to a defensive game is to create space. A fake is something that players do to make an opponent think they are doing something else. Ideally, players give themselves more time and space by making opponents think they are doing something they are not. Players can use fakes when retrieving a puck in the corner, breaking out and moving up the ice with the puck, or shooting from the point. A defensive player who adds fakes and deception to their game can drastically increase their ability with the puck. Players can work with three different parts of the body to create space with their fakes:

1. Feet
2. Hands
3. Eyes

Faking with the feet enables the player to create separation against a checker. By getting an opponent to believe they are going one way and then going the other way, the player has created space. Everything with fakes is about creating space to work in. Fakes with the hands can be as simple as moving the stick above the puck. Often, by causing an opponent to think that the puck is moving when it is not, the puckhandler can create space. Players can also open up their blade or fake a slapshot (by moving their stick back) to make an opposing player think they are doing something else. The motion of the stick creates the fake. The eyes are a powerful tool, but some players do not use them. If the puckhandler looks in one direction, the defending player will likely believe that the puckhandler is either going that way or passing that way. The defender will move their stick or their body into that lane. After they move their stick to take away a passing lane, the puckhandler has created space for what they want to do. I clearly remember a goal from a couple of years ago when Conner McDavid scored after coming down the wing looking to the middle of the ice. He kept his eyes looking for a teammate in the middle, making the goalie think he was passing the puck. While looking to the middle and moving closer to the net, he shot the puck five hole and scored. His ability to create space simply by looking caught the defending team off guard.

As players improve at manipulating space with these three factors, more work with the puck can be added. As the puck is added to players' skating, they can learn to use three categories of fakes.

Puck Fakes (Be Careful How You Say That One)

Puck fakes involve moving the puck to create more space, either laterally across the body or forward and backward. Fakes can occur on both the forehand and backhand side and should be practiced on both. An example of a lateral fake is the forehand fake (see figure 2.6). The puck starts on the forehand and moves across the body to the far foot. The player can stop the puck and pull it back to the forehand. The puck moves in two straight lines, one across the body and one back out. The puck will also start and finish on the forehand in the event the player needs to pass or shoot before or after the fake. The fake doesn't have to be too far outside the body because pulling it back to the forehand side will take longer.

One of the most useful fakes in the game, this one can be done with the toes forward toward the net or with the hips turned sideways and used more as a fake shot. During a shootout, one of the six shooters in the game will probably use some version of the forehand fake. This fake can also be done on the backhand side to counter pressure on the forehand side of the body. This action is referred to as a backhand fake. The puck starts on

Figure 2.6 Puck fake: *(a)* start; *(b)* movement; *(c)* finish.

the backhand side, is pulled across the body stopping in line with the far foot, and is pulled back to the backhand side to finish. Puck fakes can also be done moving the puck forward and then laterally to keep the goalie guessing when the player will release the puck. To practice puck fakes, players can simply work on moving the puck laterally. They can work across their body and back to where they started. They can do this both ways and practice becoming faster.

Stick Fakes

Stick fakes are very useful for defensive players. Such fakes can involve a fake slapshot whereby the stick comes back away from the puck or a forehand flash in which the blade opens up. Moving the stick is a tougher skill because players often tend to move the puck as well. If the puck is in a good spot, the player should be able to move their stick and then come back to the puck to complete the fake. A useful stick fake is the fake slapshot. Think of a player at the offensive blue line getting ready to shoot. If the player brings their stick back with the puck loaded in a good spot, they can shoot. With their head up, they can see that the defensive player is in their lane ready to block a shot, so instead of shooting, they bring their stick back down to the puck and push it to a new location where a shooting lane is available.

The forehand flash is another effective fake because it forces players to react to something that the puckhandler is doing. This fake involves simply turning the toe of the blade back away from the puck and then coming back to the puck. The fake can be done quickly and often creates space to either open a new passing lane or get the shot through from the point. A player who adds stick fakes to their game has more confidence with the puck because they can create more space for themself.

If players are looking to work on their stick fakes, they can fake a slapshot by simply winding up (see figure 2.7). Instead of coming down and exploding through the puck, they stop at the end and either push the puck or pull it into their body. The motion on the fake becomes important because the player can move into new ice. If players are working on the forehand flash, they can work to turn the toe of the blade away from the puck and back to it. The puck does not have to move to create the fake. The top hand turns the blade away from the puck and back toward it. The goal with this

Figure 2.7 Stick fake with the windup.

fake is to get the goalie to lock their inside edges into the ice. After locking their edges in, the goalie thinks that the player shooting, and the player can then either pull or push the puck to work around the goalie.

Body Fakes

The body fake encompasses anything that a player does with the body to increase the fake or make the fake look better. This movement can include turning the head and shoulders in the wrong direction, kicking a leg while using the stick to fake, or something as simple as looking with the eyes in a different area as they are carrying the puck up the ice. By adding a leg kick, a player can get an opponent to think that they are shooting. By adding a head and shoulder fake, a player can get an opponent to think that they are going one way when they are really going another. The key to executing proper body fakes is to maintain balance when skating. As players adjust their weight distribution, they can change what they are about to do as they are moving down or across the ice.

Body fakes are more simply movement or weight transfers that happen in the body. The head and shoulders move to create a fake, or weight is transferred from one leg to the other to create a fake. For example, a right-handed player can transfer their weight from the right leg to the left leg and back to the middle to sell the fake (see figure 2.8). With width between the

Figure 2.8 Body fake: *(a)* start; *(b)* movement; *(c)* finish.

player's feet, they can execute a great fake that creates space. As players start to combine puck, stick, and body fakes, they can confuse players during the pace of a game.

PUCK PROTECTION

After players have worked on basic puck skills, they can start to practice more difficult skills involving puck protection. Working with someone who is trying to check them can be difficult for players because they are working under pressure. Being able to protect the puck really means that players will be able to put the puck in a good spot even against pressure. Using the body to shield the puck is an important skill.

Mastery of puck protection for a defensive player really builds their confidence with the puck. Players who are comfortable with an opponent pressuring them can extend the time with the puck for themselves and their team. At an NHL or AHL level, players who put the puck in the wrong spot against pressure soon lose it. Players who have good range of motion with their puckhandling and the ability to react to pressure can protect the puck better when that situation comes up in a game.

Players can build a wall against pressure by placing more body weight on the side that pressure is coming from (see figure 2.9).

Figure 2.9 Puck protection: *(a)* building a wall; *(b)* starting position; *(c)* transferring weight.

They lean into pressure and shift their weight to be stronger on the leg that is closer to the opponent. Players can also shield the puck by turning their toes out and using their hips into pressure. They place the puck in a spot where it remains in front of them where the check would have to go through their body to get to the puck. Players can also protect the puck by slipping away—by moving the puck away from pressure, adjusting their feet to go inside edge to inside edge, and moving to a new space. With this move, the player protecting the puck stays facing the checker but again moves the puck so that it is harder to reach.

A good drill to work on puck protection is for players to work against another player, stationary at first. The player simply leans into the checker and moves the puck into a space that it is protected. The player resets and then does it again. After they become comfortable on one side, they try the other side. After they get the hang of shifting their weight into pressure, they can start moving. The player with the puck simply skates in a figure eight. The checker also skates in a figure eight and works to provide pressure to the puck carrier. The puck carrier starts skating and leans into the checker, moving the puck away from the defender. When they realize that they cannot get shoulder position against the defender (that is, get their shoulders in front of the defender's shoulders), they can spin away. The defender spins with the puck carrier and works to meet them on the other side. They can continue doing this drill for three full figure eights and then switch.

When players become proficient at protecting the puck, they gain a high level of confidence in their puckhandling. They can adjust to game situations quickly and take in the information that is constantly being thrown at them. Players need to have a high level of composure as they are working with the puck to be able to feel pressure and not be pushed off the puck.

MAKING PASSES

Perhaps the most important skill for players to work on in practice is passing. Brad McCrimmon used to tell me, "Passing is like brushing your teeth. When you are brushing your teeth, you don't poke yourself in the eye. When you pass, you do not miss passes—you put passes on the tape!" I was not always sure that his story made any sense, but I always remembered the importance of passing on the tape or putting the puck to spots where the team could get the puck back. Various factors can change the way that a player passes the puck, but no matter how a player passes the puck, it needs to be passed flat and firm so that the receiver can secure it. The distance between the passer and the receiver determines how hard the pass is.

Defensive players need to understand the variety of passes they might use in games. A pass used frequently in games is the short support pass. For example, during a battle in the corner, a partner comes to the close post for the pass.

All the player has to do is bump the puck 6 to 8 feet (2-2.5 m) to get it to their partner. A pass to the partner can occur behind the net, in the neutral zone, or along the offensive blue line. Players may make a rink-wide pass in the neutral zone when a defensive player goes back to get a loose puck, turns it up, and looks across the ice. Players can use saucer passes to get the puck over an obstacle to a teammate. All these passes must be firm so that the receiver has more time with the puck.

Passing Harder

One of the areas that young players need to improve is passing the puck harder. When I see younger players come to pro camp, they often need an adjustment period to learn how hard they need to pass the puck. Pro players pass the puck hard! They zip the puck from player to player as they move down the ice. I address this aspect of play when younger players are watching a pro practice. I say to them, "Watch how hard they pass the puck and watch how easy they receive it." I always encourage players to pass the puck harder.

When players are working on passing, they should try to keep the blade in contact with the puck to increase accuracy. When I tell players to pass the puck harder, they often slap the puck to a teammate. I do not want them to bring their stick back away from the puck. Instead, they should work to keep contact and push the puck to a teammate. Players can also practice using their backhand to move the puck to teammates. All the passes listed earlier can also occur on the backhand side, and players must be comfortable making passes off both sides of their blade. When making a short defender-to-defender pass or a reverse coming back in the zone, using the backhand is often a case of reacting to pressure. Depending on the game situation and based on pressure, players need to practice scenarios that come up in games and do them over and over. They can make direct passes and even indirect passes to learn the angles off the boards. Defensive players need to work on passes behind the net to a partner and up the wall to a winger.

Passing with power depends on a couple of things. The first is distance between the passer and the receiver. If the teammate receiving the pass is close to the puck carrier, they cannot throw the pass as hard as they can. The rule is to pass it firmly to get it to the teammate faster. The second is passing angle. The player receiving the pass must position their body in a way that allows them to receive the pass. If they are in a bad spot, they have little chance of catching the pass on their stick.

When players work on this in practice, they start stationary before moving on to motion and drills. They can work on passing harder dot-width apart. Player should snap the puck to their partner. The first couple times they do this, the puck will bounce off the receiver's stick and they will have to go get it. As they do this more, they will improve. They will get better at passing the puck harder and better at receiving harder passes. From there, the coach can add motion, speed, pressure, and game-simulated drills to encourage harder passing.

Indirect Passing

Another type of passing that comes up during game play is the indirect pass. This pass doesn't go directly from player to player; instead, the player banks the puck off the boards to get it to a teammate. Players can use the indirect pass behind the net or up the boards in the neutral zone. Ultimately, when players are making these types of passes, they need to be aware of a few things.

What is the game situation?

Is the opponent putting lots of pressure on the partner, or is the player moving the puck to get away from pressure? When moving the puck away from pressure, the goal is to create time and space. As the player is moving the puck to a new spot, are they creating time and space for a teammate? The goal is to allow the teammate to make the next pass quickly or be able to skate into the puck.

What hand is the receiver, and where do they want the pass?

Players do not want to give a teammate a pass that they will struggle to handle. The puck carrier wants to give a teammate a pass that is easy to handle and that they can do something with.

What is the distance of the pass?

Is this a defender-to-defender pass to the back post, a defender-to-defender pass to the close post, or a reverse to the side of the ice from which the player is leaving? These passes below the goal line can often produce a successful breakout on the first try. A player who can use the wall in the defensive zone and keep control of the puck moving out of the zone becomes more effective as a defensive player. Another option to think about with regard to distance is a breakout pass using the boards in the neutral zone to get the pass to a winger. This longer indirect pass needs to be passed harder.

Using their eyes, the player should be able to identify those areas before they bank the puck to a teammate. All these factors help players make better passes. The passer wants to avoid rimming a pass to a teammate that requires them to dig it off the boards. Instead, the pass should allow them to advance the puck and make the next play. If the player needs to advance the puck through the neutral zone with a pass, they can do that with an area pass off the wall to get it to a place where a teammate can receive the pass. If they are in the defensive zone and skating around the net with pressure either right on their hips or cutting the front of the net, they can use a reverse and bump the puck off the wall where a center or their defensive partner can grab the pass. A defensive player who can make a good first pass is a useful player for any team.

RECEIVING PASSES

Nothing is more frustrating for a coach than seeing a player make a good hard tape-to-tape pass that the receiver misses because the puck either hits their stick and goes through it or hits their stick and bounces off it. In either case, the team loses possession of the puck. Every player must work on their pass-reception skills so that the pace of the game can increase. When players can accurately move the puck tape to tape to teammates, the puck can move down the ice quickly. Players need to work on receiving both good passes and bad passes. Pucks that hit them in the feet, pucks that are behind them, pucks that are between their stick and their feet, pucks that are in the air—these are the pass receptions that players must work on in practice so that they feel comfortable receiving them during a game.

Players can work on handling poor passes by standing stationary with one player a couple steps behind the other. This positioning creates a little angle to help the player with the pass reception. The player with the puck (player behind) passes to the player in front of them, who receives the pass. The only thing is that the player passing aims for the feet. The pass receiver can take the pass on the outside of the foot, take the pass on the inside of the other foot, or reach behind them and pull the puck up. Whichever option they use to receive the pass, the goal is to get the puck from their skate to their stick with control. They can flip around and do this from the other side to get a feeling for using both sides of their body. After the player has practiced using both sides, the partners switch roles. After they get the hang of this, they can add motion and continue to put passes into the feet for reception.

Forehand and Backhand Reception

Good passes should be easy to receive. The game happens quickly, and players should be prepared to move the puck quickly after they receive it. The motion to receive the pass is with the wrists, not the arms. When receiving passes, players should be aiming to receive the pass right in front of their body. They should start with the stick on their front foot and cradle the puck with the wrists so that it does not leave their skates. By stopping the puck quickly and not allowing it to travel too far, the player can keep their eyes on the play and be ready to move the puck faster. When players receive with their arms, the puck can get into a position where it must be handled again before it can be passed. Defensemen should work to receive passes and be ready to move the puck again quickly without any additional handles.

The reception on the backhand side is a little tougher, but players should be able to stop a pass that hits their blade. They need to get their blade square to where the puck is coming from and prepare with strong hands. Think about shaking hands with someone. If they have a weak grip when they grab your hand, you can tell right away. Opposite of that is a strong grip, and you can tell that right away. Players need to have a strong grip on their stick as they are receiving passes on both the forehand and the backhand. With the backhand reception, players should start their blade on the front foot, closest to the puck, and receive the pass before the puck leaves their back foot. This way the puck is received in a small area, stopped, and controlled. The puck often bounces to a spot where the player no longer has possession of it. If the puck bounces off the stick when the player is trying to receive it, they do not have possession of the puck for that short time. The goal in pass reception is to keep possession of the puck for the team. When a pass comes to a player, they must stop the puck and be ready to make the next play.

Receiving Imperfect Passes

Puck passes that are not perfect happen often in games. Players may strive to give perfect passes every time, but it does not work like that. Players will miss their teammates or jam them, and the pass receiver must be able to receive the puck when it comes to them. Passes that are in the feet are often the hardest passes to receive. Players can use the inside part of the skate on the foot farther from the pass or the outside part of the skate on the foot closer to the puck. Whichever foot they are using, they can try to take a little weight off that foot and direct the puck out in front of them to the area where their blade is. This technique allows more control when the puck hits the foot and reduces the bounce off the foot. A more advanced move is to reach the inside part of the skate back behind the other foot and take a pass that is behind the body. This motion is tough to execute, but players can work on it in practice so that they have at least a chance on this type of pass. The coach can line up behind the player just a little bit and give them a

COMMON ERROR

A common error when defensive players are receiving passes is that their feet are standing still. Players should be moving as they receive passes. They can work on sliding across the blue line or in the neutral zone on regroups and on getting up the ice on defender-to-defender passes. In the offensive zone, they should work on timing to join the rush so that they are hitting the available space at the right time. The timing of their skating often determines whether they can receive the pass successfully. If they are too fast through the available space, the window during which they can receive the pass is often very small. The angle is poor, and they are put into a bad situation where they are not able to handle the pass. A pass may also set them up to get hit as other players quickly close the gap on them. If their timing is correct, they will have a bigger window to receive the pass and more time to react to the next play. If someone is coming to hit them or finish a check, they have a chance to fake, make a pass, or move out of the way of the opposing player.

pass that is behind them. Players work to gain control of the puck by using their feet to receive it.

Players should be able to receive a pass and position the puck to move it again without another stickhandle. This idea is a new one to many young players, but as they grow older and play at higher levels, coaches have that expectation. Many players stickhandle for the sake of stickhandling and often put the puck in a position where they cannot do anything with it. The good defensemen at the NHL level can receive a pass so that the puck is positioned to be passed again, shot to the net, or skated up the ice. Handling the puck successfully comes from not overhandling it but just working to keep it in a good spot and make the pass as it comes up in a game.

Players should be able to receive pucks that are within one stick length. That puck is theirs. When the puck hits the stick, it should stop. If the player chooses to move it again, that is their decision from their possession. The decision making for players with the puck comes from their spatial awareness and being able to scan the ice to make the next play. I try to get players to think about scanning the ice before they receive the pass. Players should begin to recognize the available space before they get the pass and identify who is open to move the puck to next. When they have spatial awareness before they receive the pass, they will have more confidence in making the next play. They will be able to keep their feet moving when receiving a pass and make better decisions moving up the ice.

Coaches should be trying to build players' confidence in their puck skills. They do this in practice by giving players a chance to handle the puck, make plays, and work on skills that are meant to make the game easier. Coaches can work to expand the comfort range of a player's puckhandling and develop their skills in passing the puck harder and receiving hard passes from a teammate. Developing these areas takes time and effort, and players, of course, must want to get better. They can work on passing on their backhand behind their own net or learn the angles off the back wall to make a successful defender-to-defender pass to their partner. But again, some passes will not be perfect. Coaches need to give players repetition in practice for the skills they will need to use in games.

The following drills are specific to passing and pass receiving. Coaches should encourage their team to pass pucks cleaner with possession. I tell players, "Pace of play is controlled by a team that passes the puck well." These drills will help players develop their passing and receiving skills.

3-4-5 PUCK WARM-UP

Level of Difficulty

Moderate

Players

Any number of players

Objectives

To warm up the hands and get comfortable with speed and range of motion around the body

Setup

Players need to have access to five pucks each or with a partner. Players can stand anywhere in the neutral zone to work stationary with their hands.

Procedure

The first step in this drill is for players to set up two pucks about one stick length apart in front of them. They move the last puck in a figure-eight pattern around the first two pucks. They start by coming toward their feet first in the under pattern. Next time they go in the over pattern. They go away from their toes and pull the puck around the other two pucks. They should try to eliminate any unnecessary stickhandling and make the movement as smooth as possible.

The next step with their three pucks is to go up, over, and down. This pattern starts with a puck on their forehand side beside their body, a puck in front of them on their forehand, and a puck on their backhand side in front of them. The first puck moves up and stops. Players then move the next puck over and stop it. They grab the third puck and move it down to the backhand side. They follow this pattern back the other way as they work their hands and try to go faster.

The next step is to add a fourth puck with one beside them on the forehand, one at 45 degrees on the forehand, one in front of the body at 90 degrees, and the last one at 45 degrees on the backhand side. The player starts by handling the first puck on their forehand toward the next puck. They stop it, grab the next one, and move it toward the third puck. They stop it, grab the third puck, and move it toward the fourth puck. They stop it, grab the fourth puck, and move down to the backhand side. They follow the same pattern on the way back. Players can get faster as they follow the pattern with control.

The last puck is added in to make a small box with pucks. Players stickhandle the fifth puck around the other four in no set pattern. They can start stationary and then move around the other four.

Coaching Tips

- Players can start slowly and then add speed as they become more comfortable.
- They should handle the puck with the middle of their blade and then move it around with good control.

Variations

- Variations can be added to make the drills more challenging as players work through them.
- If they have a partner, the second player can show a number with their hands to encourage the first player to keep their eyes up as they are handling the puck. The second player does not have to do this through all parts because the first player is focusing on their hands, but it can be done on the figure eight.

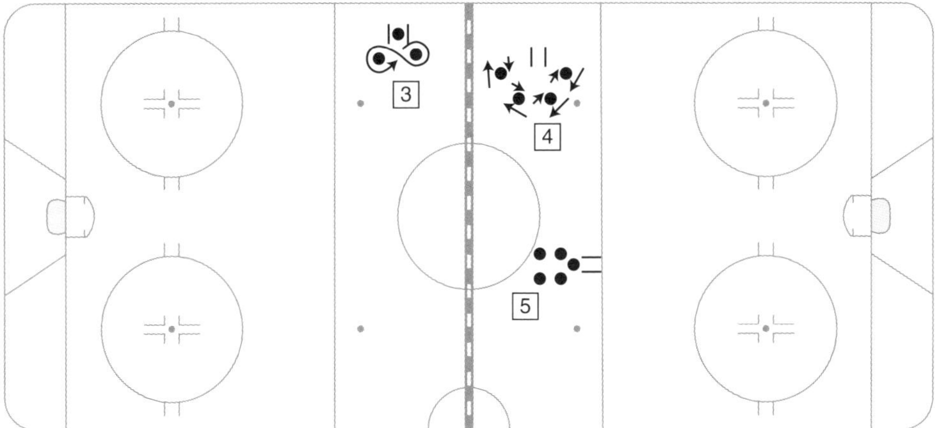

D SPIN

Level of Difficulty

Moderate

Players

Two players or one player and a coach per group, ideally groups of three

Objectives

To work on receiving passes moving backward and transitioning the puck moving forward

Setup

Players work across the ice from one side and have two lines (one on each side) to work with. Players waiting have pucks in the middle of the two lines and are against the wall. This drill can be done in one to as many as six stations depending on how many players are in the group.

Procedure

The first player moves backward away from their partner (or line). They receive a pass and give it back. The player in line gives them another pass on their forehand, and the player in the drill turns on their edges, spins (nice and big), and handles the puck around the space to pass it back to the line. They come up, pivot backward, receive another pass, pass it back, and then get one more pass on their backhand side. They then spin the opposite way of the first spin, cross their feet over, and pass back to the player waiting. The drill continues with the next player going.

Coaching Tips

- This drill is a simple way to get lots of players involved at the start of practice.
- Players should call for passes and get used to handling passes that are not perfect.

Variations

- This drill can be done with edges and crossovers as explained earlier (see 1 in diagram).
- This drill can also be done with tighter spins at the bottom of the drill (see 2 in diagram).
- Deception can be added to the drill by having players start their turn one way and come out the same way they started. This movement adds an unpredictable path to the drill.
- The player in the drill can face their partner the whole time at the bottom of the drill and pull the puck across their body before passing it back.
- Eye-hand coordination can be added by giving the player in the drill saucer passes to knock down as they are moving backward.

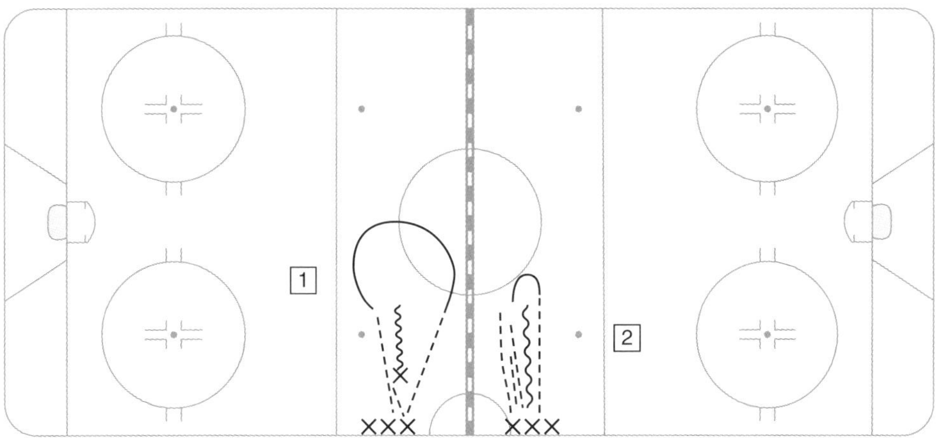

NEUTRAL-ZONE TRANSITIONS

Level of Difficulty

Easy

Players

Any number of players in groups of three

Objectives

To work on transitioning with the puck either facing up ice or escape turning to new space

Setup

The rink is divided into three lanes. The first lane is from the wall to the edge of the circle. The second lane is from the edge of the circle to the edge of the circle. The third lane is from the edge of the circle to the wall. A cone (or tire) can be placed just inside the blue line on each side in each of the three lanes. A total of six cones are used.

Procedure

Players line up behind each of the tires. The first player in each line from one side moves forward to the far blue line and pivots backward. They skate backward to the other blue line, move forward, and finish in the other line. They should move in a circle so that when they come back the other way, they can pivot and transition the opposite direction. After they have the movement down, they can receive a pass as they are skating backward from the line ahead of them. As they get the hang of the drill, they can escape spin at the bottom. Players always move in their own lane so that they do not collide when moving.

Coaching Tips

- Players must be aware of where they are on the ice and how they are moving.
- Passes should be on the tape and controlled.
- The goal here is to have players step into ice in front of them to move the puck to their teammate.

Variations

- Players do not use a puck; they just skate (see line 1 in diagram).
- Players can receive a pass from the line ahead of them while skating backward and then pass it back as they move forward (see line 2 in diagram).
- Players can receive a pass from the line ahead of them while skating backward, escape spin out, and step up to give the pass back (see line 3 in diagram).

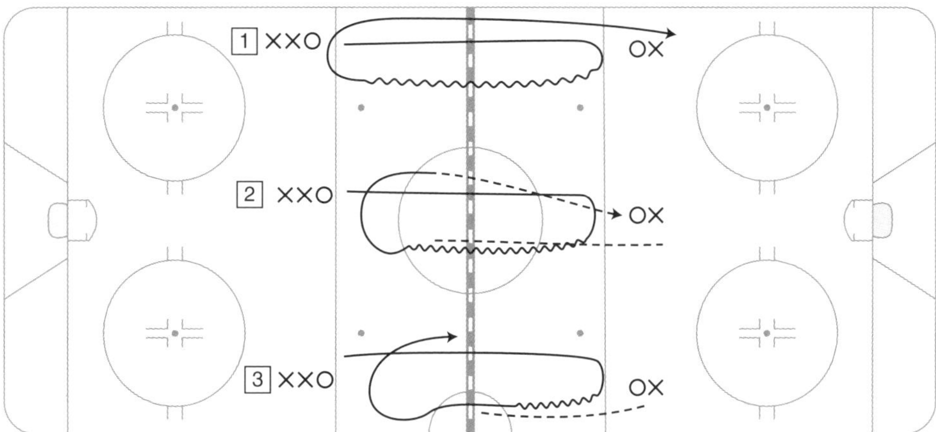

AROUND IN A CIRCLE

Level of Difficulty

Easy

Players

Any number of players

Objectives

To introduce players to the idea of not overhandling the puck but just letting it slide with them as they move around

Setup

Players line up in one corner (small group), two corners (medium-sized group), or all four corners (bigger group) with two cones in front of them. One cone is placed on the dot, and one is placed between the top of the circle and the blue line.

Procedure

The first player starts by skating and follows the circle around the cone. They come all the way around and stop at the wall, facing the line they came from. After they stop, they go back around the first cone, go around the second cone, and stop at the blue line. The next player goes when the first player comes past them and then goes around for the second time. Players come back the other way to work on the other side of their crossovers or pushes.

Coaching Tips

- Players can think there is a line to ease off the gas as they start accelerating. They can visualize a warning track in baseball in front of the wall.
- Players can push away from the wall and then slow down coming into the wall.
- Players should extend fully off their outside edge and push off their inside edge to get maximum power.

Variations

- Players can do this drill without a puck.
- Players can add a puck and work on not overhandling it. They should place the puck on their outside foot and just slide it with them as they move around.
- Players can do the drill with or without crossovers and just pushing off one side. This action closely simulates how they move in the defensive zone or neutral zone with a puck while working to beat someone up the ice.

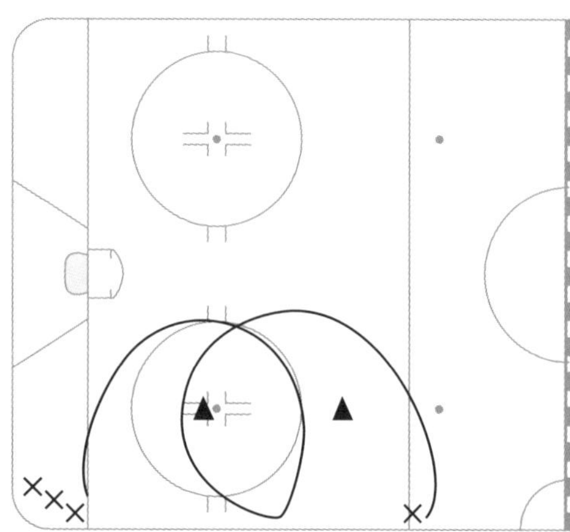

PUCK CONTROL WITH PIVOTS

Level of Difficulty

Easy

Players

Any number of players

Objectives

To work on transitioning with the puck and not overhandling it while moving.

Setup

Five cones (or tires) are set up across the ice with three slightly in front of the other two. Players start at the blue line and move through the cones.

Procedure

The first player moves through the cones, always facing one way. They move forward to a cone, pivot backward, and then move backward to the next cone to pivot forward. They do this all the way across through the five cones while carrying a puck. They make sure to have their eyes up and keep the puck in a good spot.

Coaching Tips

- Players can think about pulling the puck backward on their backhand rather than stickhandling the puck while moving backward.
- They can put the puck on their backhand and pull it with them. As they step forward, they should place the puck in a spot where they can pass it if necessary.

Variations

- Players can go straight through the cones with pivots facing one way the whole time.
- They can perform escape turns at the bottom two cones and then move forward.
- Passing can be added by having a player move across the top of the drill to give and receive passes.

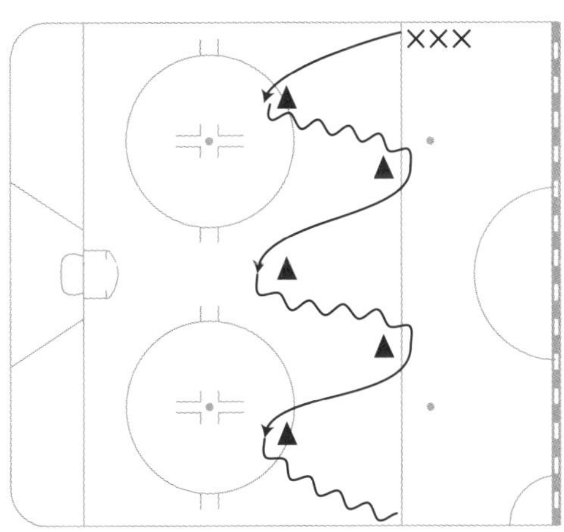

DEFENSIVE-ZONE PASSING—SIX PLAYERS

Level of Difficulty

Moderate

Players

A minimum of six players

Objectives

To work on passes that happen in games

Setup

Six players—two defensive-zone players, two defensive wingers, and two players at offensive blue line—and a coach to spot the puck

Procedure

The two defensive players who are in the drill move and follow the puck around the zone. The coach spots the puck in the corner, and D1 goes back to get it. D1 moves it to D2, who gets possession of it and moves it to the winger. The winger moves it to offensive D1, who moves it to offensive D2. Offensive D2 moves the puck to the winger, who is waiting on the wall, and they dump it in. They can go three times around and then switch. Wingers come into drills, offensive Ds move to wingers, and players that were in the drill move to the offensive blue line.

Passing sequence is as follows: D1, D2, W1, OD1, OD2, and W2, who dumps it in corner.

Coaching Tips

- Players should work on not overhandling the puck and moving it quickly.
- Every pass should be hard and on the tape.
- Communication is also key in this passing sequence.

Variations

- Back-post D to D below the goal line.
- Close-post D to D below the goal line with a little bump of the puck to the partner who is close by.
- Add reverses into the bottom of the drill so that the puck works around one way and then back the other way rather than in a circle.

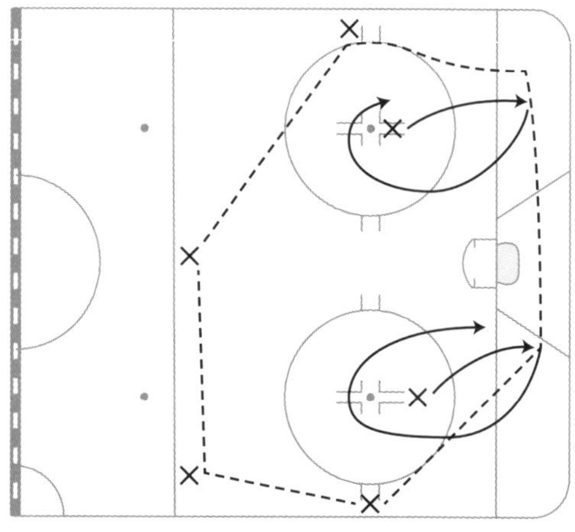

SIMPLE PASSING SEQUENCE

Level of Difficulty

Easy

Players

Any number of players with partners

Objectives

To work on giving and receiving hard passes on both the forehand and backhand

Setup

Partners spread out dot-width apart and have one puck between them.

Procedure

This simple passing drill encourages players to pass the puck rather than slap it to each other. The puck should remain on their stick and be passed hard to their partner. The passer aims first for the forehand side where the receiving player can stop the pass and move it back. The receiver returns a hard pass to the forehand of their partner. After they have shown that they can receive and make hard passes, they can receive hard passes on their backhand. Passing on their forehand, they are now passing to their partner's backhand side. When they can receive backhand passes, they can make backhand passes to their partner's forehand. The challenge in this is to (a) get their head up and put their passes on their partner's stick and (b) pass the puck as hard on their backhand as they do on their forehand. Meeting this objective will probably not happen, but it is a good goal to work toward.

Coaching Tips

- Passing is a skill that is required in the game. If players cannot receive hard passes, they are unlikely to play at a high level.
- I often tell players to pass the puck harder. Anyone who has an opportunity to watch an NHL practice will be amazed to see how hard guys can pass to each other and how easily they can receive a hard pass.

Variations

- The partner can show the passer where to pass the puck. The pass could be to the forehand or backhand side, and the passer must react to what they see and put the pass on the tape.
- Players should work to eliminate stickhandling when moving the puck. They should try to stop the puck and then pass it without additional stickhandling.

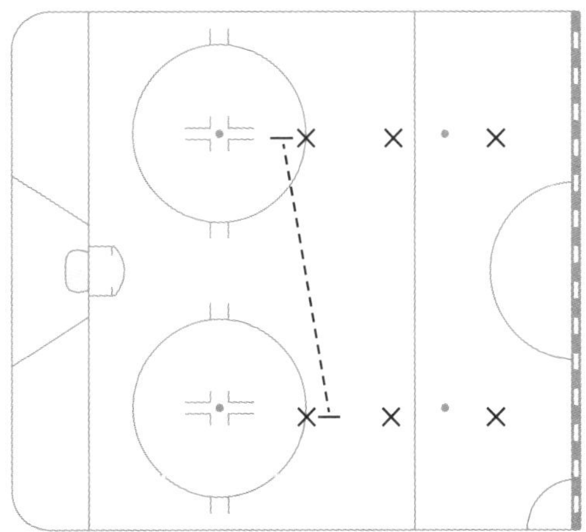

DEFENDER-TO-DEFENDER INTRODUCTORY WORK

Level of Difficulty

Easy

Players

Groups of two

Objectives

To work on both direct and indirect defender-to-defender passing, both to the close post and a harder pass to the back post

Setup

Two defensive players set up in the drill—one net front and one at the top of the circle. The defensive player (D1) at the top of the circle does the work on puck retrieval, while the net-front D2 works to support their partner. A coach has pucks at the top of the circle on the half wall.

Procedure

D1 (top of circle) goes back in the corner for a puck. The first pass is a D-to-D (direct) pass to the partner, who releases from the net front to the back post. They call, "Over" loud enough for their partner to hear. The second pass is to the D who retrieved the first puck. They go up above the top of the circle and come back to get a second puck. The supporting D moves back to the net front and then back below the goal line. The coach spots a second puck, and the retrieving D now passes D to D (indirect) to their partner. The third puck starts the same way with the retrieving D going up and coming back to get the puck spotted from the coach (shown in diagram at opposite end, just for clarity). This time the supporting D is on the close post and releases below the goal line after the puck is spotted to skate out the other way. Players should go as both retrieving D and supporting D. Two new players do the next rep.

Coaching Tips

- The puck must be spotted in the right place for this drill to work properly.
- Puck 1 should be below the goal line, and puck 2 can be above the goal line.
- Puck 3 should be outside the dots to allow space for the D to make plays.

Variations

- Other retrieval options like reverse or wheel can be put into place.
- Players should react to the puck and the call. The coach should not use a set pattern of three pucks; instead, players should have react to what they hear from their partner.
- The coach can pressure the D and force them to make a play to get the puck past them.

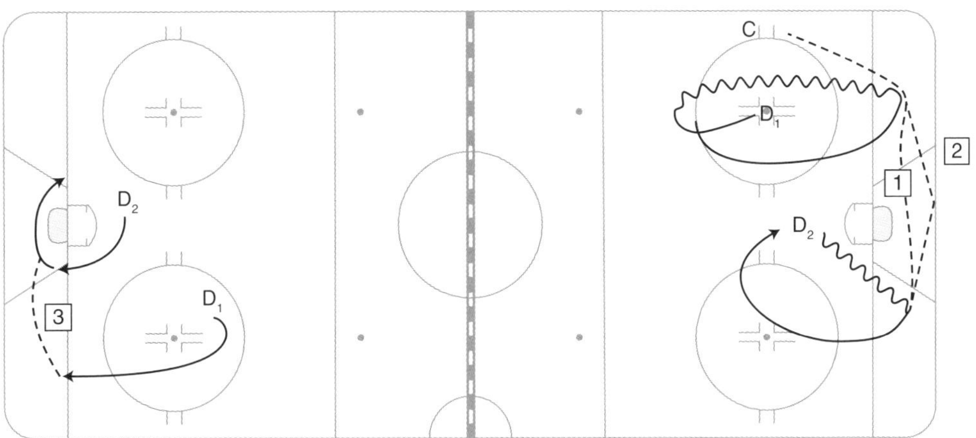

STICKHANDLING WARM-UP LINES

Level of Difficulty

Easy

Players

Any number of players

Objectives

To work on handling the puck with the eyes up and using a variety of patterns

Setup

Players line up at the blue line with pucks facing the neutral zone.

Procedure

Players move across the blue line, up to the red line and across the red line, and then up to the far blue line and across the far blue line to finish. Players can start between their toes with their eyes up on the blue line, change to the forehand side (forward and back) on the red line, and finish with the backhand side (forward and back) on the far blue line.

Coaching Tip

- Coaches should give players constant feedback in this simple stickhandling drill to build their confidence with the puck.

Variations

- Players can add width to the stickhandling by sliding the bottom hand.
- Players can add fakes to the motion—forehand fake, backhand fake, fake shot, and more.
- Passes can be added to the drill if three coaches are available. Players skate backward away from one coach and give two passes to the coach at each line. Timing is important for this sequence to work properly.

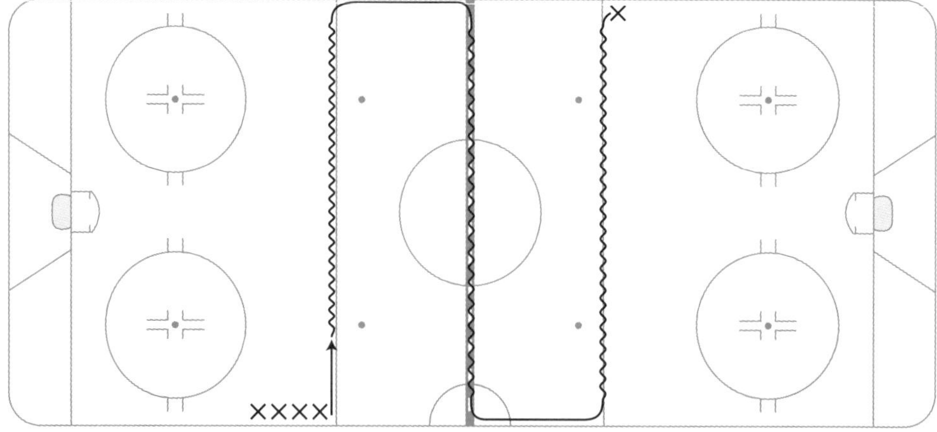

CHAPTER 3

Shooting From the Point

Working from simple puckhandling and passing (also receiving passes), the next step in developing defensive players is to work on shooting. Players love shooting the puck, and one thing I know for sure is that if you are working on a shooting drill, you will get more attention from the players compared with working on a tracking drill or defensive-zone coverage drill. Players love scoring, so the work on shooting comes easy. In saying that, players can work on specific areas with shooting to create more consistent shots. A specific thing that players should think about is to shoot with their head up. This starts with loading the puck into a good spot and seeing the net with their eyes. The result is either getting a shot through to the net or getting a shot blocked. Having defensemen that can get shots through from the blue line to the net is an effective way to create more offensive chances and more time in the offensive zone.

Good, consistent shooting from the point comes with practice. Players need to practice getting a pass and shooting without extra stickhandles. They need to practice getting their eyes up and reading what type of space they have to shoot. The space they have will help them decide what type of shot they can fire. If space is limited, they may be looking just to get it through to the net. This type of shot may not have the maximum power they were looking for, but it can get the job done. Often, this shot comes with their hips facing the net instead of being turned to add a weight transfer. If more space is available, players can rotate their hips and decide whether to shoot a wrist shot, snap shot, or slapshot. Wrist and snap shots can be effective in finding sticks or putting the puck in a specific area, whereas the slapshot is the hardest shot with the most power.

Whatever shot the player selects, it should get down to or around the net. Getting the puck around the net is OK because the shooting lane is often blocked.

When working with defensemen, I always ask, "What is better—the shot getting blocked and going back the other way or the shot getting close to the net and giving the forwards something to work with?" The discussion always helps them understand that shooting from the point is not always about scoring. Many times, the shooter may be giving the forwards something they can use when looking for a deflection. When working with forwards about screening the goalie, I tell them they have two jobs, which are equally important:

1. *Screen the goalie.* Take away or change the goalie's sight lines to the puck. Make the goalie look around you to see the puck. Make them react to a shot that comes rather than let them see it all the way to them.
2. *Deflect pucks on net.* Work to get every deflection on the net. Nothing is more frustrating for a coach than seeing a shot get through from the point only to be deflected wide by the forward. The forwards need to know where the net is behind them and work to get pucks to the net. If the puck is coming at them, they may not want to deflect it because they may deflect it wide. They can stand in there as long as possible and just rotate their hips to get out of the way of the puck as it comes through. In this case, the forward has done their job by screening the goalie and helping the puck get to the net. Shot that are headed outside the posts are the shots that the forward needs to bring back to the net.

Defensemen who can consistently work with passing from low to high or from D to D and get shots through to the net under pressure from the opposing team will play at a high level.

TYPES OF SHOTS

Players can work on a variety of shots and release points. The more options that players have with the way they release the puck, the more dangerous they are as shooters. The same applies to a defensive player who is shooting the puck. They should be able to shoot with their hips facing the net or their hips turned. They should be able to release the puck off either foot and while sliding one way or the other. As players work through shooting, they should try to identify the areas in which they are strong and the areas that need some work.

Wrist Shot

When working on shooting in practice, starting with the wrist shot is a good first step. Whether players are learning to shoot or are working to improve an already effective shot, they can always take something out of a session focused on the wrist shot. This shot allows contact between the blade and the puck until the puck is released to the net. The puck starts on the heel of the stick, and as the blade moves forward, the puck spins off it. This spin is important in getting the puck to travel harder to the net. The faster that players can move through the shooting zone from loaded position to released position, the harder the shot will go to the net.

One common error that players make is moving the puck too slowly from the loaded position through the shooting zone to the release position. They then try to lift the puck at the end to raise it. I tell players to shoot the puck as hard as they can first: "Shoot the puck, don't lift the puck." When players try to lift the puck, it goes up instead of forward. Often, the error here is releasing the puck too far in front of the skates. With the wrist shot, players should be trying to release the puck before the front foot so that they can use weight transfer, the technology of the stick from a strong bottom hand, and explosive speed through the shooting zone to shoot the puck harder.

Hand Position

Hand position is important in shooting. Players' top-hand position should have the area between their thumb and pointer finger on the thinner side of the knob (see figure 3.1*a*). The top hand should hold the top of the stick, and the bottom hand should at a distance of roughly shoulder width. I say roughly shoulder width because some players like their hands closer together and others like them a little wider. Many younger players (and some older players) hold their stick incorrectly, which makes shooting the puck more difficult. If the top hand is rotated under the stick when they shoot, they will not have sufficient wrist mobility to release the puck with power (see figure 3.1*b*). Players should be able to go from stickhandling to shooting in one smooth motion without rotating the stick in their hands. Their wrists can turn and load the puck to their back hip with their top hand coming in line with their belly button.

Figure 3.1 Wrist shot hand position: *(a)* correct; *(b)* incorrect.

Timing and Balance

As the puck moves forward, the player transfers their weight from the back foot to the front foot as the puck is loaded and released. This weight transfer turns a wrist shot into a full-body shot, allowing the player to use the legs, hips, core, arms, and stick when releasing the puck. In golf, even smaller players can hit the ball more than 300 yards off the tee. The exquisite timing of their body enables them to make a perfect, powerful swing. The same thing occurs with hockey. Whether a player is small or big, they can shoot the puck hard with a simplified and smooth shooting motion with either a wrist shot or a slapshot.

I work with many players who are simply not comfortable shooting off their front foot because they do not (yet) have the timing with their body to release the puck with balance. When players develop the necessary balance and timing, they can typically shoot the puck harder in stride. They also have more options in the way they release the puck. They can load the puck and push it, they can pull it, they can fake it, or they can shoot it directly. Having the ability to change the way they release the puck gives players more options to get the puck through from the point and to the net.

The stationary shooting drill is always a good way to work on becoming more explosive through the shooting zone with good timing. Working with the feet turned sideways and transferring body weight is a great position to start in. Players can also work with their hips facing the net and shooting off their inside foot. From there, they can add motion to drills. The motion does not have to be fast; they can simply glide in toward the net if they are on the ice. With the gliding motion, players can work to aim pucks to specific spots such as the area that the goalie has not reached yet (long side) or the area the goalie came from (short side or back across the net). Accurate aiming keeps pucks out of the middle of the net and forces goalies to make tougher saves. If players can shoot at home, they can add a stickhandle to load the puck quicker. The stickhandle can be away from them or coming back toward them to change the release point of the shot. This action will change the balance point and force the player to work on keeping their weight in a good spot to shoot the puck harder.

Snap Shot

The snap shot is effective because it comes off the stick quickly and the release point can be changed before releasing the puck. Players usually develop the snap shot after they have learned to take wrist shots. They learn to snap the puck with their wrists to increase the velocity of the shot. Many players are now using a snap shot more than they do a wrist shot because stick technology continues to advance. Players can change the kick point in their shaft to match what they think gives them the best release of their shot. Players can shoot off one foot, the foot

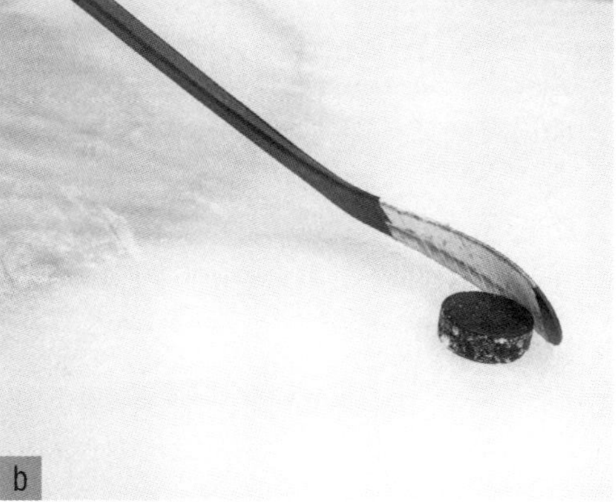

Figure 3.2 Snap shot: *(a)* puck loaded on toe; *(b)* blade position.

closer to the puck, and really snap the puck to shoot it harder (see figure 3.2). The other option would be to set up the shot similarly to the wrist shot but instead snap it off two feet (with weight transfer). The difference between a snap shot and a wrist shot comes in two forms.

1. With a wrist shot, the puck starts on the heel and rolls to the toe of the blade. With a snap shot, the puck starts on the toe and is released with contact at the middle of the blade.
2. With the wrist shot, contact is constant between the blade of the stick and the puck. With the snap shot, the puck is released off the blade very quickly before contact is made again to shoot it.

When looking at game play and deciding which shot is better in a given situation, players must look at time and space with regard to other players. A wrist shot can be extremely effective from the point when the player is trying to get the puck through a lane. A snap shot can be effective when the player needs to shoot the puck quicker and get it to the net. Snap shots can be effective when the player is coming down the ice off the rush, and wrist shots can be effective when moving across the slot when the hips are turned. Each shot has a place in the game depending on the space that players have and the direction they are moving. Players need to choose the one they like better.

The snap shot can be very effective in games because players can release the puck off either foot and still shoot it hard. Players can improve the accuracy of the snap shot through practice when they have possession of the puck and can shoot with their eyes to the net. Their hands can be strong and push down through their bottom hand to work on using their flex.

Having the ability to use either the wrist shot or the snap shot and release the puck off either foot allows players to pick which shot works best at the particular time of the game.

Puck Release for Wrist Shots and Snap Shots

When looking at wrist and snap shots, players can also work on changing the way they release the puck. They can push or pull the puck in toward their feet to change the angle of the release, but they can also change the way they shoot the puck and release it off different feet. They can use a weight transfer from back foot to front foot to engage more of the body or snap the puck off the foot that is closer to the puck. The foot they use depends on the game situation, where the shooter is, and the position of their hip. I encourage players to be balanced and work to shoot the puck as hard as possible. Being able to change the way they release the puck with both wrist shots and snap shots allows players to keep goalies guessing about when and how the shot will come. Being able to pull the puck with a snap shot or push the puck with a wrist shot causes the goalie to adjust their weight and footing. Shooters gain an advantage if the goalie does not have their feet set to make the save.

When talking about balance with players, I address the amount of space available if the opposing team moves into their space (and possibly hits them). Players should not be off balance when shooting because they will not get as much on the shot and their momentum will likely carry them to the corner or away from the net. When the player releases the puck off the stick, they should try to finish in a position where they can see where the puck goes. A situation that often comes up in practice is the way in which the player finishes when shooting from the point. Defensemen often shoot and turn quickly toward the neutral zone. They have no idea where their shot went because they are getting ready for their next shot. I encourage players to follow their shot to the net and know exactly where it goes. Players should be able to keep their eyes on the puck and be aware of the possible plays that result from where that puck goes.

Having the ability to change the way they release the puck adds another layer to a player's shooting repertoire. They will be less predictable and more able to react to the game situation. Always a consideration in shooting is the power that players can generate from the front-foot release (weight transfer) versus the inside-foot release (foot closer to the puck). The front-foot release generates a good amount of power from the blue line to the net, whereas the one-foot release is a little quicker. Defensemen who are adept at taking both types of shot can choose the shot that works better for them based on the amount of space available in the offensive zone.

Backhand Shot

Defensive players rarely use the backhand shot from the blue line, but if they activate into the zone they can use the backhand shot on their way to the net. The backhand shot is similar to the wrist shot because players turn their hips and transfer their weight from back foot to front foot as they release the puck (see figure 3.3). The puck is loaded to the backhand side of the body, and contact is kept between the blade and the puck until it is released as a shot. The biggest thing to work on and focus on with the backhand shot is balance. Players should practice transferring their weight from back foot to front foot and snapping the puck to the net. At first, they should not worry about how high the shot goes but instead try to shoot the puck harder. After they attain velocity on the shot, they can start adjusting blade angle to elevate the puck.

A common mistake made by players who are learning the backhand shot is following through very high and keeping the arms straight. Players should shoot with their wrists, not their arms. If they use their arms to shoot, they will typically finish high and be unprepared for a rebound. When players use their wrists to shoot, they do three things that will benefit them:

1. First, they can snap the puck off their stick to generate power.
2. Second, they can release the puck to a variety of spots. They can choose to elevate the puck or shoot it hard and low.
3. Third, they can be ready for a rebound after they release the puck.

The backhand shot becomes an especially effective tool as the player gets close to the net. For defensive players, depending on the situation in the game, having the backhand as a tool can help significantly. The backhand clear is an effective use of the backhand from the defensive zone to get the puck down the ice under pressure. The backhand clear allows players to elevate the puck quickly (like a flip) and get the puck into the neutral zone and away from pressure. The clear can be used when nearby opponents prevent the player from getting back to the

Figure 3.3 Backhand shot: *(a)* hips forward; *(b)* hips turned.

forehand side. Being able to shoot the puck on the backhand side allows players to feel comfortable lifting the puck out of the zone. The blade on the stick stays open, and the puck is elevated by the wrist and arms working together.

Slapshot

The slapshot comes into play when players have a little more time and space at the blue line to shoot. Every young player wants to master this shot. They want to shoot the puck hard and really wind up to do that. But players do not need a big windup to shoot the puck hard because they generate their power from explosive motion toward the puck, not their backswing. To start, players should position their hands about double the width of their shoulders and their stick across the thighs (see figure 3.4*a*). This position allows them to start with their stick flat, or parallel to the ice. With this position, players can keep the face of their blade facing the ice to ensure that the contact between the blade and the puck is square to the net.

As players take their stick away from their body, they should think about moving it straight back (see figure 3.4*b*). Having the stick come straight back enables them to engage their legs, core, and upper body to shoot the puck harder. If players are having trouble with this movement, they can move to the boards and put their hips against the boards. Players should be able to wind up and shoot through a spot without their stick hitting the boards on either the windup or the follow-through. The stick does not need to go back beyond an imaginary line drawn through the hips.

Figure 3.4 Slap shot: *(a)* set up; *(b)* movement; *(c)* finish.

Players can also work to think about keeping both arms straight in the windup phase of their shot. Many players make the mistake of either bending their top arm into their belly or bending their bottom arm to bring the stick up. I again tell players, "Get rid of things you do not need." Bending the bottom arm is not something they need to do. If players want to hit the puck with good contact, their arm will be close to straight at contact. Why bend it and then straighten it on the way to the puck? Keeping it straight (or almost straight) and then pushing through the bottom hand is much easier. The top hand can come back to the back hip to get ready to shoot.

From this position, players can prepare to push toward the puck. They should be as explosive as possible with the movement down toward the puck. Their weight transfers, their core rotates, and their stick contacts the ice just before it hits the puck. Players should work to hit the puck in the middle of their blade at contact to generate power on their shot as well as hit the shot with some accuracy.

When players are starting to work on their slapshot, they should place the puck in the middle of their skates. Players can thus work on making contact with a square blade and getting the puck to the net. As they become a little more advanced, they can move the puck around a little closer to their back foot or a little farther forward to their front foot to make sure that when the situation comes up in a game, they are still comfortable shooting the puck.

As players progress with practicing slapshots, they should work on generating power with their shot before worrying about raising the puck. Players can work on shooting low and hard and really driving the puck to the net. As players get the hang of recognizing space, they will see this before they release the puck. As they get better, they will learn to get the puck set up quickly and shoot with their eyes to the net.

Slapshots are a tough skill to work on, but for players who want to get better at it the best way to start is with stationary drills. Players can work to get their hand position correct, get the puck in the middle of their skates, and make contact in the middle of the blade. The goal with the slapshot is to hit the ice just before hitting the puck to allow the player to flex down on the stick. This technique helps generate more power as the player transfers their weight to the front foot. After the stationary player can hit the puck hard, they can begin to move into a puck that is stationary and work for the same contact. As the player begins to shoot the puck hard while skating into it, they can then begin to carry the puck and set it for a slapshot. The setting of the puck is difficult because it must be set in front of the body where the player can skate into it. For this reason, players must develop their puckhandling before they work on shooting.

One Timer

After players have developed a consistent slapshot, they can start to work on their one timer. This process involves the same shooting mechanics as the slapshot only now the puck is not placed in a spot to shoot from. Instead, the puck is passed to the shooter. The goal with the one timer is to get the puck to the net before the goalie has a chance to set their feet. As players get older, the goalie who can set their feet on the pass across has a good chance of making the save. But if the shooter can get the puck on to the net before the goalie can set their feet, the chances of scoring increase.

One-Timer Preparation

A crucial aspect of the one timer is the pass that is coming to the player who is preparing to shoot. I tell players all the time, "Good passing leads to good shooting, and bad passing leads to no shooting." This pass must be a good one. Players must learn how to pass to someone who is ready to shoot. The passer must put the puck into an area where the player receiving it feels comfortable getting the puck to the net. The pass must be hard enough to get to the player quickly, and it must be flat on the ice. If the player has to wait for the pass, they will likely not get a shot to the net because the pass will either be picked off or blocked. If the pass is firm and in a good spot, the shooter can be prepared to shoot.

One-Timer Setup

One thing I tell players is to relax before they shoot. Players often get tight well before the puck comes to them. If they are flexed or tight, at some point their muscles start to fatigue and they cannot produce as much power. If players are relaxed (think of Alexander Ovechkin on the power play, standing straight and waiting for a pass), they can start to prepare as they see that they are getting the puck. I tell players not to be as relaxed as Ovechkin but to relax and prepare to shoot. The stick of the player shooting should already be back and ready to unload. Their movement down toward the puck is the same as with the slapshot, and contact should be the same. The shooter is looking to make contact between their feet and hit the puck with the middle of the blade. Players can push down through their bottom hand to generate power from the shaft of the stick. As the puck is coming to them, they can grip down their stick a little tighter, load their back leg, and start to get their hips ready to rotate.

One-Timer Release

The idea of releasing the puck quickly with a one timer goes hand in hand with the idea of releasing the puck quicker to get it to the net. In some situations, the player can stop the pass and release it to the net without stickhandling. This concept is a good one because the puck gets to the net faster, often as the goalie is still adjusting to the play and before they can set their feet. Defensemen can do this off a hard defender-to-defender pass or by joining the rush and shooting.

Much of the success of a shot has to do with the player's hand placement and ability to prepare before the pass comes to them. Players need to get their hands, hips, and feet ready to shoot before the pass comes to them. Theirs hands should be away from their body so that they can tuck their top hand into their belly button on the shot. Having the hands ready also means having their stick ready with the blade of the stick perpendicular to where the pass is coming from. This positioning helps stop the puck when it hits the blade. If the blade is angled at all, the puck will bounce, especially on a hard pass, and rarely will it go exactly where the shooter wants it to go. The hips prepare either to rotate to transfer weight or sink into the shot. The feet prepare to shoot by not crossing over and getting into a position where the puck can be released.

After the puck hits the stick on a pass, the player can quickly turn their hands into a shooting position and look to get the puck through. When players are shooting, they should think about getting the puck to the net quickly. Often, a quick release will be better than holding the puck and looking for a perfect shot. A puck that is released quickly and is a perfect shot is a great combination, of course, but only if we can get there.

Game Scenarios

When Paul Maurice was the coach of the Winnipeg Jets, I asked him what skill young defensemen who are close to making the NHL can work on. His response was to work on one timing the puck off the pass from low to high when it comes indirectly off the wall. This is one way that players can use one timers in games. Here are some others:

- Off a defender-to-defender pass
- When joining the rush on the strong side
- In the rush as a dot-lane player
- Attacking the dot and a pass from below the goal line

These areas can be addressed in splits at the beginning of practice, end of practice, or during practice. A specific shot can be added into a drill to allow players to focus on that example and gain confidence in using it in games. For

COMMON ERROR

A common error that occurs when players are learning (or getting ready) to one time the puck is adding an extra motion over the top of the puck. They add an extra move forward, so the count is one (forward), two (back to wind up), and three (forward to the puck). Players should be back and ready with the stick so that in one motion (forward), they can drive to the puck.

example, for players to work on joining the rush on the strong side, a coach can have pucks near the hash marks and the defensive players can line up on the close neutral-zone dot. Players skate into the zone and receive a pass from the coach. If players are on their one-timer side, they can look to one time the pass. If they are on their offside, they can look to stop the puck and shoot it. Coaches should switch sides so that all players get a chance to one time pucks. The other option is to have right-handed players on one side and left-handed players on the other side so that they are working only on their one-timer sides. They can also do this from the opposite side, taking passes across the seam to the backside dot as they enter the zone. Coaches can get creative with options and allow players to work on each shot.

When players get comfortable one timing the puck, they have added another shot to their bag. They become more dangerous offensively when shooting from the blue line or from areas where they are joining the rush. I believe that players should work on consistency with their shot before they work on accuracy. When players can consistently hit one timers hard and get them on the net, they can start to work on placing the puck to various areas of the net.

RELEASING THE SHOT AFTER RECEIVING THE PASS

Quick wrist shots or snap shots often result from passes that come from low to high, go from defender to defender, or go to a player joining the rush. When shooting a slapshot with a quick release, players can think about a concept called "get it, set it, shoot it." The player receives a pass and sets the puck in front of their hips (see figure 3.5). From the set position, the stick comes straight back into the windup and the shot goes to the net. This smooth motion of catching the pass and delivering a shot to the net without stickhandling allows defensive players

Figure 3.5 Releasing the shot: *(a)* blade position; *(b)* squaring up for the pass.

to add another layer of offense to their team. Right-handed players can do this moving to the right, and left-handed players can do this moving to the left. This simplified motion of setting the puck and moving straight into a windup eliminates the need for additional stickhandles. This way of setting the puck allows players to get their head up and get the puck to the net quicker.

If right-handed players are moving to the left (or if left-handed players moving to the right) and the pass is behind them so that they cannot one time the puck, they may be able to "soft set" it. To do this, they receive the pass and in one motion set the puck between their feet so that they can wind up and hit it. Players must be able to slow down the pass enough so that the puck stays between their feet for the slapshot. As players get better at the soft set, they can add in a "soft touch," meaning that they simply deflect the pass into an area where they can wind up and shoot. This skill is tough to learn, but when players get the hang of it, they can get the puck to the net quickly from the blue line. Players can practice the soft set by working across the blue line and receiving passes from their partner. They can do this repeatedly to work on the accuracy of the shot. They focus on receiving the pass, setting the puck, and shooting it with their eyes up.

Whether players are working to shoot the puck with a wrist shot, snap shot, or slapshot, the key to releasing the puck quickly is the reception of the puck. Players should be able to receive the pass and get the puck into a spot where they can shoot it all in one motion. Players should try to eliminate stickhandles and work to control the puck in a way that gets the puck to the net quickly. In some situations, the player may add a fake before they shoot or change the angle of their release with the shot, which could require adding a stickhandle to the release. The difference is that their handling of the puck is done with the intention of faking, not just stickhandling.

SHOOTING FROM THE BLUE LINE

The next aspect of shooting to discuss is shooting from the point. Many young players work constantly on moving in because they want to get the puck to the net in the air. The problem with that approach is that space is rarely available in games because opponents will be in their defensive-zone positioning. Instead, players should slide laterally and work to shoot from the blue line. They should shoot the puck hard enough to get it to the net with something on it. Taking the puck closer to a checker makes their job easier. Shooters can make their opponent's job harder by making them come out and challenging them to stay in the shooting lane. The shooter does this by moving laterally, which forces the opponent to move laterally. If the shooter is standing still, the checker has an easier job to block the shot because the shooter will be stationary. If the shooter can put the puck in motion and slide (even a little bit), they make the opposing player's job much harder.

COMMON ERROR

An error I often see when players are working on shooting from the point is that they overhandle the puck before shooting it. This issue is especially common with young players learning to shoot because they think that they must set up the puck perfectly to shoot it. As players become stronger and their puck skills start to come around, I encourage defensemen to work on receiving passes and getting the puck into a shooting position without stickhandling it. The faster they can get the puck off their stick, the less time an opposing player has to get into the shooting lane and block the shot. If the shooter can combine a lateral slide and a quick release, the opponent's job becomes much harder.

Offensive Zone

In the offensive zone, defensive players typically receive passes from specific spots. The first one is low in the corner to the blue line, either straight up the boards or an indirect pass off the boards. This pass is effective in the offensive zone because it forces the defensive team to stretch out their defensive-zone coverage. The defenseman who receives the pass can work to get off the wall and move toward the middle of the ice. The second pass that typically happens in the offensive zone is the defender-to-defender pass across the blue line. This partner-support pass is another effective one because it forces the defensive team to move in the offensive zone and adjust to the play from one side to the other. As defensemen become proficient at handling these passes, they can begin to look at the shots that come from each one.

Low-to-High Passes

In games the low-to-high pass sometimes opens up a shooting lane right away. The defensemen must be able to get their eyes to the net before they get the pass and know that a shooting lane is available. By doing so they can take one step toward the middle to get their hips around the puck and shoot it toward the net. Players can use wrist shots, snap shots, or slapshots in this one-step slide and work on looking for sticks for deflections. The one-step slide is effective when the defensive partner is not an option and the puck needs to get to the net quickly.

A challenge with the one-step slide is that if a player shoots the puck hard and misses the net on the long side, they are helping the other team potentially break out of the zone because they are on the far boards. Players should ideally shoot for the close side of the net if they are shooting from the boards, but if they must shoot for the far side (maybe they are shooting for a deflection), they should work off the wall and quickly get back into the middle of the ice.

Shots off Defender-to-Defender Passes

This play happens often in games when the defensive player sees that their partner is available and moves the puck across the blue line to them. A player who makes a defender-to-defender pass should do it before the dot as they move off the wall. The partner can then stay in a good lane to the net close to the middle of the ice as they start to slide. The goal is to work to get the puck quickly through to the net off the pass. If a player is on their strong side, they can continue to the pass. This is known as a soft catch, and the puck is quickly loaded to shoot it. If the player does not like what they see, they can place the puck into the corner. If they like what they see, they can work to get the puck to the net.

The defensive partner has two options off a defender-to-defender pass. First, they can accept the pass with a soft catch and be ready to shoot it. This option stretches the coverage in the defensive zone and forces the defensive player in the slot to slide with the attacking player as they move. The second option is to attack the pass. The partner is going to shorten the distance of the pass and skate into the pass to accept it quicker. This movement can confuse the opposing team and forces them to adjust their coverage. This can happen if the defensive partner is maybe a little wider than normal or they see available ice to move into. Either way, the partner should look to get the puck into a shooting position quickly.

GETTING OFF THE WALL

As players receive a low-to-high pass (from the corner to the blue line), they are looking to get off the wall. The goal with this movement is to avoid being boxed in by the defending team so that the only option is to throw the puck back down the wall into the corner. By getting off the wall, the player has more options and can start to generate offensive chances or sustain time in the offensive zone. Players can move off the wall in a few different ways to look to shoot.

Sprint

Sprinting is especially effective on the power play when a player needs to get to the middle quickly. Players essentially turn and skate across the line without worrying about any crossovers. This sprint can really open up various lanes for the player as they are working to get into the middle of the ice.

Slide

Moving in this way allows players to keep their hips and shoulders facing the net so that they can see everything happening in front of them. They can minimize stickhandling and work to keep the puck on their forehand so that they can pass to their defensive partner or look to shoot the puck. The footwork is important because players do not want to take too many crossovers. Players can push, cross over, and move to get off the wall. As players get their foot work down, they should be able to move efficiently into the middle of the ice. Typically, with this slide, the defender-to-defender pass happens before they get to the dot. The player receiving the pass then has space to analyze what they see, and the player who passed the puck can follow into the middle of the ice.

Flip the Hips

This is a quick shot coming between the boards and the dot. Players will recognize the space in front of them and see that there a lane is available as soon as they get the pass. They can quickly flip their hips on their strong side of the ice to get into a shooting position. This works well if the offensive team can move the puck low to high and catch the strongside winger out of position. If players are playing their offside (right-handed player playing the left side or left-handed player playing the right side), this move is a little easier because they are moving the puck in front of them across the blue line and it is already loaded.

USING THE LANE YOU CREATE

As players move laterally across the line, they can use a concept called "use the lane you have created." This concept helps players get the puck through to the net more often, and it allows forwards to anticipate where the puck will be coming to the net. Think for a minute about the nonverbal communication that occurs between a pitcher and a catcher in a baseball game. If the pitcher sees that the catcher wants a fastball, the pitcher throws a fastball. If the catcher wants a curve ball, but the pitcher throws a fastball, the catcher typically comes out to talk to the pitcher to get back on the same page. Likewise, if the forward can anticipate where the puck is coming to, they will have a better chance to deflect it on the net.

Let's say that a right-handed player is moving across the line and an opponent is trying to block the shot. If the player tries to go back across the net, they bring that player back into the equation when they try to get the puck through to the net. If they move the puck to the right, there should be a lane to the right side of the player. That is the lane they will use to shoot the puck on the net. The player should shoot the puck to the right side of the net (when looking at the net). If players frequently use the lane they have created, the forward will start to understand where the puck is coming to and prepare for it. This idea enables players to get through from the point and have fewer shots blocked.

Heads Up

The idea of shooting and using the lane that teammates have created allows players to get pucks through to the net. To do this effectively, players need to have their head up so that they can scan their options. With the head up, players can see shooting lanes and see what other options are available as far as shooting for sticks. They may have an option to get the puck through to the net. At other times, however, the opposing team may have done a great job of not giving up a lane to the net. In that case, the defensemen may need to shoot the puck wide on purpose. This safe option ensures that the puck is deep in the zone and does not getting blocked and directed back the wrong way. Players can work on shooting off the close post so that the puck comes back out in front. This option works well if the shooter is established in the middle of the ice but does not have a lane to the net. If players are shooting from the boards, they can look to shoot off the back wall so that the puck kicks out off the back boards to the backside post. Players can read that shot and be prepared to jump onto a rebound.

The important point for a defenseman who is shooting is to get their head up when shooting from the point. When players have their head up, they can more easily recognize options. They can see where the lanes to the net are and who is in the lane to block the shot.

With their head up, defensive players can recognize where the shooting lane is and what options are available to get the puck through to the net, whether shooting for a stick or a deflection. The idea of shooting for a stick puts pressure on the defensive team. They must be super aware of all the players around the net and make sure they have the attackers' sticks tied up. When a defensive player with the puck at the blue line can see a lane with a teammate's stick in it, they should shoot it hard enough to get it to the forward. All that player has to do to create a great scoring chance is touch the puck to deflect it on net. This slap pass can be done with a slapshot. Just at the end, right before contact, the shooter adjusts their hands and aims for the stick on the ice. This can be an effective way to get a shot through to the net when someone is blocking the shooting lane.

Shooting in the Air

The other option for a defenseman who has the puck moving across the blue line is to shoot the puck in the air, aiming for a stick to have someone deflect it. The player can do this with a wrist shot, snap shot, or slapshot to give the forward something they can use to get the puck to the net. The defenseman's eyes must be up so that they can see the available lane and put the puck through to the net for the forward to deflect it. When I teach this skill, I tell the defensemen to shoot between the knees and waist of the forward in front of the net. Placing the puck at this height allows the forward to deflect the puck down (more common) or up (less common) and makes it more difficult for the defenders to block. If the puck is on the ice, the defending team may step in front of the pass and move out the other way. If the puck is in the air, a defender must decide to try to get in front of it. If the shooting defenseman can work to get the puck off their stick quickly and with their eyes up to see the available lane, they have a good chance of creating a scoring opportunity.

Communicate With Forwards

One thing that comes up a lot when shooting from the blue line is helping the forwards understand where the shot will be coming to. What does not work is having a forward in front and blasting the puck by their ears, which is a quick way of discouraging teammates from standing in front of the net. The forward has a couple of jobs in front of the net, and the defensemen must be quick in getting the puck through to the net for them. If the forward has to take a beating in front of the net (the other team's net front should be the hardest spot on the ice for the attacking players to occupy), they are less likely to want to go in there if there are no shots coming through from the back end.

If the defensemen can get the puck to the net quickly and trust that the forwards will be there for their shots, the team can start to create a cohesive unit on point shots. By being able to anticipate where the shot is coming from the point, forwards will have a better chance of getting their stick free for deflections. The key is to keep it simple. The shooter uses what they see from the back end and gets the puck through to the net. The player may have to shoot the puck wide because that is the lane that is available, but part of the forward's job is to deflect pucks to the net. Players must work to get on the same page so that the forwards receive something they can use. In practice, defensive players should work on shooting the puck hard from the blue line and using the lane that is available to get the puck through to the front of the net. Forwards need to understand what the defensemen see from the back end.

MOVING IT BACK TO THE FORWARDS

At times in games the defensive player with the puck at the blue line may have neither a shooting option nor an opportunity to pass to their defensive partner. But they may have an option to come back to a forward who is supporting them in the area they just left. Forwards giving this type of support need to support high enough to be a viable option. A defenseman who is sliding on their strong side—that is, a right-handed player on the right side or a left-handed player on the left side—has two options. The defenseman who is sliding can either turn their hips and move it on their forehand back to the forward or move it on their backhand back to the forward if they are confident with their backhand. Some coaches tell players not to make this backhand pass, but I believe it is a pass that must be made. Players must practice it so that they have multiple options. As players reach a higher level, they may need to use a saucer pass, slip the puck under a stick, or hook it under a stick to get it back to the forward. Defensemen must be able to make all the passes.

As soon as the defensive player passes the puck to the forward, they should prepare for a pass to come back to them in the middle of the ice. A common mistake that players make is drifting and going beyond the midline of the ice. If they drift, they cause a pass back to them to be longer and less likely to happen. If they do pass the puck back to the forward, they can stop in the middle and be prepared for a pass back. If the pass is perfect, they can look at one timing it or, if they are on the other side, "getting it, setting it, and shooting it." As the player is becoming a threat in the middle of the ice off the pass back to the forward, the weakside defensive player can become a threat as they start to activate down the back side. The forward then has options with the puck, and any player who has options is much more dangerous. A player who has only one option often sees that option taken away. A player who has multiple passing options can choose which one they like best and make the play.

The pass back to the forward should be relatively short because the player is sliding and pulling someone with them, creating space for the forward to move into. If the player can move the puck back to the forward and then turn and face them, they can become a good shooting option from the blue line.

Moving the puck into the space vacated by a defender can open up a lane for the player who receives the pass or for the defender as the puck comes back to them.

SHOOTING OFF THE BACK WALL

A topic that comes up for defensive players is the concept of shooting a puck wide on purpose. This happens when an opposing defensive player has done a good job of getting in the lane and the player with the puck wants to get it through. The shooter can do this by aiming just wide of the net and shooting the puck hard so that it hits the back wall and kicks back out in front of the net. The shot must be on the ice because if the puck hits the boards in the air, it will die behind the net. By hitting the boards on the ice, the player will get the kick they are looking for to get the puck back to the net front.

SHOOTING FOR DEFLECTIONS

An important area for defensive players as they start to build confidence in their shooting is shooting for deflections. When players start shooting the puck harder and getting shots through from the top, they create more offense. The idea of shooting for deflections can help create a lot of chances and will cause many problems for the defending team.

If the forwards are working to get to the net, the shots will need to come quickly from the top. Players can shoot on the ice or in the air to get pucks to sticks for deflections. Slapshots should be low and hard, and wrist and snap shots can be up between the knees and the waist. Hard slapshots can act as slap passes to be redirected to the net, and wrist and snap shots can be deflected on the net by the forwards. A puck in the air is more difficult to block, and the forwards can deflect it up or down. The forwards can be in front of the net, on the strong side, or on the back side. The shooter has the job of recognizing where the forwards are and using the kind of shot that gets pucks to the net.

If the forward is net front, the player has options to get the puck to them. The defensive player can shoot on the ice or in the air on either their forehand or their backhand. They can even shoot the puck outside the post and let the forward do their job and deflect the puck back to the net. If the defensive player shoots it directly at the forward, meaning it could hit them, the forward can stand in as long as possible and then simply slide their hips out of the way to let the puck through.

If the forward is on the strong side, they could be looking for a deflection with their stick in front of them or possibly a wedge deflection in which their hips are facing the shooter and they are simply angling their blade to try to score. This type of deflection requires the shooter to shoot the puck hard and look to have the forward deflect it.

If the forward is off the back post, they should be positioned inside it where all they have to do is deflect the puck. If they are outside the back post, they need to shoot the puck back to the net, which sometimes works. But to execute a deflection, where they stand is important.

A forward in the higher slot may be looking for a high tip. This positioning means that they have found some ice and are making their stick available. The job of the defenseman is to shoot the puck hard enough that the player deflecting it only has to touch it to get it to the net. The velocity of the shot can be enough to produce a score. This approach works great on a power play in which the puck can come to the net without a direct shot. Many NHL teams use their bumper on the power play as a high-tip option for their defensemen to get pucks to the net.

When the defensemen are shooting for deflections, they have their head up and can get pucks through. Being able to recognize time and space and having a variety of shots and releases are key components to shooting from the point.

I tell players all the time to continue working on their shooting at home, in practice, and in games to build a more consistent shot. Players can choose something specific to work on and challenge themselves to get better at that skill. They can work on simple mechanics like hand position and puck position or more advanced areas like changing the angle of release or shooting off one foot. Whatever they decide to work on, they should shoot pucks as hard as they can. The best way to develop a harder shot is to practice shooting the puck harder.

The goal of this chapter is to help players and coaches understand how they can shoot and how they can generate more offensive chances for their team. Thinking about these topics from a team perspective is useful. Defensive players who have offensive skill are valuable to any team.

STATIONARY SHOOTING

Level of Difficulty

Easy

Players

Any number of defensive players working on shooting from the blue line

Objectives

To work on shooting the puck harder and with more control

Setup

Players work on shooting individually from the blue line with a pile of pucks in front of them.

Procedure

Players can work on their wrist shot or snap shot by loading the puck and moving it forward to the net. Their feet are turned sideways. Beginners can shoot to the side of the pucks. More advanced players can shoot over the pucks. As they get stronger and more skilled, they can add one stickhandle to push the puck or one stickhandle to pull the puck. As they become more skilled after working on changing the angle, they can add a fake and shoot off the fake.

Coaching Tips

- This drill can be done from different angles and different distances from the net. Beginners can be at the top of the circle so that they have a chance to get the puck to the net in the air.
- Stronger players can move all the way to the blue line and shoot from there.
- Beginning players do not need to shoot from the blue line. They can move closer to net to build confidence.
- One thing to add to this drill is to shoot with the head up so that the player can see the opponents looking to block the shot.

Variations

- Wrist shot
- Snap shot
- One stickhandle to push the puck away
- One stickhandle to pull the puck in
- Forehand fake and shoot
- Pull the puck back in, forehand fake, and shoot

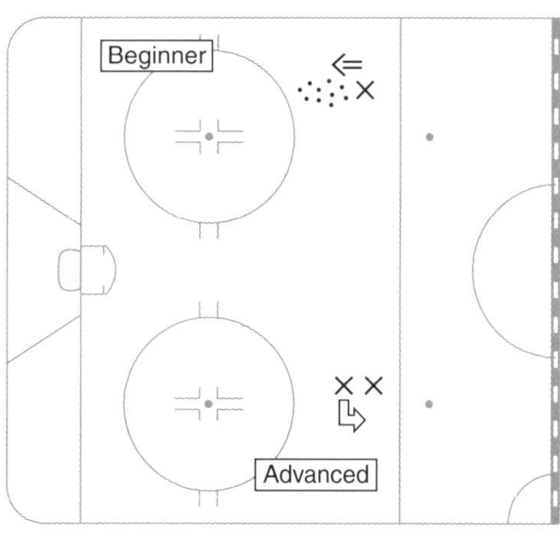

USE THE LANE YOU CREATE

Level of Difficulty

Easy

Players

Three players per group

Objectives

To work on getting the head up and shooting the puck past a shot blocker

Setup

One player is at the blue line with pucks, one player is in the high slot as a stationary shot blocker, and one player is at the net as a player looking to deflect pucks.

Procedure

The player with pucks slides one way or the other and looks to get pucks through to the net past the player who is stationary in the slot as a shot blocker. The player can start by sliding to their forehand side and shooting to that side of the net. The player who is in front of the net can anticipate the puck coming to that side and get ready to deflect it. The shooter can then grab a puck and slide the other way to shoot to the other side of the net. The goal is to get pucks through without hitting the player in the high slot. Players can repeat the pattern for four to six shots on goal.

Coaching Tips

- I did this drill with Team Canada Women before they played in the World Championship one year, and many of them realized that they do not shoot with their eyes up. The shot may be going wide of the net, but the player in front can bring it back to the goal.
- The job of the shooter is to get the puck through from the blue line by not getting it blocked.
- Players should continue to face the net after they shoot and not turn into the neutral zone.

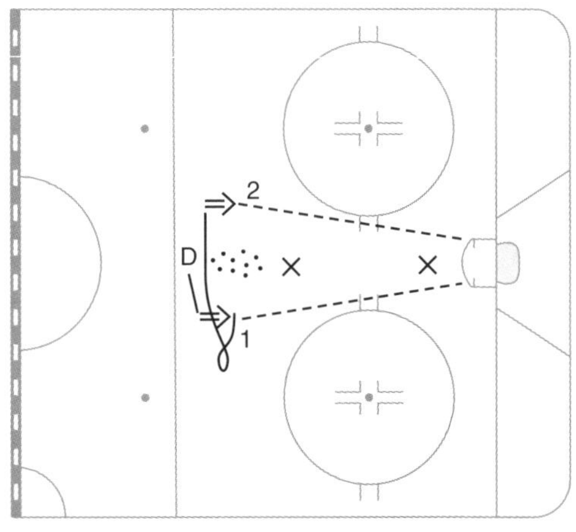

Variations

- With a small group, the net can be placed in the middle of the ice where it is normally set up.
- With a big group of players, three lanes (with three nets) to the net can be set up because the focus of the drill is shooting with the eyes up.

SHOOTING PARTNER WORK

Level of Difficulty

Moderate

Players

Two players for this passing and shooting sequence

Objectives

To work together with a partner and move the puck properly and in good spots for them

Setup

A coach has pucks at the half wall, and the line is at the blue line. Two players are ready and waiting—one at the blue line and one in the middle of the ice.

Procedure

A coach spots pucks up to the strongside defender who is at the corner where the blue line meets the wall. The first puck is collected and then with one step to the middle, the shot comes to the net. The second puck is moved from one defender to the other for a shot. The player who shoots slides into new ice. The third puck is moved player to player, and the player who receives the pass slides and works to turn the corner. The player who started the passing sequence slides into the middle to support. The player with the puck can add a fake shot and then pass back to the middle of the ice to the waiting partner. The player who started gets the last shot in this rep. As the first player moves off the wall to replace the player in the middle, a new player slides into the blue line.

Coaching Tips

- If a goalie participates, they should have a chance on every shot.
- With no goalie, this drill can go quickly because two shots can be coming at the same time.

Variations

- Players can work on one timers if the pass is good and the receiver is on the correct side.
- A fourth shot can be added by having the backside player activate down the backside lane. A passer can be added on the goal line to give them a pass across to the activating player.
- A third player can be added to the drill to take away the goalie's eyes and make them look around for the puck.

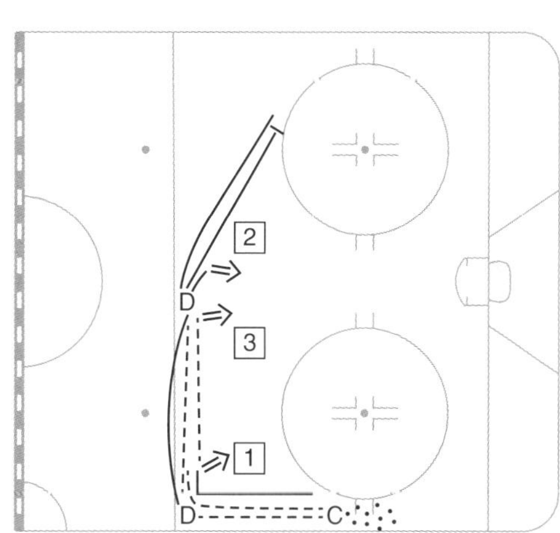

SHOOTING FROM THE OFFENSIVE-ZONE BLUE LINE WITH ACTIVATION

Level of Difficulty

Moderate

Players

One to six players

Objectives

To work on getting the head up and making plays by shooting for deflections

Setup

One player is in the high slot, and one player is on the strong side at the blue line. The coach has pucks at the top of the circle.

Procedure

This is a three-shot drill for the player at the blue line. A coach spots the pucks. Puck 1 is placed so that the player can shoot right away. The pass can be an indirect pass off the boards so that the player must collect the puck and look to shoot. Puck 2 is a hard shot on the ice to give the player in the high slot a chance to deflect it. Puck 3 is an activation into the zone from the player at the blue line. They can slide in down the wall where the coach steps off the wall and leaves a puck for them. The player in the slot can either pop out or go to the net. The active player must recognize where they are and make a pass to them. After the player shoots and makes plays, they rotate to become the player in front of the net.

Coaching Tip

- This drill encourages defensemen to be active in the offensive zone by jumping down the wall and teaches them to get their eyes up to find a supporting player.

Variation

- Pucks 1 and 2 can be changed by the player in the high slot with their stick up or down. If their stick is down, they want a shot pass for a deflection. If their stick is up, the shot should be coming through. This signaling encourages the player on the blue line to get their eyes up.

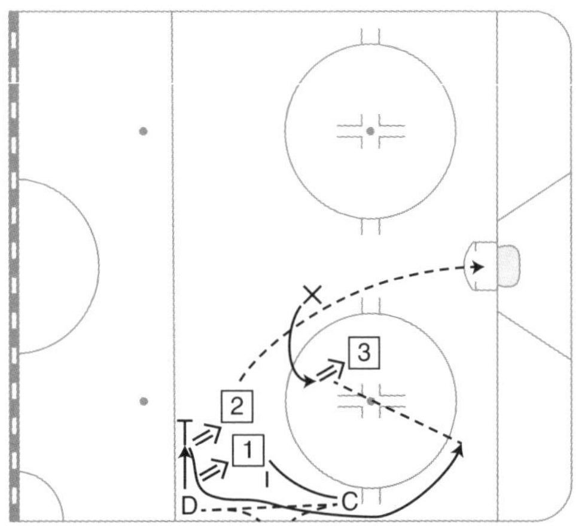

DIVING WITH PUCK MOVEMENT

Level of Difficulty

Hard

Players

Two to three players

Objectives

To work on being an active defensive player by diving down the middle and filtering through to the back side

Setup

A coach has pucks on the half wall, and two players are at the offensive blue line.

Procedure

This is a two-shot drill in which passing must be on and support must be in good spots. The strongside player jumps into the middle of the ice and receives a pass from the coach for the first shot. With the player diving in, the offside player moves into the middle, supporting over the top of them. The coach passes to the player at the blue line, while the diving player moves out to the other side. The player who dove down the middle finds available ice on the back side, and the player with the puck looks to pass for a one timer or quick shot. The rotation is to have the player who passed dive down the middle and to have a new player start in the middle of the ice and support over the top.

Coaching Tips

- This drill helps create movement in the offensive zone and quick-strike offensive chances.
- The passes must be good, and the player who dives in must get high enough to support the puck with a clean passing lane.
- To execute this advanced play, players should be able to one time the puck.

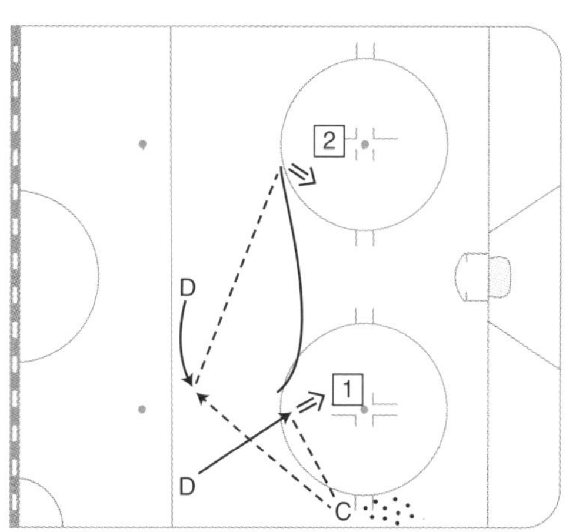

Variation

- The player at the top can fake a pass to a one timer and wrist a couple of shots in. The variety of shots that can come from this play makes it more effective because space will be created.

BACKDOOR ACTIVATION

Level of Difficulty

Moderate

Players

A maximum of four players (or one or two coaches)

Objectives

To work on short one timers and quick release shots from the back side

Setup

This drill can go quickly because both players have pucks at the blue line with a passing player down low on the goal line.

Procedure

One player starts with a puck and passes down to the goal line. As that is happening, the backside player starts to move and comes down the backside seam. They should try to position their body so that their stick is lined up on an imaginary line between the dot and the post. The passing player passes the puck to the back side, where the activating player tries to shoot it quickly. If they can one time it, they should try to hit it quickly. The pass should be hard but might also be a saucer pass to avoid the obstacles that come up in games. For players on their one-timer side, the shot can be a short one timer, meaning that players do not bring their stick up off the ice but instead simply push into the puck to shoot it. If players are on their opposite side, they can simply stop the puck and release it to the net.

If six players are available, they can work with two in each line at the blue line and two down low. The passers can pass 10 to 12 pucks before rotating back into line to keep the drill moving.

Coaching Tips

- Passing to a shooter is a tough skill to master. Players work on passing the puck hard, and shooters work on releasing the puck quickly.
- The goal of this drill is to make the goalie move post to post, so players should shoot to a spot that is harder for the goalie to save.

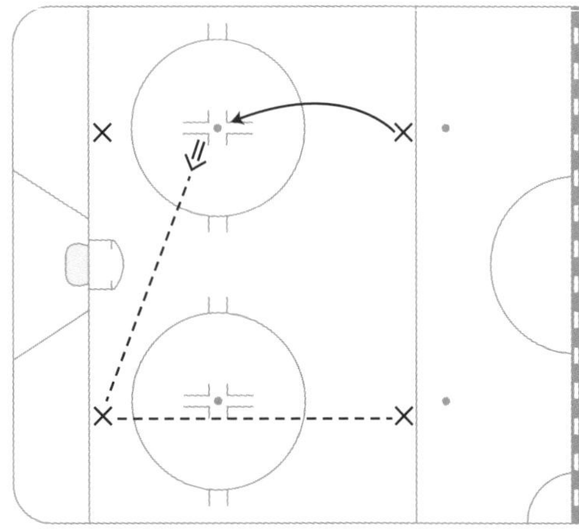

Variation

- The puck can be moved down to the goal line, and the passer skates the puck behind the net. The active player moves into the play and looks to receive the pass at the dot. This shot can be effective in a game because the player can shoot the puck really hard.

SHOOTING WITH A PURPOSE

Level of Difficulty

Moderate

Players

Two to three players

Objectives

To work on receiving a pass and shooting with the head up to recognize the placement of the stick of the player in front of the net

Setup

A coach (or player) has pucks at the corner of the blue line in the offensive zone. One player is in the middle of the blue line, and one is in front of the net.

Procedure

The intention of the drill is to have the player who is shooting recognize the location of the stick of the player in front of the net. The coach (or player) starts the drill with a defender-to-defender pass. The player who receives the pass looks to shoot. The player in front can pick from one of four spots with their stick—on the ice on their forehand, on the ice on their backhand, in the air on their forehand, or in the air on their backhand. The goal is to have the shooter recognize where the stick is and put the puck into that area. If the stick is on the ice on either side, the shooter can take a slapshot (slap pass). If the stick is in the air, the shooter can wrist (or snap) the puck to the net. The shooter can take five or six shots for one rep and then switch and move to the net.

Coaching Tips

- The shooter must get their head up quickly before shooting.
- The shooter can also slide one way away from the puck or attack the puck to make it more difficult for the player who will be blocking their shot in a game.

Variation

- Passers can be on either side, and passes can alternate coming into the middle to the shooter.

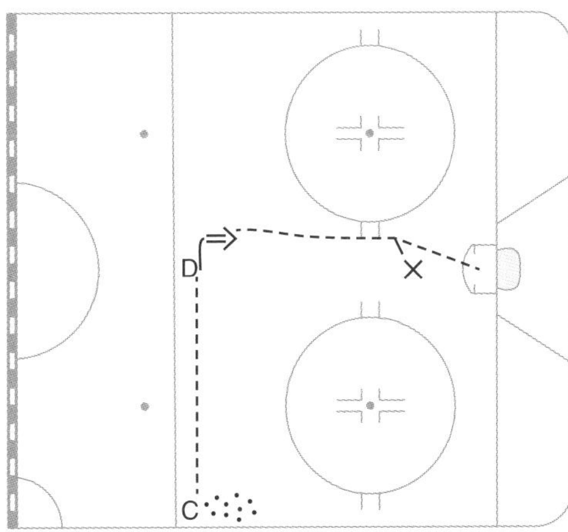

SHOOTING WITH CONTROL

Level of Difficulty

Moderate

Players

One to three players shooting with no goalie

Objectives

To control the hips after the shot and face the net

Setup

Pucks are placed in a pile at the blue line with two cones (or tires) in front of them. The player starts behind the cones at the blue line facing the net.

Procedure

The player shooting grabs a puck and moves to the forehand side to shoot. After shooting, the player faces the net and moves back to grab a second puck sliding the other way. After taking that shot, the player repeats the drill once or twice, grabbing a new puck before each shot.

Coaching Tips

- Players can think about using the lane they have created to emphasize where their shots are going into the net.
- Players may also shoot the puck wide of the net to have a forward deflect it back to the net.
- Players should focus on completing their weight transfer by setting their feet and facing the net after their shot.
- A common error is turning into the neutral zone after shooting.

Variations

- To accommodate multiple players, the drill can be done with stations closer to the wall on each side.
- The players waiting to shoot can be in a line in the middle of the ice and give passes to the shooter.
- Another defensive player or forward can be in position in front of the net to work on deflecting pucks on the shot. This drill progresses into Use the Lane You Create with a player in the high slot and a player in front of the net.

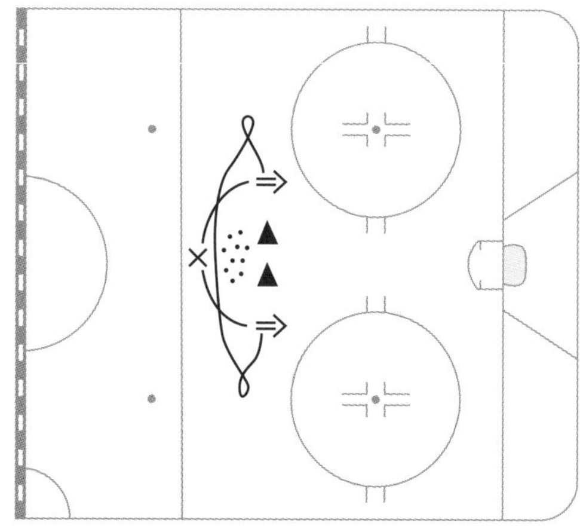

D THREE SHOT

Level of Difficulty

Moderate

Players

Three players and a coach passing

Objectives

To work on using a partner at the blue line with defender-to-defender passes

Setup

Players are positioned at the blue line. One is at the wall, and one is in the middle of the ice. A coach has pucks at the top of the circle, and another player is down low on the goal line.

Procedure

The coach starts with the puck and passes it up the boards to the player at the wall. The player passes it across to their partner, who slides out wider for a shot. The board-side player comes back to the wall and receives a second pass from the coach. Again, the player moves the puck to their partner. This time the player from the middle of the ice who is sliding out moves the puck back to the starting player, who is now in the middle of the ice for a shot. The coach then passes a puck down to the goal line, and that player passes across the crease to the backside player, who is activating down the back side.

Coaching Tips

- This drill works on timing and spacing. The players must move together and support each other.
- The last pass across the crease should come to a player who is moving into that space. When they shoot, their stick should be on an imaginary line between the dot and the post.
- A common error occurs when players come back into the slot, which will be occupied in games.

Variations

- Players can shoot with wrist shots, slapshots, and one timers. If they are one timing the puck, they can add short one timers on the last shot as they get closer to the net.
- The player who is down low can skate the puck around the net and make a pass up to the dot to simulate a different game situation.

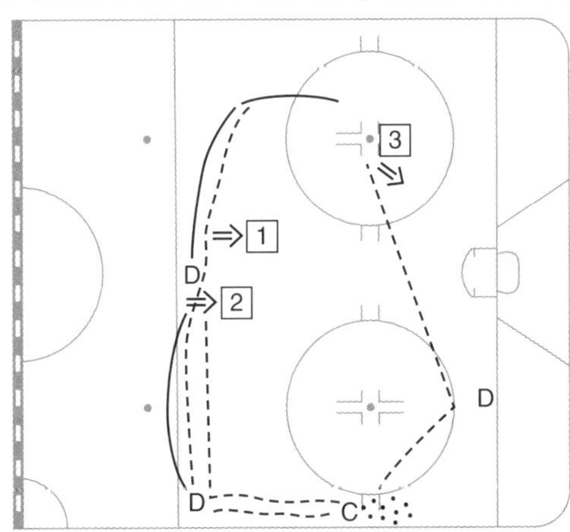

SHOOTING FOR STICKS—DECISION MAKING

Level of Difficulty

Hard

Players

One or several players working with a coach

Objectives

To challenge players to get their eyes up before they shoot to recognize what is in front of them

Setup

Pucks are placed in line with the dot and just inside the blue line. A player waits at the blue line with the pucks. A coach (or player) waits at the offensive-zone dot in the circle.

Procedure

The player at the blue line passes a puck down to the coach at the dot and then gets a pass back on the outside of the pucks. They move to the middle and look to see the coach, who has turned to the net. The coach has their stick either up or down. If their stick is up, they are not available, so the player shoots to the net. If their stick is down, the player shoots for a shot-pass deflection. The player who is shooting can shoot four or five shots, making a decision on each one. Each shot starts with a pass down and a pass back up.

Coaching Tips

- This drill forces the player to get their head up before they shoot.
- The coach can stay out of the way if their stick is up to allow the player to shoot the puck hard without worrying about hitting the coach.
- If the player is sending a slap pass to the net, they can shoot the puck as hard as they can on the ice.

Variation

- A player can replace the coach, make passes, and roll to the net.

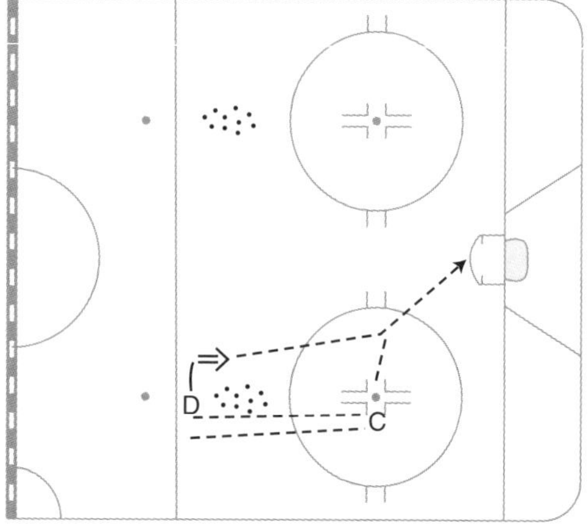

CHAPTER 4

Stick Position

Skating may be the most important skill for defensemen, but stick position comes close. Players should learn to use a good stick position when they are learning to work on edges, when they are learning to work on their forward and backward stride, as well as when they are learning to play 1 vs 1 or in the defensive zone. A good stick position makes a player appear bigger. A player who has the stick in the correct lane will force opponents to work around them and compel them to make tougher decisions. A good stick will start the checking angle and steer opponents into an area of the ice where they must make plays they do not want to make. Players can learn about all these areas in practice long before they get into games.

When players work on their stick position, they begin to take their game to another level. Having their stick is in the correct lane allows players to break up plays. Whether players are working in their defensive zone in tight spaces or in the neutral zone where more space is available, they need to learn where their stick should be to make the situation easier on themselves and their teammates.

SETTING UP OTHERS FOR SUCCESS

Take a forward on a neutral-zone forecheck in a 1-2-2 system as an example. Their job is to angle and steer the opposing defensemen one way. Some teams take away the defender-to-defender pass and steer the puck up the wall. Others allow the defender-to-defender pass and then force the puck up the wall, not allowing another defender-to-defender pass back to the other side of the ice. This will depend on how close they are to attacking and where the puck is on the ice. If the forward can angle with their stick on the ice, they can take away the option and force the player to go to spot where they want them to go. As this is happening, the other four players (including the two defensemen) can start to slide over or anticipate the puck coming up one side of the ice or the other. If that same forward tries to angle without their stick on the ice or in the correct lane, the puck can be moved through them or around them without fear of being turned over.

This starting angle for the forwards in the neutral zone is a big part of a team's chances of recovering the puck from the neutral zone. When a player starts to understand how important their stick is to what happens in this type of play, they will start to play at another level and help their team have more success in turning pucks over. When the defensemen can anticipate and read where the puck is going, their gap can be tighter and they can close off the space quicker. When the forward uses a good angle and a good stick and the players behind them read and adjust their positioning, a great neutral-zone forecheck is possible.

ANGLING TO DENY SPACE

When players get good at angling, they can come from a little bit behind the attacking player. The reason they come from behind is to deny the option to cut back into the middle of the ice. They continue to force them to eliminate space. When players eliminate space, they are better able to predict where the puck will go next. They should start their angle with their stick and force the player with their feet through their skating. Players can use their skating to come at an opponent and steer them into a space that will eventually run them out of room. Players should not come straight at an opponent. Instead they should come underneath them and skate beside them, focusing on their body position against them.

A good angle allows a player to go to hip to hip and stick to puck. Having their body going hip to hip will help a player control where the opponent goes, and having their stick to the puck makes it harder for the opponent to pass the puck through their stick. With their stick to the puck, the player can deflect the pass or eliminate passes to the middle of the ice. This defensive body position allows the player who is angling the puck carrier to continue to eliminate space and keep their stick in a position close to the puck. Players can imagine the difficulty of stopping an opponent from passing the puck past them if they had no stick and could use only their body. If the body is in the correct spot but the stick is in the wrong spot, the offensive player has options to move the puck. If the defensive player has both their stick and their body in the correct spot, the offensive player has limited options or must work around the defender's stick. By taking away the offensive player's options, the defensive player can force them into choosing a less desirable play. They may chip the puck forward or try to stop up, but either way the angler and the players who are supporting them are prepared to get to the puck.

By forcing an opponent with the puck to work around the stick, the defender requires them to make a tougher decision with the puck. The puck carrier must look for available space to make a pass or advance the puck. Do they pass it around the defender's stick in front of their body? Is the passing lane better between the defender's stick and feet? Or is the saucer pass over the defender's stick the best option to get the puck to another offensive player? The defender's stick position to the puck is what forces the offensive player to make these decisions. The offensive player's job is much harder when the defensive player has their stick to the puck and is working to take away time and space.

COMMON ERROR

An error I often see at a high level is players pushing all the time with two hands on their stick on the puck carrier's back, which allows the offensive player time and space when they have the puck. I saw the Kelowna Rockets work on this years ago. They had a player with the puck working against a defensive player in the corner. The defensive player was required to hold a puck, which prevented them from going to two hands on their stick. The player had to work with one hand on their stick and go stick to puck while pushing with their free hand (while holding a puck). I have used this coaching method from time to time if I notice that a player is having trouble in the defensive zone with their checking or stick position. When players learn when to go to one hand with good stick position and then change to two hands to battle for pucks or make a play, they become more effective defensive players.

DENYING PASSING OPTIONS

Moving down into the defensive zone, forwards can take away passing lanes to the offensive defensemen by using their stick. The way that they are facing and the placement of their stick either allows or takes away passing options. The same applies for the defensemen who are either in front of the net or in the strongside corner where the puck is. The stick position is important in taking away options for the puck carrier or denying passing options. The strongside defenseman can have their stick in one hand and on the ice to make themselves appear bigger and take up more space. The net-front defender can have one hand on their stick to take up more ice and work to deny passing lanes. Each player can have one hand on their stick and their stick on the ice until they need to battle with two hands on their stick.

TIGHT-SPACE STICK POSITION

Even in the tight spaces in the corner in the defensive zone, defensive players can think about stick position and what their angles will allow. A good angle will not allow the offensive player many options. They can keep skating and eventually be eliminated to the boards. If they try to make a pass, they will have to make a pass where the defender wants the puck to go, and other defensive players are often able to anticipate where the puck will go. The defensive player who uses a poor angle allows the offensive player multiple options. They can continue to skate and move into available ice, or they can cut back against the defender's angle into more open ice. The offensive player can also make a play because the defender is likely are not close enough with their angle to steer the offensive player where the defender wants them to go. If the defender's angle is correct and their stick is in the correct lane, the offensive player who chooses to cut back should run right into the defender. If hitting is allowed (at the older ages), the defender will get a good hit by not doing anything except being in the right spot.

One thing that the defensive player should think about when playing in a tight space is always being able to see the offensive player. If the offensive player cuts back and tries to work against the defender, they should stop (or turn) and keep their eyes on the offensive player. A common error in defensive-zone coverage is turning the wrong way against a cut back. The goal is to continue to work to take away space when an opponent cuts back. As they cut back, the defender turns and keeps pushing toward their hips. They continue to use the stick to eliminate passing lanes and deny an easy lane to the net. Players often have trouble with cut backs and stick position because they do not lead with their stick. They let their stick trail behind them or bring it over the top of their head. This action as the stick recovers to get back into position is called the helicopter. Players can think about sliding their hand back and keeping their stick to the ice to bring it back out in front of them. With young players, I tell them that their stick is like a magnet to the ice and that they should not let it come up in the air. This idea helps them understand that their stick is useful all the time.

KNOCKING DOWN THE PUCK

Players can work on having a good stick in many ways. Checking is one way, deflecting passes and breaking up plays is another, and knocking pucks out of the air is perhaps the most fun way to work on stick position. Think about a 2 vs 1 rush against a defensive player. If that player does their job correctly, no passing lane should be available through them to get the puck from the puck carrier to the player on the back side. The only passing option (unless they move the puck early) will be a saucer pass over the stick. If the defensive player is confident in their abilities, they should be able to knock the puck down and get a piece of it so that it does not land flat for the player receiving the pass. This kind of play can be important in the outcome of a game. The action happens quickly and is largely a reaction play, but the defender who can knock the pass out of the air with their stick eliminates a scoring chance.

Players can work to improve their eye-hand coordination so that they are better at it come game time. This type of play can happen in various situations:

- In the defensive zone from below the goal line to the slot
- On the rush and a 2 vs 1 against the defender
- In the neutral zone playing against the rush
- In the offensive zone knocking down a clearing

Working to practice each scenario can come in handy come game time. Coaches can spend time with defensive players in their splits and give them specific things to think about. For example, a saucer pass can be attempted through the defensive players, who work to knock the puck down.

PRACTICE METHODS FOR STICK POSITION

The following steps outline the ways to work on stick position during any practice. Consider using this practice method for skill development:

- Stationary
- Add motion
- Add speed
- Add pressure
- Add game-simulated drills

By following this outline, coaches can teach players the skill of using a good stick. These options can be added to drills in practice. Defensive players should be challenged to think about using their stick to break up plays and deflect passes.

Stationary

The progression should begin with stationary drills. Players get into a group of three and pass back and forth. The only difference is that the two outside players try to saucer pass the puck to each other while the third player in the middle tries to knock it down. The player in the middle can use a small motion with their wrists to try to get a piece of the puck. Many young players (or players who are not confident) swing at the puck with their stick and occasionally hit the odd one, but they miss many more. Players who track the puck with their eyes to the end of their stick and make a small motion with their wrists will have more success in knocking pucks down.

Motion

After players work on stationary skills, movement can be added. A good approach is to do this around the blue line by having a player try a saucer pass from just inside the dot line to the outside lane. The defensive player skates backward close to the dot lane and works to break up the pass as it comes through. The passer can throw a saucer pass or a hard regular pass (on the ice) to keep the defensive player reacting to the pass and not knowing what is coming next. This drill is typically done a little slower when players are working on the skill.

Speed

A similar drill can challenge players to move a little faster by adding more speed. This can come up in full-ice drills with pace and can be a regular part of practice. Players should react to what happens based on where the puck carrier is. Players should have to work at game pace on their stick position and knocking down pucks that are coming faster. This can be done in the same way, or players can attack on a 2 vs 1 with players making a pass across the slot. The goal is to have the defensive player break up passes that come across the slot through their stick position.

Pressure

Pressure can be added to drills to require players to make plays quicker. Players should be challenged to get every puck with their stick. They should work to prevent shots on goal and to have their stick always in the correct position. Coaches could say, "Do not let pucks gets through" or "Get a piece of every puck" to players as they are working on this skill. Adding a game to the practice can be a fun way to add pressure. A fun game is to have players skate down the wall (in the neutral zone) and to have a coach try to saucer pass the puck from the bottom of the circle to the boards (aiming for the red line). If the players can stop the puck, they get a point. If the coach can saucer pass it past them to boards, the coach gets a point. If the players deflect the pass and it hits the wall, both the coach and the players get a point. The game is typically up to 10. To make the game more challenging, the coach can tell the players if they get to 10 they win, but if the coach gets to 5 the coach wins. Players then must make a play on every puck that the coach saucer passes for them.

Game-Simulated Drills

The players have now worked on the skill and are ready to use it in drills. Coaches should be vocal with players and let them know whether they are using the proper stick position to break up a play. If a puck gets past them, they should hear that they could have used that skill with their stick. Players should be challenged to react to game situations. Coaches can give players different options on the rush, out of the corners, and from below the goal line. The defenders should be challenged to react to where the puck is and where the opposing players are and then make plays by deflecting pucks to deny scoring chances.

An important aspect of stick position on the defensive side of the puck is protecting the triangle. Offensive players are always looking to expose the space between the defender's stick and their toes by slipping pucks through. If the defensive player can protect their triangle, they can deny its use as a passing option. They can do this by keeping their stick close to their hip and being able to extend their hand. Players often skate with their stick extended and give the puck carrier the option to slip the puck in front of their toes where it is hard to get to. If the defensive player can keep their hand close to their hip, they make that space a little smaller. This type of play is often seen on 2 vs 1 against the defender when offensive players are looking for passing lanes through the defender. Players should learn to take away options

1. in front of them with a good stick,
2. between their toes and their stick, and
3. over their stick with a saucer pass.

When a player can take away the passing options through them (or over them) with a good stick, they become a better defenseman.

Players who have a good stick can frustrate opposing teams. Few quality scoring chances will occur when pucks are always deflected, knocked down, or picked off. When players work in practice to have a consistently good stick and understand how their stick can influence the play, they will become better defensive players in games.

Drills to improve stick position are challenging for players at first because many will have never worked on this skill in detail. They may have been told to have a good stick or they will hear about having a good stick on TV or from their coaches, but many will not understand what that means until it is explained to them. With young players, coaches should start slow and introduce the idea of where their stick should be. As players get older, they can be challenged to do things quickly and work to take away space. Many NHL players I have worked with comment about how good opposing players are with their sticks, especially the defensemen.

STATIONARY POKE CHECKS

Level of Difficulty

Easy

Players

Two players working together

Objectives

To work to have the defensive player use an active stick to poke pucks off an attacker

Setup

Partners set up in the neutral zone. One player has a puck, and the other does not. The player with the puck faces their partner and stickhandles in front of them. Extra pucks can be behind each group of players.

Procedure

On the coach's whistle, the drill starts. One player stickhandles, and the other player works to poke the puck off their stick. The player who is poke checking can extend their stick and then bring it back, or they can track the puck to keep their stick in the way. If the puck goes too far away, players turn around, grab a new puck, and keep going. On the next whistle, the players switch roles.

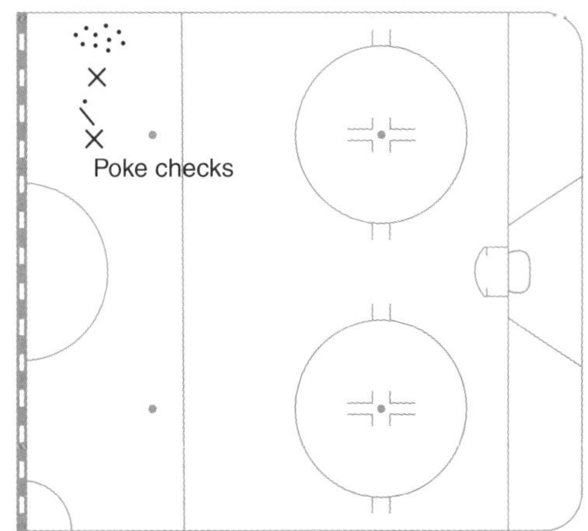

Coaching Tip

- The defensive player in this drill works to keep their eyes on the attacking player and their stick in front of their body.

Variations

- Motion can be added to the drill to have a small area where players can move around.
- The offensive player can turn their back and work to protect the puck, while the defensive player works to go stick to puck.

NEUTRAL-ZONE STICK WORK

Level of Difficulty

Easy

Players

A group of three players or two players and a coach

Objectives

To work on using the stick to break up plays across the slot

Setup

One player is net front as a defensive player, and one player is on each side of the net. Players should be almost in a line with the defensive player one step back and their stick in the lane between the two offensive players.

Procedure

One player starts the drill and works to pass the puck to their teammate. The defensive player works to poke the puck away. The first player passes four to six pucks, and then the other player passes four to six pucks. The goal for the defensive player in the middle is to get a piece of every puck. Players do both sides and then switch around.

This drill works well as a station or after practice when other players are working in the end zones.

Coaching Tip

- Players should always remain balanced because the only way a puck should get through is if they are off balance and do not have their stick positioned correctly.

Variations

- Motion can be added, and players can attack the net.
- Saucer passes can be added so that the defensive player can work on knocking pucks out of the air.

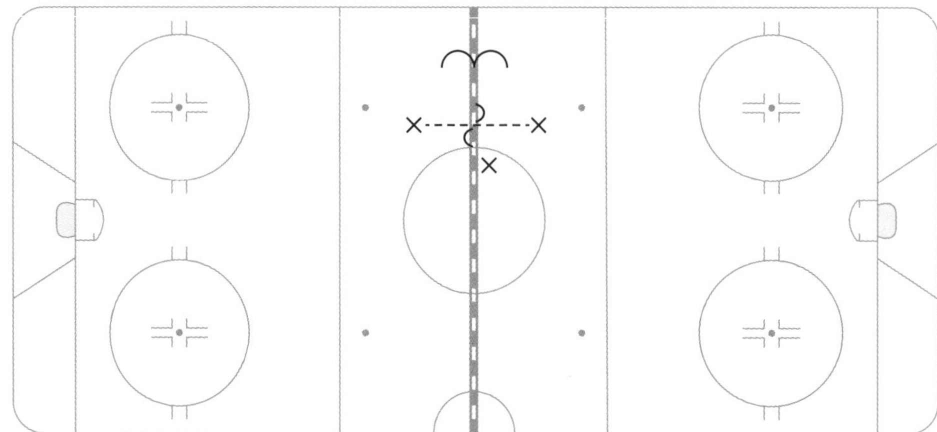

STICK POSITION AROUND THE CIRCLE

Level of Difficulty

Easy

Players

Two players working together

Objectives

To have players always move with their stick in front of them

Setup

Two players set up on the outside hashmarks.

Procedure

The players move across the circle with their sticks touching. They pivot backward, push away from each other around the top or bottom of the circle, and then meet up again at the hashmarks. They move across the hashmarks with their sticks touching again. Players go three or four times around the circle. They should go both ways before moving on to the next drill in practice.

Coaching Tip

- Players should think about always keeping their sticks in front of their hips and on the ice. This drill will help them go stick to puck more frequently.

Variation

- One player can carry the puck while the other player keeps their stick to the puck. They can pass it as they move around the circle, so that the other player has the puck the next time around.

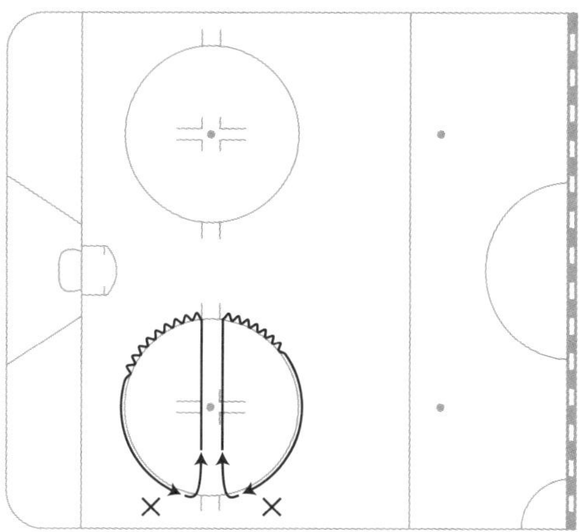

DEFENSIVE STICK WORK TO PUCK

Level of Difficulty

Moderate

Players

One player at a time working on stick position

Objectives

To work on deflecting pucks with good stick position and going stick to puck in the corner

Setup

Pucks are placed behind the net with the coaches. Three cones (or tires) are placed up the wall toward the hash marks. A puck can be placed at each cone.

Procedure

One player starts in front of the net with their stick on the ice. The coach passes a puck, and the player deflects it away. The player then heads to the corner and the first cone, going stick to puck and stopping. They then move to the next cone, go stick to puck, and stop. They go one more time up the wall to the next cone and go stick to puck. The player then rotates with their stick on the ice (not above their head) and skates back to the front of the net. The coach passes three more pucks to the net front, which they must deflect away.

Coaching Tips

- The footwork in this drill is important. As players improve at the drill, they will find they do not need to cross over much to move.
- The stick should always be in a good position in this drill.

Variations

- Saucer passes can be added, and the player in front should knock the puck down to gain control of the pass.
- This drill can be done on both sides if six players are participating because there is no shooting.

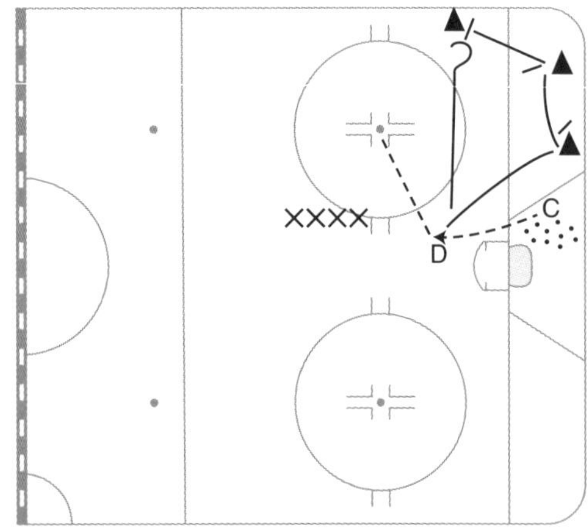

DEFENSIVE BLUE LINE STICK WORK

Level of Difficulty

Easy

Players

Any number of players from one to six

Objectives

To work on not allowing pucks through from the outside to the inside

Setup

Pucks are set up outside the blue line, and a coach and a player are set up just inside the blue line on the dot line. Another player can be inside the blue line and inside the first player.

Procedure

The coach tries to pass pucks under the stick from the outside to the inside, while the player tries to poke it away. The coach can go slowly at first and then speed up to make the player react quicker. The coach throws 8 to 10 passes before players rotate.

Coaching Tips

- Players should relax their hands and leave room to extend their stick.
- They should not play with their stick fully extended.

Variations

- The coach can add saucer passes that the player must knock down or deflect.
- Motion can be added to have the player backing up, with the support moving as well. The player must get up the ice after each puck, so this variation is a little harder than standing still.

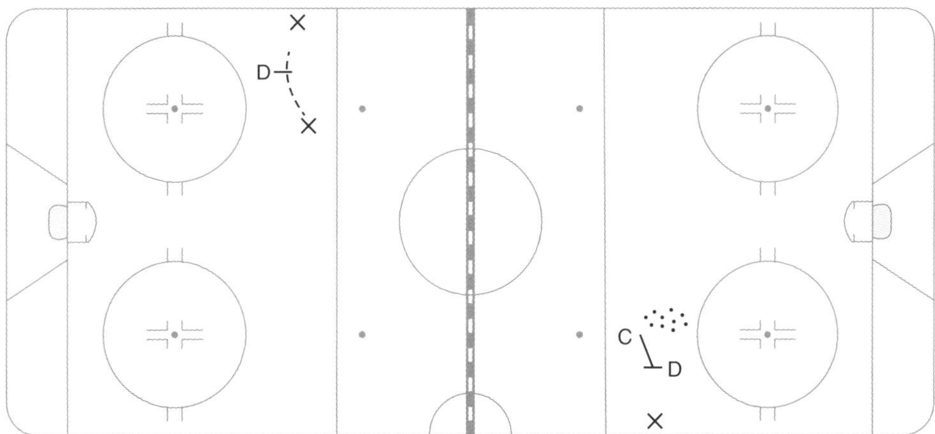

KNOCK IT DOWN

Level of Difficulty

Moderate

Players

Any number of players from one to six

Objectives

To work on eye-hand coordination and knocking pucks down moving backward

Setup

Use groups of equal numbers. With four players, use two groups of two players. With six players, use two groups of three players. The groups start on the wall and can move with lines on either side of them. Between the blue line and red line is a good example of the space that players need. Another group can be on the other side between the red line and blue line. With a large group, players can be spaced out down the ice with lines on each side of them. The lines keep players from running into each other.

Procedure

The player in the drill moves backward away from their partner. Their partner tries to saucer pass the puck past them on their forehand side. The defender who is moving in the drill knocks the puck down and then passes it back to their partner. The player comes up again, pivots backward, and does the same thing on their backhand side.

Coaching Tip

- This drill is tough, so players will miss the puck. Make sure that each group has multiple pucks with the passer so that they do not run out.

Variations

- The player can add a pass to a partner, get the pass back, and then throw the saucer pass to them.
- Players can go multiple times on each side before rotating out. Going twice on each side is a good number of reps before switching out.
- The player can pass the puck back to the player in line with their eyes on their partner the whole time (if the puck stays in front of them), or they can escape spin away from them if the knocked-down puck gets behind their hips. The defender works on both knocking down pucks and quickly recognizing where the puck goes.

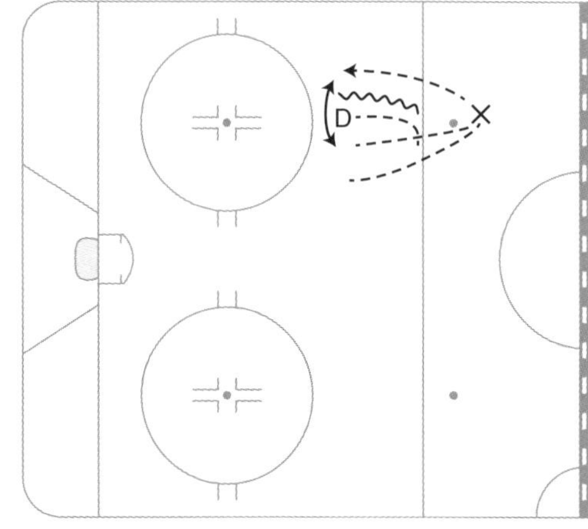

CHAPTER 5

Puck Retrievals

Puck retrieval should be one of the starting pieces to any programs or sessions that coaches use to develop defensemen. A player who can retrieve a puck in their own corner under pressure and make a play will help their team spend less time in their own zone and move the puck out of the zone more cleanly. Whatever option the player has when going back in the corner to get the puck, they can do some things every time that will help them move the puck on the first touch and limit the amount of stickhandling they have to do.

Doing fewer stickhandles allows the player to move the puck faster by either skating the puck, passing the puck, chipping the puck out into the neutral zone, rimming the puck (putting the puck around the boards), or eating the puck and keeping it on the wall. One of the first things to work on with players as they start going back for pucks in the corner is the footwork to get back to the puck quickly. A common error that players make is not really working quickly back to the puck. The quicker they can get back to the puck, the more time they will have to make the next play. As they turn, they must keep moving their feet. If they take three or four good strides forward to the puck and work to turn so that they can see it, they are starting themselves off on a good path.

BE SPATIALLY AWARE

Many coaches tell their defensemen that they need to shoulder check as they are going back for the puck. I take this one step further and work with defensemen to improve their spatial awareness and understanding of their surroundings. I learned this idea from Paul Boutalier, an outstanding coach who I met with the U17 Team Canada program. He talked about how quickly players could count to three. He referred to the time that players were not involved in the play as shift downtime and encouraged them to always be taking pictures and understanding where the other team's three forwards were. I found this information helpful when I worked with defensemen. I encouraged players to scan the ice before they turned and to take in information as they were facing up the ice. The idea of taking in information helped the defensemen I was working with. Most of them just turned and chased the puck.

When I got players to see things before they turned, they understood earlier where the pressure would be coming at them. As they were turning and going back for the puck, their shoulder check was now to confirm what they already knew. When players look at the ice before they turn, count to three to identify the forwards as Paul suggested, and then turn and keep that picture in mind, they get an idea of the options they will have on their recovery of the puck.

SHOULDER CHECKS

Every player should work on the concept of the shoulder check. Gaining spatial awareness and understanding options based on pressure is something that defensemen in particular need to practice. Turning and looking over the shoulder as they are skating is a hard skill for players to learn. Most players quickly turn their head, and some will be able to take in information as they do this. Some players turn their head and do not see anything, whereas others can see players coming behind them. Players can work on this skill in practice by going back to the boards with someone behind them, chasing them from one side or the other. Players can learn to ***feel*** pressure and ***see*** pressure.

Feeling pressure means understanding when pressure is on them and knowing what side of the body pressure is coming from.

Seeing pressure means making visual confirmation that a player is coming and recognizing what side of the ice the pressure is coming from. As players start to understand what pressure feels like, they will be able to avoid it better. As they start to understand what pressure looks like, they will no longer just turn their head for the sake of turning their head—they will turn their head and look for pressure. With a good shoulder check, players should be able to identify both pressure and support. Pressure is who is coming at them, and support is where they can move the puck to a teammate coming to help. By working on their shoulder checking, players can recognize situations quicker.

As players reach higher levels, they can learn to turn their body before turning their eyes. This technique allows them to keep their eyes up the ice a little longer to see if the forechecking players are changing anything along the way. The forechecking players may make a line change or change the angle at which they are attacking. The sooner the defensive player recognizes that, the sooner they can get the puck moving out of the zone. The process of turning the body while keeping the eyes up ice can take defensive players some time to learn. But being able to see the play for just a split second longer will make their decision making on the retrieval that much smoother.

APPROACH ANGLE

As players come back for the puck in the corner, they should avoid going straight back. The angle at which they come back to the puck is their approach angle. A good approach angle allows teammates to support the puck and enables the player to keep the puck moving. Taking a good approach angle also allows players to skate through the puck. Players often glide to the puck and potentially get pinned to the boards. If players skate through the puck, they can often skate through the first forechecker's pressure or make themselves harder to check. Players need to practice setting up the right approach angle because if they take too much of an angle, they may give up a line to the puck. So, without giving up a line, they set up their angle and leave themselves multiple options. They can continue toward the net, bump the puck back to the wall, or move the puck to center support. The defensive player who has options with the puck off their retrieval creates problems for the forecheckers.

RETRIEVALS ALONE OR WITH PARTNERS

Anytime a defensive player retrieves the puck in the corner, they need to have options with the puck. Options fall into two categories:

1. Options by themselves
2. Options with their partner

A big part of puck retrievals is communication by the offside defenseman to the player chasing the puck about what their options are. This problem is huge with younger team as they work on retrievals. The defensive partner should help the player going back for the puck by supporting them but more important by yelling to them what they should do with the puck when they touch it. The goal for the player going back is to get the puck moving on the first touch so that the opposing team cannot establish any sustained time in the offensive zone. Communication from the partner (and goalie) should be the start of the puck-retrieval sequence.

Options by Themselves

As players work in practice on options by themselves, they can start to think about identifying pressure through their shoulder checks and then reacting to what is coming at them. Teams use different terminology for the options, but I refer to these as "wheel" and "up." The wording is simple to facilitate communication from the defensive partner to the player retrieving the puck. The partner should not be yelling a paragraph to the player chasing down the puck; the partner should be saying one simple thing, and the retrieving player should know what they are talking about.

Wheel

When the retrieving player hears "Wheel," they know that pressure is coming from behind them and they need to skate from the corner around behind the net and be prepared to move the puck. As they are skating, they are trying to skate through the puck and keep the puck protected with their body. If the check is coming behind them, they can work to cut the net at the back post, so that the opponent does not get an opportunity to get their stick and body back to the inside of them. When they are skating behind the net, they should try not to overhandle the puck. Instead, they should just let the puck slide with them. Doing this is harder on the backhand side, but it may be required to prevent the puck from ending up in the inside of the ice where it is exposed. The defensive partner stays in front of the net as the player wheels around behind to provide some safety in the event that the player falls (or the puck is somehow turned over). The partner can also be a passing option if the puck moves up the wall or to the center so that they can be active in the rush.

Up

When the retrieving player hears "Up," they know to get the puck up the ice as quickly as possible. Typically, players turn the puck up away from the net and move it up the boards or to the middle of the ice. This happens when pressure is coming from the front or the opposing team is cutting off the net. Sometimes, the play is a short pass to the winger who is on the wall. They can then make the next pass to the center, weakside winger (who is either staying wide or skating across the ice), or the net-front defensive player. The quick up may at times allow the team to stretch out of the zone. One player gets out ahead of the puck and works to push the other team's defense back. This stretch pass could be made when the opposing team is changing and the retrieving team has time to get back to the puck, turn it around, and move it quickly out of their zone. At other times, no passing options may be available, so the defensive player may need to chip the puck or elevate it into the neutral zone.

Stop and Go

The last option by the player retrieving the puck is to start wheeling behind the net and then stop as they get to the net. I call this a stop and go. This play is an option when pressure starts behind the player retrieving the puck and then cuts in front of the net to meet them on the other side. The puck carrier can use the net as protection and scan the ice to see where they can move the puck. This play is often a result of the player's shoulder check and awareness of where pressure is coming from. When the player has the composure to stop behind the net, they must be sure they are ready to step out and make the next pass because they will be stationary and the checker may be coming at them hard. An error that players often make with the stop and go is stepping out from below the goal line to make a pass and dropping one hand off the stick. They are thus unable to do the one thing they need to do—pass. When they have the puck in the defensive zone, defensive players must have two hands on their stick so that they can pass the puck. They should never put themselves in a position where they cannot make the play they need to make.

Options With a Partner

Adding a partner to the equation is a big advantage for any defenseman. Having someone who the player can move the puck to, who is supporting them, and who is helping them make a decision by communicating is a big help in a game. Working on partner retrievals is a significant part of the game. Players should learn where their partner is moving and how hard they need to pass the puck to them. Defensemen should learn to pass the puck hard, learn to bump the puck 8 feet (2.5 m), learn to bank the puck off the back wall (learn the angles of how the puck will bounce), and work on putting pucks in a spot where a teammate can do something with it. The defender off the puck should consider several points when going back for a puck in their own zone:

- Decide where they can provide the best support for their partner and work to get there.
- Communicate to the partner as they read what is coming at the partner.
- Predict what kind of pass is coming at them. Is it a direct pass or an indirect pass? Is it going to be something they can do something with, or is it a puck that will require them to work a little harder?

Gauging Position Against the Dot Line

As I work with defensemen, I try to get them to understand where the dot line is and how that will affect their play with the puck. As they go back to retrieve a puck, the dot line becomes important. If the retrieving player is outside the dot line (an imaginary line through the dots to the end boards), a partner cannot stand in the other corner and wait for a pass because they will leave the net front wide open. In that case, the partner should stand in front of the net and be an option off the close post for a little bump or soft over. If the retrieving player is inside the dot line, the partner can start to move to the other corner because the player is closer to the net and working away from pressure will be a little easier. If something goes wrong with the player's pass to the partner, the player is closer to the net to recover back in front. This idea starts the partner thinking about where they should go to support the retrieving player.

Defender-to-Defender Pass

The first option with a partner is a good hard defender-to-defender pass. This direct pass to the partner could come below the goal line, in front of the net, or in the neutral zone (on a retrieval). Making it a hard pass is important because the partner wants to receive the puck sooner. The partner should be a little bit behind the passer so that the passing angle is easier for the passer and less susceptible to pressure. If the partner is below the goal line and waiting for a pass, they should position themselves so that they can receive the pass and prepare to move the puck up the ice. They should shoulder check before receiving the pass so that they know what their next play is going to be. Their call to the puck carrier should be "Over" or "D-to-D" loud enough for the puck carrier to understand.

For defender-to-defender passes, a direct pass is better than an indirect pass unless the player must use the wall. Learning the angles off the back wall can be tough for some players. If they bank it too early, the puck can kick out in front of the net. If the net is in the way of a direct pass, the space behind the net typically offers a good angle from the dot line to bank the puck to the partner. This pass can be helpful when the puck is close to or above the goal line and the passer is under pressure. This goal-line rule helps players understand that if they are below the goal line they can make a direct pass and if they are above the goal line they can make an indirect pass. This rule helps to eliminate all the unnecessary bank passes when a direct pass could have been made.

A more advanced kind of over has the defender with the puck pass it to space while another player skates into the puck. The net-front defender holds the net front, releases after the puck is passed in front of them, and continues skating with it. This is a great skill for direct or indirect puck movement to have players work on moving the puck cleanly to get out of the zone.

Close-Post Over

The next pass is a shorter but a highly effective pass known as a close-post over. The puck carrier is outside the dot line, and the partner is net front. The player could be in a battle for the puck, which is jammed up along the boards. The partner is yelling, "Over." When the player battling for the puck hears this, all they need to do is bump the puck behind the net, and the partner can leave the net front to skate into it. A common error with this play is that the net-front player leaves too early and is standing behind the net. If the puck does not come to them, a big problem occurs if the puck goes to the net front. Players must be patient. When the net-front player sees the puck go, they can skate into it, and their motion starts them getting behind the net and out the other side.

This play can also be used off faceoffs if the team has set up that play on the defensive-zone draw. For this short pass, players need to think, "Just put it to an area." The area where they are putting the puck is behind the net. Players can also spot the puck off the wall behind them, but it should not be a rim. The partner should not have to dig a puck off the wall. The play should be as smooth as possible for players to get out of the zone. Putting the puck off the boards also places the pass around the checker's sticks if pressure is coming down on the

Is It a Bump or a Pass?

The difference between a bump and a pass is simply how fast the puck is moving. A bump is a short pass, sometimes off the wall, to an area where a player can skate into the puck, grab it, and continue to skate away from pressure. A pass can be harder and to the tape. Adjusting the velocity of a puck when passing is an important skill for defensive players to learn as they get older. Being able to snap a puck hard to the tape is a key part of puck retrievals because the player is looking to beat a forechecking forward. But when a teammate is close by or the passer needs to use the boards, a snap pass will be difficult to receive. The bump is effective against pressure because the player can absorb the pressure and bump the puck past the checker to a teammate. All defensive players should learn to judge the distance and passing angle.

Players who are in a good spot can make a hard pass on the tape. They should not have to take something off the pass so that the receiving player can accept it. The job of the passer is to pass the puck, and the job of the receiver is to receive it, no matter how hard it comes. In NHL practices, players pass the puck extremely hard to each other, but the most impressive thing is how easily they receive the hard pass. Players who are close to the passer may need a firm pass, but not as hard as the passer can deliver it. Players may call for a chip that will require the passer to bank it off the wall to where they can skate into it. If the passer banks it too hard, the puck will slide away from the receiver. By knowing when to use the pass and when to use the bump, players will be more adept at escaping pressure.

puck carrier. Players must learn that when they get pinned to the boards, their partner may still be in position to support the puck. When they hear "Over," they may not move the puck right away, but they can move it when they are able to, knowing that support is ready for them.

Reverses

Another option that is helpful for players to have in their back pocket is a reverse. This play is used when pressure is coming from behind the puck-carrying defensive player and the support player notices that ice is available behind the pressure. Just before the puck carrier gets to the net on their wheel, the support player calls, "Reverse" (or whatever the team decides it is called). When the puck-carrying defender hears that call, they simple aim the puck back away from the net and lay it off the boards. The objective is to get the puck away from pressure and into a space where the supporting partner can move into it. Higher-level players will be able to elevate the puck just a little bit as they reverse it to prevent the puck from hitting a forechecker's stick on the reverse. Again, as with the close-post reverse, a common error is that the partner at the front of the net leaves too early and has to wait for the puck. The player at the front of the net calls for the reverse because they are facing up ice and can see everything developing. The player with the puck is listening. When they hear the call, they reverse the puck. After they reverse the puck, they quickly fill the net-front area to be an option as the puck moves.

Rims

One last option for the defenseman going back to get a puck is a rim. The rim is used to beat forecheckers and keep the puck moving. A solo defender can use this retrieval option if they are under pressure and need to get the puck moving past the opposing team's forecheck. This might come up during a penalty-kill scenario or in a situation in which multiple players are on the forecheck and the defenseman needs to get the puck past them. The rim play can also come up with a partner because they can recognize that no other options are viable.

The partner yells, "Rim" as loud as they can so that the puck carrier is clear that the puck is going around the wall. As the retrieving defenseman goes to shoot the puck, they should aim for the point where the corner of the turn starts. This shot allows the puck to hug the wall and keep moving rather than hit the boards too early where it will bounce and then bounce again. When the puck rims around, it should stay on the yellow part of the boards for a while.

Building on rimming the puck is the idea of keeping it moving, in which case it serves almost like a defender-to-defender play. But the second defender is simply keeping the puck moving to trap a forechecker and then possibly jump past them. This play is effective against an aggressive forechecking team; the defensemen simply rim the puck past the opposing players. In most cases this play is not ideal because retrieving rims is a tough skill to pick up. Sometimes, however, rimming the puck can be an effective option.

Second Quick

As players get older and into contact, the pressure from forwards increases and the defenseman must make a play with an opponent right beside them. An option that has recently become recognized is having the defender slow down to allow the forechecking forward to come closer to them. This play allows the player going back for the puck to absorb the contact from the first forechecker (F1) and keep their body in a position where they will still get the first touch of the puck. This option becomes effective against an aggressive team because it can trap an opponent in the offensive zone as the retrieving team moves the puck past them. This play works well if there is a space between F1 and the other forwards or if the defenseman has close support and can bump the puck to them.

Some teams call this "second quick." A teammate is quickly supporting the player on the puck or is second to the battle. Having a teammate nearby allows the retrieving defenseman to bump the puck one way or the other depending on where the pressure is. They keep control of the puck and prevent the forechecking player from gaining possession. This skill is tough to learn because the body must be sideways to absorb the contact. The player does not want to go into the boards facing the wall or get hit from behind. Players need to practice to develop this skill, but when they get good at it, they can reduce the speed at which they get hit and slow the pace of the forechecker. This ability to absorb contact is a high-level skill on puck retrievals.

Forwards

As players reach a higher level, a forward could be a passing option as a support player down low on a retrieval. The forward's job to track the puck back and backcheck. They might at times support the defenseman on either an over (or defender-to-defender pass) or a reverse. All players should know what these types of retrievals look like and how they are executed. The timing on the play, the velocity on the pass, the passing angles required (wall, middle, or over), and the communication are all skills that forwards should learn so that if the situation comes up in a game, they are able to support the defenseman in getting cleanly out of the zone.

GOALIES

A key player on breakouts and puck retrievals is the goalie. The goalies are vital to communication as the defensive players are skating back to the puck, and the goalie often stops a puck to play it or sets it for their defensemen. The goalie and defensemen should meet at the start of the year to make sure they are clear what the calls mean and where the defenders will go when the goalie handles the puck.

When I got to Team Canada in my first year, we naturally met with the players to work on the communication aspect of retrievals. We faced the additional obstacle of having players who spoke only French and not English. We had to come up with words that were easy enough for the French players to yell to the English players and be understood. Likewise, the English players had to yell to the French players and be understood. Through some simple meetings with players, we decided on what the communication was going to be between goalie and defense.

Dump-Ins

When goalies handle dump-ins, they have a few choices with the puck:

- They can set it
- They can play it strongside.
- They can play it weakside.

If the goalie is playing it to either the strongside or the weakside, they will have the choice to rim it up the wall or to pass it to a supporting defensive player. If they are making a pass to the defensive player, they should aim for the goal line. The defenseman will know where the puck is going and will be prepared to receive it if that is what the call is. They can get there early and get their hips and skates facing up the ice so that the puck is in front of them. Even when the defenseman is late, they can still call for the pass. The goalie knows that the defenseman is aiming for the goal line and will skate into that space, moving the puck away from pressure.

Set It

When the goalie is setting the puck for the defense, the defense is coming back for it and the goalie is behind the net. The goalie should try to leave the puck in a spot that is safe for their defenseman to pick it up. Behind the net and between the net and the wall is a good spot. A common error made by the goalie is leaving the puck along the wall or along the back of the net. Either location makes it more difficult for the defenseman coming back in the zone. After the goalie leaves the puck for the defense, they should get back in the net and stay clear of the defenseman as they are coming back for the puck.

Play It

If the goalie chooses to play the puck, they need options. The defensive players are heading back into the zone to provide options. Typically, one defender heads to each corner to be available for a pass. Goalies should always work on their puckhandling so that they can help on rims and pucks that are dumped in and be like a third defender back below the goal line. They can pass the puck up the strong side or go back the other way to a waiting defenseman. If the defense has time, they can make the next play. If they are under pressure, they may need to keep the puck moving and rim it around.

Whatever play is happening, the defense needs to shoulder check to make sure they know what is coming at them before they get the pass from the goalie. At times, the goalie may bypass the defender and either rim the puck around hard or move it up to the winger to beat the forecheck. To do this, the goalie must be able to handle the puck and move it cleanly, but communication among the players on the team also plays an important role.

INSIDE DEFENSIVE RETRIEVAL

This last situation in the chapter happens often games but is rarely practiced, especially at the U18 level and younger. This scenario occurs when the defense has a tight gap in the neutral zone and the defender who is on the puck forces the offensive puck carrier to dump the puck into the defensive zone. The strongside defenseman stays up, and the weakside defenseman must go back to get the puck in the corner.

I believe that coaches do not practice working with this different angle to the puck from the middle of the ice. Because the defenseman's approach angle to the puck is different, they have different options when they go back for the puck. The best part about this is that the defense has forced a dump into the defensive zone and a forward is likely tracking the puck and can now work as a defensive forward to help on the breakout. The defensive player who is going back for the puck has options. They can either use the net to get the puck around to the other side, come back up the strong side, or use the middle of the ice to a supporting forward.

Supporting the Weak Side

Teams use various strategies to support the weak side. When a plan is put in place, the game becomes easier for the defensemen who are going back for the puck. One team in the NHL used a quick up to move the puck back up the strong side every time the puck was chipped into the corner and the weakside defensive player went back to get it. That play gave the strongside defenseman who was in the neutral zone a clear understanding of where the puck was going to go next. Rather than head straight back to the net, the defenseman who stayed up in the neutral zone could go back down the dot line and expect the puck to be coming back up the wall either with possession, as a pass, as a bump, or as a clear off the glass.

If that weakside defender has the support of the forward, the forward should be yelling loudly for the defensive player going back for the puck because they will be under pressure. The forward should be telling their teammate where the available ice is so that they can either move into it or move the puck into it to get away from pressure. The retrieving player can wheel around the net and cut the net to shake a checker, make a support pass like a defender-to-defender pass only now to the forward (in the defender's place), or execute a little bump to get the puck past the first forechecker and allow the weakside defender an option with the puck.

Whatever the option chosen by the weakside defender retrieving the puck, teammates should provide a heavy amount of communication and the defender should get back to the puck quickly. Teams need to work on scenarios that come up in games. They should work on situations in which support is needed, when support is nearby, and when support is across the ice. Players must practice retrieving pucks on their forehand and their backhand. Coaches want players to have the puck on their forehand as much as possible, but in some situations putting the puck on the forehand will expose it to the forechecker, whereas putting it on the backhand will protect it. Better that the puck be protected than exposed and turned over. Likewise, players need to be able to pass on both their forehand and their backhand so that they can move the puck past pressure. Little bumps either direct or indirect (off the wall) should be practiced so that the defensive players become proficient at moving pucks to support. These skills must be developed in practice before they can be executed in games.

First-Touch Retrieval

As players continue to develop and the pace of the game increases, coaches can start to encourage their defensemen to move the puck on their first touch to get it moving quicker. They could use a defender-to-defender pass, rim, little bump behind the net, reverse, pass to the wall, or pass to the middle. This play happens often when the defenseman is under pressure and needs to move the puck before they get hit or absorb pressure. The key to first-touch retrievals is to have support off the puck. Players need to work off the puck to get into a position where they give the player with the puck someone to pass to. When players get back into their zone quickly, the defender who is retrieving the puck has more options. A good first-touch retrieval can trap the forecheckers and catch them going the wrong way.

One of the best parts of a good first-touch retrieval is that the puck will be heading back up the ice quicker. When the defensemen struggle with retrievals, their team will spend more time in the defensive zone than their coach would like. The goal of any retrieval is to get the puck moving back up the ice quickly and out of the defensive zone. Clean exits out of the defensive zone allow the defensive players to join the rush and get involved in the offensive play.

NEUTRAL-ZONE SHOULDER CHECK

Level of Difficulty

Easy

Players

One to six players, on both sides of the neutral zone for four to six players

Objectives

To introduce shoulder checking and reading pressure on the way back for the puck

Setup

The setup depends on the number of players in the group because the drill can be worked on with forwards as well. Groups set up between two lines in the neutral zone or end zones. Pucks are placed in the middle of the two lines. For one group of three, players use the red line for the pucks and work between the blue lines. For six players, players use the red lines with pucks and work both ways.

Procedure

The first player skates forward to the wall, and the second player (in line) spots a puck past them. The first player shoulder checks on the way back from the puck and then picks up the puck using a good approach angle. Whichever way they take the puck, they should try to avoid overhandling it before passing it back to the line. They continue in the drill and go again, this time the opposite way from the first time. Players can go two or four times so that they make multiple forehand and backhand passes.

Coaching Tips

- Players should be able to put passes on the tape when given both forehand and backhand passes. Players should pass the puck hard (or firmly) to their partner.
- The shoulder check is the toughest part of this introductory drill. Players must look with a purpose.

Variations

- The player in line can direct the retrieving player which way they are going. When the player going to get the puck shoulder checks, this time they are looking to see which way they will be going.
- Pressure can added by using another player from the line. The pressure comes from one direction behind the player who is going to get the puck. This time the shoulder check is actually identifying pressure.
- Players can also cut back after they pick up the puck. The player picks up the puck in the corner and then looks at the line. Nothing is available, so the player cuts back and makes a pass back to the line.
- The player in line can have their stick up or down to direct the retrieving player to pass directly or cut back. If the player in line has their stick down, the player passes to them right away. If the player in line has their stick in the air, the player cuts back and then passes. This is a good decision-making option for the puck retriever.

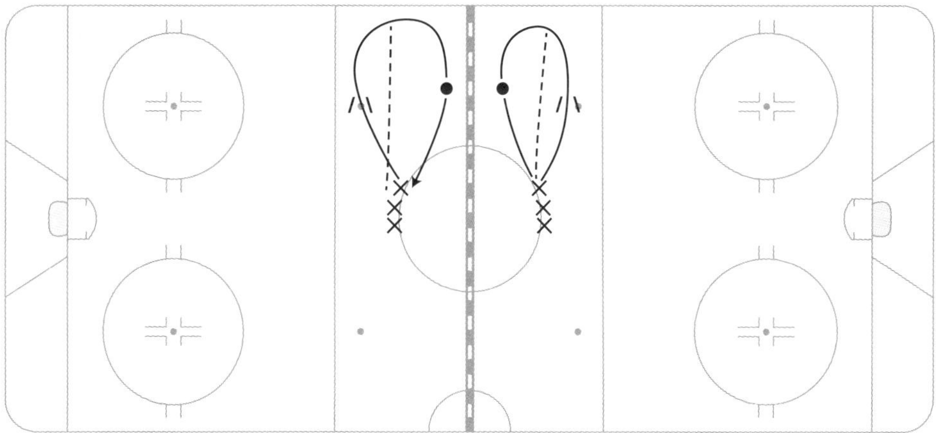

SOLO PUCK RETRIEVALS

Level of Difficulty

Easy

Players

One to six players

Objectives

To work on introducing or cleaning up specific parts of solo puck retrievals

Setup

A coach has pucks at the hash marks on one side, and a player is ready to go in the circle.

Procedure

The player takes one step up and pivots backward, and the coach lays the puck into the corner. The player turns and shoulder checks to go back to get the puck (1 in diagram). They set up a good approach angle, turn the puck up, and pass to the coach. They continue up above the top of the circle and pivot backward again. This time they turn and start to wheel the puck behind the net. They imagine that pressure goes in front of the net, so they stop and pause for a second. They can take a breath, step back out on the same side they came in, and make the outlet pass to the coach (2 in diagram). They come up a third time, pivot backward, and then open up as the coach spots (or rims) a puck into the corner. This time they wheel around the net and cut the net to come out to the middle of the ice (3 in diagram). They skate the puck to the top of the circles. The next defenseman goes as soon as the first player starts to wheel the net because they will start with a quick up.

Coaching Tips

- The details of this drill are important. Coaches should remind players about shoulder checks, approach angles to pucks, and protecting the puck as they pick it up.
- Players should be careful about moving their feet through the puck, not overhandling it, and passing the puck hard.

Variation

- Players can add in deception with their eyes, hands, and feet in this drill to be more evasive. They can add toe turns or stick fakes as they are picking up pucks below the goal line.

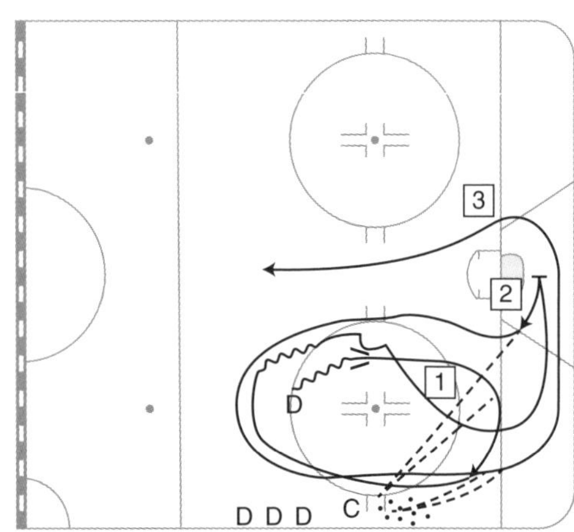

BIG CIRCLE

Level of Difficulty

Easy

Players

Three to four players

Objectives

To work on passing and skating the puck around behind the net

Setup

Two players are in the drill with two passers, one on each half wall. One player starts behind the net, and the other starts at the blue line. The two players in the drill have pucks and are going to skate in a big circle.

Procedure

When the coach blows the whistle, the players in the drill start by making a pass to the players on the wall. One player on the wall bumps their puck into the corner, and the other player on the wall holds on to it and lets the skating player transition to backward skating close to the blue line. That player receives a pass again, now moving backward. The other skating player retrieves the puck in the corner and wheels around the net (see 1 in diagram). Both players again pass to the players on the wall and repeat the drill before switching. Player should work both ways in this drill.

Coaching Tips

- This drill starts to put things together into a game-simulated situation.
- Players must communicate, shoulder check, set up a good approach angle, and skate through pucks.
- Players can work on not overhandling pucks.

Variation

- Players can turn the puck up quickly in the corner and then escape turn at the top (see 2 in diagram). For this to work, one player should be in the corner and another in the neutral zone. Passes to the player near the blue line should always be on their inside shoulder, forcing them to spin toward the wall. This variation will also help them learn to receive passes that are not perfect.

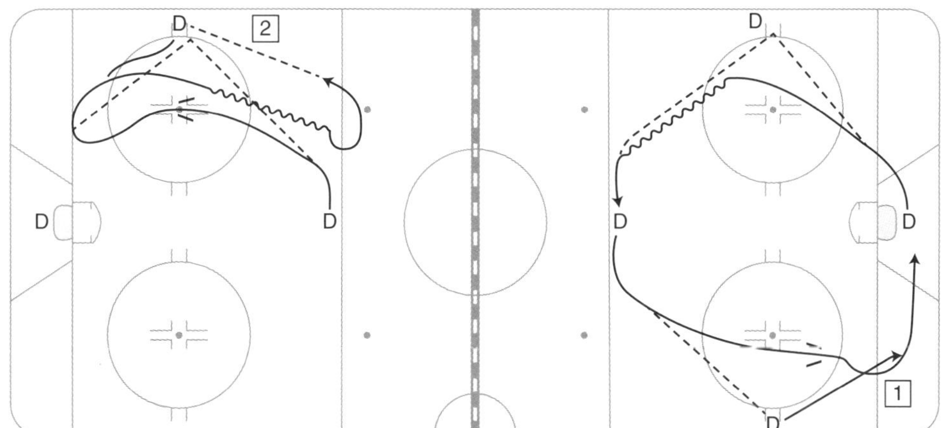

SHOULDER-CHECK RETRIEVALS

Level of Difficulty
Easy

Players
One to six players, on both sides with four to six players

Objectives
To work on shoulder checking on the way back for the puck and bringing the puck up the wall

Setup
A player (or coach) has pucks at the top of the circle in the high slot. A player is lined up at the hash marks. The lower player does the drill for three or four retrievals.

Procedure
The player at the top of the circle spots a puck in the corner. The low player goes to get the puck and must shoulder check while skating to it. They set up a good approach angle and turn the puck up the wall, passing back to the player in the high slot as a middle option. This player continues around the line and heads back into the corner to grab another puck. They shoulder check on the way back to the puck and again bring it up the wall, passing to the player waiting. They rotate after doing this three or four times. If four or more players are participating, they can be going on both sides. Players switch sides after they finish one side.

Coaching Tips
- Performing shoulder checks is hard for defensemen, but when they can scan the ice and recognize what is coming at them, their job becomes much easier.
- Some coaches want their players to check multiple times (once on each side), but if players scan before they turn, they should know where the other team's players are.
- If a player is under pressure, they may be able to shoulder check on one side.

Variation
- This drill has players turning pucks up the wall only so that both sides can go. Players can pass to the players waiting on their backhand if that is the pass. Players should use both their forehand and their backhand as they move up ice. They have a development opportunity to work on both passes, forehand and backhand.

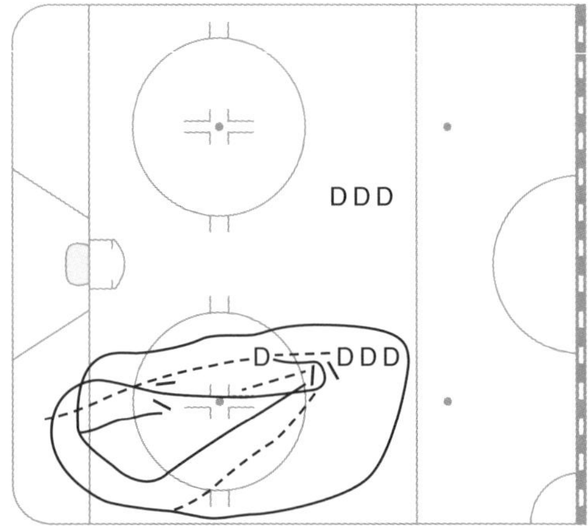

D RETRIEVALS

Level of Difficulty

Hard

Players

Two to four players

Objectives

To work on taking pucks around behind the net and making a good first pass to the winger, to work on moving across the blue line with good puck placement and good footwork

Setup

A coach has pucks on the half wall on one side. A player is at the center of the circle, and a second player is on the opposite side at the half wall.

Procedure

D1 starts up the wall and pivots backward. The coach spots a puck in the corner, and D1 starts to wheel to the net and stops behind the net. They step out and pass back to the coach. D1 continues to move up the ice, around the circle, and then back into the corner. The coach spots the same puck back into the corner again. D1 wheels around the net and passes to D2, who is waiting as a winger. D2 leaves the puck and goes backward to the blue line. D1 comes and grabs the puck and then passes to D2. D2 then slides across the line with the puck loaded and adds fake shots. D2 passes the puck back to the coach. The drill then continues with a new player starting.

Coaching Tips

- This drill works well because players get going quickly.
- As the first player moves the puck up the wall, another player can start.
- Players do not shoot in this drill, so players can be behind the net without fear of being hit.

Variations

- If shots are added to the drill, no one should be standing behind the net while the shot is coming.
- A shot can be added for the second player, who is moving across the line. Alternatively, a third player can be added, and the second player can pass to the third player (in the middle of the ice) for a shot.
- The second player can move laterally across the blue line. When they reach the middle of the ice, they pass to the coach, who serves as a winger.

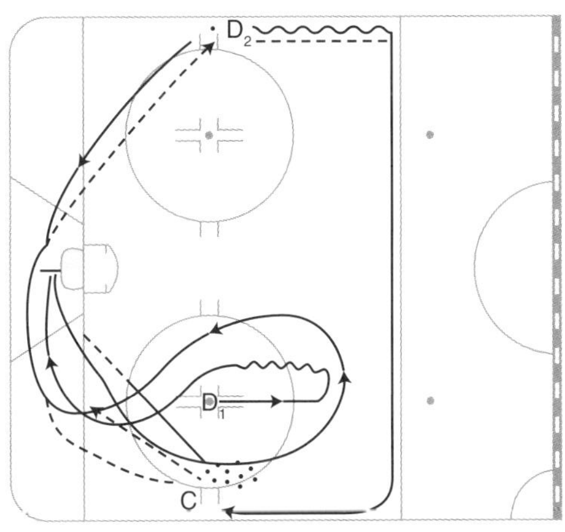

UP UP WHEEL—ONE D

Level of Difficulty

Hard

Players

Full team

Objectives

To work on either quick ups or wheels and reacting to what is seen and heard

Setup

A coach has pucks at the half wall on opposite sides of the ice. Defensive players are with the coach on the same side, and forwards are waiting at the wall at both ends of the blue lines. Tires can be placed down the middle of the ice to divide the ice in half.

Procedure

The head coach shows either stick up or stick down. Stick up means to do a quick up, whereas stick down means to wheel to the net. The players must communicate to the defenseman what they see from the head coach. The coach blows the whistle to start the drill. A defenseman retrieves the puck in each corner, while the forwards make their way back into the defensive zone.

If the play is a quick up (see 1 in diagram), the defenseman turns the puck up quickly. The forward on the strong side gets ready to receive a pass from the defenseman and then passes to the forward in the middle. The defenseman follows up and becomes available at the blue line for a rim from the coach.

If the play is a wheel (see 2 in diagram), the defenseman carries the puck around behind the net and passes to the forward on the far side. The forward passes to the player in the middle, who enters the zone with a shot. The defenseman becomes available at the blue line for a pass from the coach for a second shot.

Coaching Tips

- In this communication drill, the defensive players must react to what they hear and see. The goal is to have players yelling to each other to tell them where to go.
- If someone makes an error (which will happen), the coach should stop the drill before players collide. The coach can then restart the drill.

Variations

- The best way to do this drill is to do several reps as a wheel and then several reps as an up.
- The drill becomes more difficult as the coach starts making changes for each rep. This is a good approach to use for the last couple of reps for the group. The coach must keep in mind that both ends must do the same option for the drill to work.

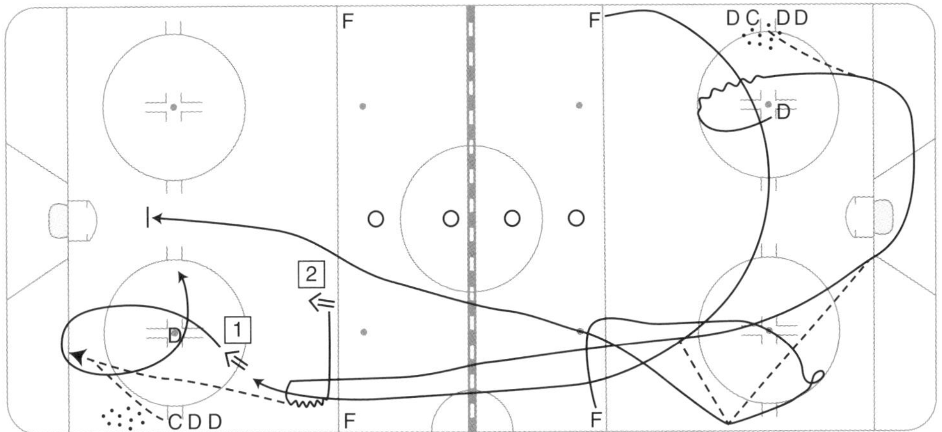

CONTINUOUS REVERSE

Level of Difficulty

Easy

Players

Six defensive players

Objectives

To work on reversing the puck and leaving it in a good spot

Setup

Defensemen line up in front of the net with the coach. One puck is in the corner, and one player is on the hashmarks on the boards.

Procedure

The player on the boards starts the drill by moving back into the corner and grabbing the puck. They are thinking to skate behind the net but will hear their defensive partner from the front of the net yell, "Reverse." When they hear the call, they put the puck off the boards so that it bounces away from the net toward the corner. The defenseman from the front of the net picks up the puck, and the player who reversed the puck heads back to the net front. The player with the puck skates up to the top of the circle and lays the puck back into the corner, and the drill starts again. Players switch sides after each player has gone four or five times.

Coaching Tips

- The defensemen can work on leaving the puck in a good spot for their partner. The partner does not have to leave early and can wait until the puck is in front of them before skating to go and grab it.
- All players should be checking where pressure is coming from and listening for their partner.
- Players should not put themselves in a dangerous position if pressure is coming from the front just to reverse the puck. They must be aware all the time.

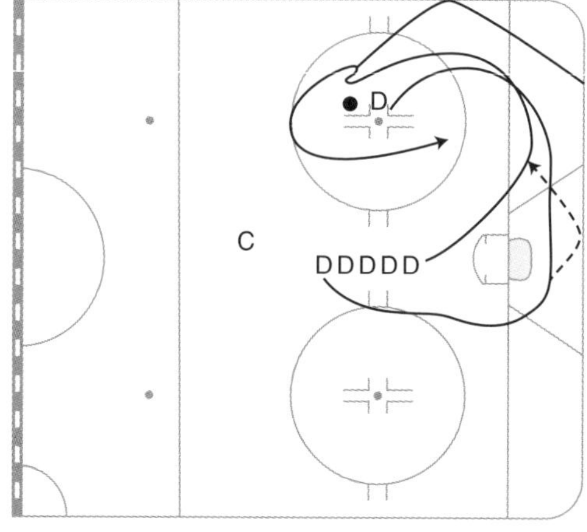

Variation

- The defenseman can elevate the puck off the yellow dasher in games if a forechecker is coming at them. The elevation of the puck will get it over the stick and prevent a turnover.

CHAPTER 6

Joining the Rush

One thing that every player wants to do is contribute offensively, to be part of the offensive side of the game. I ask players after the game, "Did you contribute to the outcome of the game in a positive way?" What I mean when I ask this is: Did they do something every shift to help the team make plays? They might have made a defensive play in the defensive zone, chipped a puck in the neutral zone, or gotten a shot through in the offensive zone. All coaches should encourage their defensemen to be active in the rush and try to outnumber the opposition going back to their own zone. Any player can be integral in the rush if certain things happen in the game. In the rare event that a defenseman carries the puck through the neutral zone, they should have the confidence to make a play. A defenseman could be a secondary player through the neutral zone and end up driving to the net. They might be a third or fourth player on the rush and be either in the far dot lane or on the puck side. Whatever the situation is, defensive players need to recognize their chance to get up in the rush and create offensively.

When I talk with defensive players about when they might get up in the rush, I teach them to recognize two game situations quickly:

1. *Does their team have clear possession moving up the ice?* If the answer is no, this is not the time to jump up in the play. If the answer is yes, they can look to be active in the rush.
2. *Is a player from the other team behind them?* If the answer is no, the opposing team has done a good job of tracking back and staying over the top of the player. This is not the time to jump into the play. If the answer is yes and an opponent is behind them, the time might be right to beat the other player up the ice and be a threat in the rush.

If the answer to both questions is yes, the defensive player should be looking to get up in the rush and working to find an available lane to become a passing option for the puck carrier. If the defensive player is up in the rush and does not happen to get the puck, they can simply stop at the blue line or move back to it to be in a good position to play in the offensive zone.

If the answer to either question is no, the defensive player should remain patient and wait for another opportunity to get up in the rush.

Defensive players who are effective at joining the rush can immediately change the success rate of a team's rush attack against the opposition. When defensemen learn to pick their spots quickly and become available for passes, the forwards will have another pass option on the rush.

SKATING SKILL WHEN JOINING THE RUSH

Skating is always important for defensemen. A player's ability to join the rush is largely determined by their ability to get up the ice through their skating. Players must be able to change gears and accelerate quickly. Their separation speed is an important part of being able to get to top speed quickly. By combining power and quickness in two or three quick steps, they can start to gain separation from other players. With the understanding of positioning in the defensive zone and how it changes as the puck leaves the zone, players who can accelerate quickly can get ahead of the opposing team and become involved in the play.

The ability to read available ice and move into it is a key part of joining the rush. Players need to be good on their edges and be able to generate power through their forward strides. Often, when players are looking to join the rush, they are too fast. Being too fast can eliminate that player as a passing option for the puck carrier as they skate into traffic. When players join the rush effectively, they are an option for the puck carrier. They can find available passing lanes where their stick is available to receive a pass. At higher levels, players should be looking to one time the puck to the net or, on the other side, get the puck off their stick quickly. At a younger age, players can work on receiving passes and getting the puck off their stick with no stickhandles. The goal with the quick release is to get the puck to the net before the goalie has a chance to set their feet and get square to the shooter. If the player joining the rush can get the puck to the net before the goalie sets their feet, they will significantly increase their chance to score on the shot.

COMMON ERROR

Players may get to a spot where they think they are open, but only their body is available while their stick is not. When they learn to time the play properly, they will put themselves in the appropriate lane where a pass can get to them and they can make their next play, either to pass or to shoot.

DEFENSIVE BREAKOUT

Defensemen can become active on the rush in several ways. The first is being an option on their team's breakout out of their own zone. The defenseman might have the first touch on the puck and move it by jumping past the opponent who is checking them. Or the defenseman might be an option in front of the net for the next pass from their defensive partner who has moved the puck quickly up the boards. More teams are using their defensemen on breakouts because they can find open ice and passing lanes. Teams are using their forwards for support of first-touched pucks by defensemen and allowing their weakside defender to remain as an option.

A common passing sequence to activate the defenseman on the breakout is a defender's pass to a winger, who passes to the weakside defender in the slot (D to W to net-front D). This sequence can happen in several ways, but if the team can find that defender in a good passing lane, they can often escape out of the zone quickly.

A strongside defender who stays up in the neutral zone often either finishes a check or forces a dump-in. (This situation was discussed in the chapter Puck Retrievals as well.) In this situation, the weakside defender is now going back for a puck without the normal support from their partner. Some teams have rules for this play when the weakside defender touches the puck. Some teams always bring it back up the wall where the puck was dumped in from. The defender than know that if the puck gets dumped past them, it is coming back up that side of the ice. Other teams have their first forward back (not just the centerman) being support and allowing short bumps with the puck, either toward the net, to the middle, or back up toward the wall. If the forward is the next touch, the defenseman who was in the neutral zone can now be an option on the breakout. If the breakout is clean and a player is behind them, the defenseman can be active in the rush. The idea of having active defensemen in the rush starts in either the breakout or the transition attack. Puck movement and reading are two big components to defenders being active.

After the defenseman moves the puck in the defensive zone, they should remain in support in the event the puck is moved back to them, but they should also get their eyes up the ice as well as behind them to see where the other team is. The idea of scanning the ice is a big development component for defensemen. By understanding where players are and how they can be an option, the defenseman gains a big opportunity to get up in the play.

READING THE CONDITIONS

Defensemen will join the rush far more than they will lead the rush. As defensemen are jumping up in the play, they have a choice to be either in the far dot lane on the rush as the third player in the attack or on the strong side closer to the puck carrier as the fourth player in the attack. To execute properly at the offensive blue line on offensive-zone entries, teams need to have three things.

1. *Speed on the rush.* The speed on the rush can come from either the puck carrier or the net-drive player. If the speed is coming from the puck carrier, the options include net drive, shots, passes, or delays. If the puck carrier must slow down, the options change. The speed now must come from the net-driving player to push the opposing defense back and open up passing lanes.
2. *Width.* The width on the attack comes from a puck carrier entering the puck on the outside lane and teammates being spread out to create movement when the puck moves. One player to think about is the opposing goalie and the way in which they must move to react to a pass. The opposing defense is also reacting to the attack. If the attacking players are all close together, the attack is easier to defend. As players get older and can pass the puck harder, they should think about moving down the dot line to force the goalie to go post to post off a pass. If the attacking team can get the shot to the net quickly before the goalie has a chance to set their feet, they get the advantage back on their side.
3. *Depth.* The puck-carrying team should try to change the passing angles by creating depth on the attack. For example, the net-driving player is ahead of the puck, the dot-lane width player is behind the puck, and the fourth player (typically a defenseman) is in a good spot to receive a pass on the strongside dot line. The attacking team does not want to have all three players in one line across, an attack that it is easy to defend.

When these three things are happening on the offensive rush, the puck carrier has options. When the puck carrier has options, they are more dangerous in making a play. When the puck carrier does not have multiple options, the opposing team can take away the one option they do have and look to force a turnover.

PROVIDE OPTIONS FOR THE PUCK

An offensive defenseman who is active in the rush is there to provide an option to the puck carrier as they enter the zone. If three forwards are in front of them and they are the fourth player in the rush, the player should know where to go. If the forward in the neutral zone chips the puck and gets hit (or falls), the offensive defenseman can now be the third player in the rush and fill the wide lane to the net. If the offensive defenseman moves the puck up to the forward and is the second player in the rush, they may be the net-driving player who works to push the opposing defenders back. The ability to recognize how many forwards are in front of them is a defenseman's key skill in scanning the ice. A defenseman who can move the puck up to the forwards and work to join the rush is more valuable than a defenseman who carries the puck and leads the rush. Leading the rush may occasionally happen in a game or during the season, but defensemen will have many more opportunities to join the rush from good puck movement. When a defenseman is comfortable reading the play and reacting to their position in the rush, they will contribute more to their team.

TIMING

One key for the defenseman to consider when joining the rush is the point at which they get the puck in the offensive zone from a pass from the forwards. If the rush is successful and the player is in a lane to get a pass on the rush, they should be ready to shoot. To do this, they must be preparing to shoot before they get the pass in the offensive zone. As they enter the zone, they are scanning the ice to see what type of passing angle they have and where the opponents who could block their shot are. Of course, players should know where the net is so that as they get the pass, they can react quickly.

A big part of releasing the puck quickly is being prepared before the puck comes to them. Having their hands, hips, and feet ready to shoot the puck before they receive the pass will speed up the release of the shot. Eliminating stickhandling when receiving the pass will help the shooter release the puck quicker. Players need to understand the difference between a stickhandle and a fake. Those who have to stickhandle because they cannot receive passes cleanly can work to eliminate that problem and try to take passes in a spot where they have no need to stickhandle. If players are stickhandling to sell a fake, that situation is different and may be required if a defender gets into the lane. When working with players on this point, I constantly remind them to eliminate things they don't need. If they do not need to stickhandle, they shouldn't do it. Players should be able to pass the puck hard, receive the pass, and shoot the puck all without stickhandling the puck.

Being able to get the puck off the stick quickly gives the shooter an edge in the race with the goalie. The goalie wins the race if they can set their feet. The shooter wins the race if they can get the puck to the net before the goalie can set their feet. The player may not score, but if they hit the net, the puck has a chance to go in on either the first shot or possibly a second shot.

Another possibility that comes up on entry passes to late players is the option to hesitate before shooting. To do this, the player receives the pass cleanly but does not shoot right away. The player can stop the puck and hold it as if they are planning to release it. The goalie must hold or move just slightly as the player holds on to the puck. The hesitation is hard for the goalie because they do not know when the puck will be shot. NHL players successfully use this type of shot to create good scoring chances.

A shot that players may want to develop is the one timer off the pass on the rush. If they are on the correct side (a left-handed player down the right side or a right-handed player down the left side), they can look to one time the puck to the net off the pass. They can do this by either flipping open their hips and slowing their forward momentum or opening up their front foot and gliding toward the net. In either case, their hands, hips, and feet need to be ready to shoot as the pass is coming to them. Their objective is to shoot the puck hard to the net and get it off their stick quickly. When learning this skill, players should work first on shooting the puck hard and then on shooting it accurately.

WHERE TO SHOOT

On passes that come across the midline of the ice, players need to understand where they are shooting. One thing I tried to tell the Manitoba Moose this season was to force the goalie to make saves, not hit the goalie with shots. By adhering to this simple concept, players can keep the puck out of the middle of the net. The middle of the net width-wise is where the goalie's body is, and they eat up pucks that hit them. The middle of the net height-wise is where the goalies' hands are, and they either catch the puck or block it to the corner. Therefore, players should shoot either to the area that the goalie has not yet reached (or short side) or to the area that the goalie came from (or far side). Either way, players shoot to score on passes that come across the slot and are tape to tape.

If a player is getting passes when joining the rush in the width lane, meaning that passes come across the midline of the ice, they are more likely to have a clear shooting lane to the net. Traffic is less likely in front, and the shooter can work to get the puck to the net quickly. If a player is joining the rush on the strong side as the fourth player in the rush, they are more likely to have to shoot through traffic, meaning that more players are in front of them. Players can work on shots for both scenarios in practice.

Players can start at the blue line on the dot line and simply jump down the dot line to receive a pass from a coach who is at the top of the circle. Players can be in one line because this drill goes quickly. Players should work from both sides of the ice because they cannot predict what the situation will be in a game or where they will attack from. Players could be on their strong side attacking down to the net or on their off wing where they have a one-timer option. With the coach in the same spot, players can come down the close dot line to simulate a fourth player in the attack when three forwards are ahead of the player. Simple drills to re-create game situations can be used in practice to build confidence with these types of plays come game time.

HOLDING WIDTH

When players are coming down the backside dot line, they can continue down the line rather than attack the pass and move back into the slot. This option will cause the goalie to move post to post rather than shorten their route, which would happen if the player moves back across the slot. A 3 vs 2 rush works best when there are direct lines to the net. The direct lines create options for puck movement, shots, coverage of ice, and scoring chances. If players start to move laterally across the slot on the initial attack, they give backcheckers time to get into the play and break up passing options. When defensemen join the rush, they should always work to be an option.

With younger players, the third player may be a little closer to the puck based on passing ability, but the fourth player, who could be a defenseman, can still be on the backside dot line. With older players who can pass the puck harder, having the width on the attack allows more ice to be covered. Keeping width is a great way to spread out a defending team and open up scoring options. Defenders need to understand what holding width looks like for them.

Coaches must recognize that having active defensemen could have consequences coming back the other way. The team must know the risks of turning the puck over. Turning the puck over in the neutral zone can quickly produce opportunities going the other way. Players on the offensive rush must make good plays with the puck and recognize when no play is available. Offensive players can get the puck in behind the opponent's defense to generate time in the offensive zone. The net-driving player can do this by getting on the puck and working to create puck possession. The width player can support the puck, and the defenseman can return to the offensive blue line to be an option for the next puck. Things do not always go as planned in games. Teams must be prepared to read when plays break down, make a play to keep possession, and advance the puck. In chapter 8, we look at what happens when teams must accept a rush by the opposition.

RECEIVING PASSES IN THE RUSH

Level of Difficulty

Easy

Players

Any number of players

Objectives

To work on receiving passes to simulate dot-lane passes coming in games

Setup

A coach has pucks on the wall, and players line up on the far neutral-zone dot.

Procedure

A player moves into the zone and receive a pass from the coach. The player's goal is to receive the pass and shoot the puck all in one motion without any stickhandles. The shots can go either to the area the goalie has not yet reached or to the area where the goalie came from. Where the shot goes depends largely on how hard the pass was and how it was received. Players should make hard passes and achieve clean receptions.

Coaching Tip

- The goal is to get the puck to the net quickly to make the goalie move across the crease.

Variations

- The coach can give passes that are not perfect so that players must work to receive them. Perfect passes rarely occur in games.
- Players can look to one time the puck when they can perform the shot comfortably.

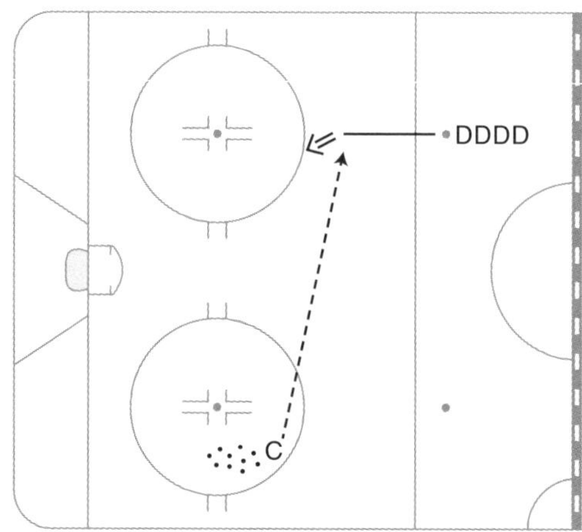

YALE CONNECTION

Level of Difficulty
Moderate

Players
Full team required

Objectives

To work on defensemen being active in the rush with forwards attacking over the blue line

Setup

Forwards line up at the top of the circle on opposite sides, and defensemen are in the middle of the ice. Forwards have pucks with them to start the drill. This drill can start on one side, and then both sides can go at the same time.

Procedure

F1 leaves from the start of the line with D1, and they exchange the puck a couple of times. When they get back inside the blue line, D1 passes to F2 from the other line, who passes to F1 coming across the middle. F1 enters wide, F2 drives the net, and D1 joins the rush. F1 can find D1 with a pass in the offensive zone for a shot. D1 can stay on the close dot line or flare out to the backside dot line.

Coaching Tips

- This drill works well when players can pass effectively.
- F2 should stop at the net and at the back post to allow another option for D1 if the shooting lane is not clear.

Variations

- Both sides can go at the same time with players communicating and staying in the correct lanes up the ice.
- Offensive entry does not always end up to the defenseman, with shots coming from the wing, hitting the net-drive player, or seam passes. The defenseman is active in the rush regardless of what happens.

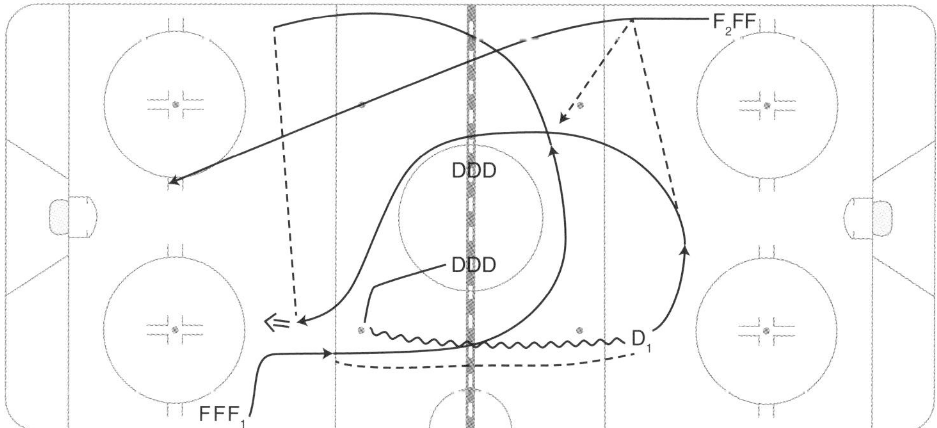

UP UP WHEEL—TWO D

Level of Difficulty

Hard

Players

Full team required

Objectives

To work on taking pucks around behind the net and making a good first pass to the winger, to work on moving across the blue line with good puck placement and good footwork

Setup

A coach has pucks on the half wall on opposite sides. A defensive player is at the half wall, and another is net front. Forwards are at both ends of the blue lines.

Procedure

The coach blows a whistle and spots a puck. D1 retrieves the puck, and D2 calls over and receives a pass. D2 moves the puck to F1 coming back on the wall, who moves the puck to F2, the forward in the middle of the ice. D1-D2-F1-F2.

F2 carries the puck through neutral zone, and D2 joins the rush. F2 enters wide, F1 drives the net, and D2 can either stay strong side or fan out to get outside of F1, who is driving the net.

The same thing happens on both sides of the ice. D1 becomes D2 for the next rep on the other side.

Coaching Tips

- This communication drill builds on Up Up Wheel—One D.
- Communication and passing must be good for this drill to work well.
- Both sides go at the same time, so lots is going on in this drill.

Variations

- The defender-to-defender pass can be direct or indirect depending on what pass is available.
- The defender-to-defender pass can be hard to the back post or a little bump to the close post. The coach should be specific about what they want like to see.

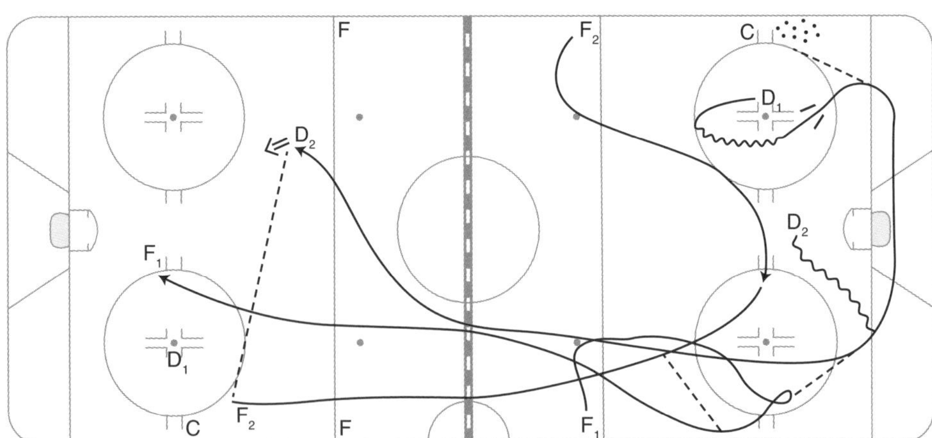

DEFENDER-TO-DEFENDER NEUTRAL ZONE (HIGH LEVEL)

Level of Difficulty
Hard

Players
Full team required

Objectives

To work on passing and having defensemen up in the rush as an option entering the offensive zone

Setup

Players are at both ends of the blue lines. Forwards are opposite each other, and defensemen are opposite each other. Pucks are placed at the red line on each side.

Procedure

This drill is continuous. A coach starts one defensive player on one side. D1 starts skating, and D2 (from other line) moves out to the middle of the ice to support D1. D1 moves the puck to D2 and moves underneath them. When D1 goes past the forward line, two forwards leave the line. The first one supports underneath the blue line in the middle of the ice, and the second supports up and across between the red line and the blue line. D2 passes to F1, who turns up ice and hits F2. F2 enters wide, F1 drives the net, and D1 coming down the backside dots is up in the play. F2 passes to D1 behind the net driver for a shot on goal.

As this rush is happening, D2 waits for them to go and then starts the drill again the other way.

Coaching Tips

- This drill is a timing drill as much as it is a passing drill.
- With good timing, the passing lanes will become better. Players should be in good lanes and call for passes.

Variation

- The player driving wide (F2) does not have to make every pass to the defenseman. They can shoot with a net driver. They can slip it to the net driver for a shot. They can slip it to the net driver, who then finds the backside defenseman. The options make this drill more realistic.

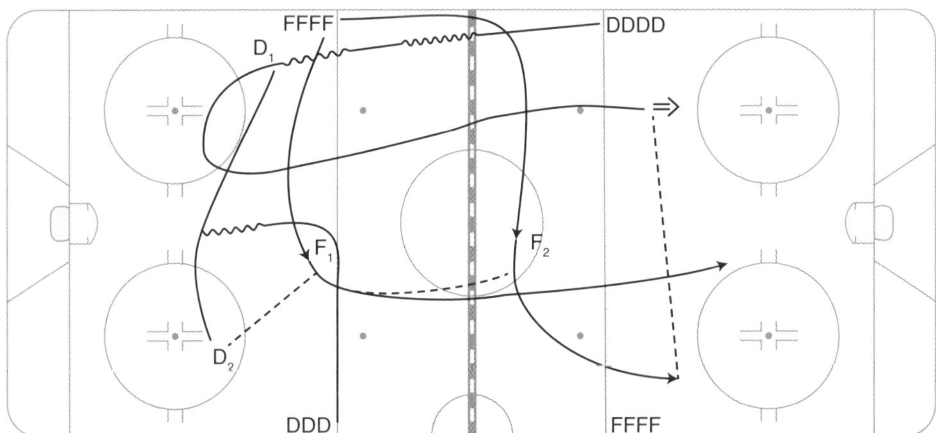

SKYREACH SHOOTING

Level of Difficulty

Moderate

Players

Full team required

Objectives

To work on passing and timing to have support and a defenseman joining the rush

Setup

Forwards line up at the red line on each side. Defensive players are in the middle. Coaches have pucks on opposite sides between the blue line and top of the circle. One puck stays in the middle with defensive players on each side.

Procedure

On the whistle, one forward from each line leaves and one defenseman leaves each way. The defenseman receives a pass from the line of defensemen and gives the puck back to them. The defenseman then receives a pass from the coach and passes to the forward line on the wall, who passes to the forward coming through the middle underneath the puck. The forward enters down the wall and delays (turning toward the wall). The defenseman goes around the neutral-zone circle and enters the zone as a late attacker to receive a pass from the forward. The defenseman then grabs a rimmed puck from the coach and passes to the forward coming off the wall so that both players get to shoot in the drill.

Coaching Tips

- Players can switch around in this drill. Forwards can play as defensemen at the start of the drill so that they are entering late into the zone and defensemen are carrying the puck making plays.
- The second puck can come low to high for a point shot if the second shooter is a defenseman.

Variations

- This drill also works by having the defenseman at the start of the drill hit the swinging forward through the middle to simulate a middle support pass. The middle forward can either move it to the line or skate it and enter wide.
- Two forwards can go and the defenseman can pass to the second forward, who then passes to the first forward. The drill now has a wide entry and a net driver. The defenseman is no longer required to go around the circle and can get up to fill the far dot lane, adding width.

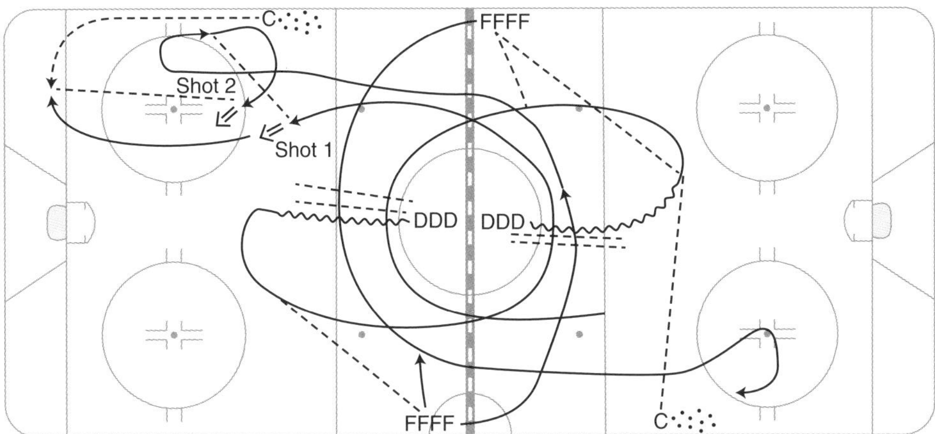

CHAPTER 7

Accepting the Rush

This chapter focuses on playing defense against the rush. Previous chapters have highlighted the importance of skating. Players who skate well can cover ice effortlessly as they move around. Their positioning on the ice is built on their understanding of what is happening and where they need to be at that time. As mentioned in chapter 6, Joining the Rush, the idea of not turning the puck over is fundamental. If the puck is in the offensive zone, the shift seems easier. When a team has the puck, they have no worry about the other team scoring. But if they turn the puck over, the situation changes. The team must now defend and protect against the opposition's attempt to create a scoring chance or get the puck into their offensive zone, where the team now defending must work to get it back.

INSIDE THE DOT LINES

A good place to start when thinking about accepting the rush is players' positioning relative to the dot lines. These dots in the neutral zone provide more than just a spot to drop the puck. They can also be used as landmarks on the ice. Because hashmarks, dots, offensive-zone dots, goal lines, and so on do not change from ice surface to ice surface, they can give players a reference as to where they should be. As defensive players are accepting the rush, they should try to be inside the dot line to protect the inside of the ice. The attacking forwards always try to move the defenders outside the dots to allow a teammate to skate inside the dots to the available ice. I refer to this idea as working into available space. The defenseman's goal is to push the puck wide in the neutral zone, allowing their team's forwards to track the puck back through the neutral zone. They then push attacking opponents to the outside, either before the blue line or after the blue line, trying to get them to give up the puck as they enter the zone. The offensive team is always trying to gain the blue line in the offensive zone with possession of the puck. The defending team tries force them into making a play they do not want to make so that the defending team can regain possession of the puck and start a breakout.

Using the Dot Lines As a Guide

As the opposing team is attacking, the dot lines (or "rails" as defense coach Eric Dubois of the Manitoba Moose calls them) are a good indicator for positioning while accepting the rush. As mentioned earlier, the dot lines are imaginary lines that run down the ice through the end-zone dots, neutral-zone dots, and end-zone dots in the other end. Defenders can use this landmark to ensure that they do not give up the middle of the ice. Defender should work to be on or inside the dot lines and adjust to what they see coming at them.

OUTSIDE THE DOT LINES

If defensive players are continually getting caught outside the dot lines, they will most likely get beat, which can happen in several ways. All three of these ways can lead to scoring chances for the opposing team.

Getting Beat to the Inside of the Ice

To guard against getting beat inside, defensemen must use good angles when they are closing on the puck and no teammate is back to the inside. The defenseman's stick goes to the puck, and their body lines up with the opponent's body. The defenseman can then force the opponent where they want them to go. The opponent who thinks they can cut back to the inside will run into the defenseman's shoulder.

Getting Beat With an Area Pass or a Hard Pass

The passing option is a tougher one to defend against because every team will try to have puck support. Players off the puck will work to get into available space. Defensive players should continue to work on their stick position, eye-hand coordination, foot position, and ability to break up passes. Defensemen should not let anything get through them to possession for another player. If the opponent passes it, the defenseman should make them put the puck into an area where there is no possession and they can battle for the puck.

Getting Beat to the Front of the Net

Getting beat to the net happens often in minor hockey. This can occur when the defender checks an opponent and somehow ends up on the wrong side of the battle. When battling, the defenseman should stay on the defensive side, that is, closer to the net than the offensive player. If the offensive player wants to get to the net, they must drive through the defender to get there. A defender who is consistently in the way of the attacking forward is in a good spot defensively.

SHUT DOWN THE WALL

Defensive players need to have or develop the skating ability to get from the dot line to the wall quickly. The defender who takes a long time to move from the dots to the wall allows the offensive player more time to make a play. Offensive players want time and space through the neutral zone to make a play. Shutting down the wall can happen in one of two ways: angling over backward or angling from back to front.

Angling Over Backward

To angle backward, the player turns their supporting leg and pushes multiple times off the same leg to move toward the wall. Players must be able to do this both ways so that on either side of the ice they can move quickly over and close off the space. If players are older (and have body contact in their game), they can move over with the intention of finishing a check. When players angle over backward, they must move with their stick in front of them and on the ice to prevent the offensive player from cutting back into the middle of the ice. They should start to angle over when the forward has committed to going wide down the wall. The time to move over laterally is when the offensive player is skating down the wall and the puck gets between the defenseman's stick and their feet. The defender can then maintain body position (protecting the middle of the ice) and angle the offensive player to run them out of space.

Angling From Back to Front

The second way to shut down the wall is to use a linear transition whereby the defensive player skates backward and opens up their hip on the board side, turns their skate heel to heel, and accelerates forward to the wall. The change from backward to forward should be done smoothly without missing a stride. Players who can do this well do not need to cross over. To use this skating technique, players can take weight off the foot that turns and point the toes on that leg to the direction they want to go. They should be able to do this without crossing over; instead, they push and get right into forward skating. The stick is important in this movement because it takes away space and helps to shut down the wall quicker.

CONTROLLING THE GAP

Defenders can improve their ability to accept or break up rushes by gaining better understanding of gap control. Skaters who do not trust their skating ability give up bigger gaps through the neutral zone, typically to avoid getting beat on the rush. The flip side of that is that if they worked on their skating and had a tighter gap, they would not get beat either. If a player is backing up into the zone to avoid getting beat back to the net, they will be leaving a lot of space in front of them. A good team will use that space for seam passes, cross and drops, one timers, or simply shots with the defender who is backing up and serving as a screen. Defenders can minimize that problem by having a tighter gap through the neutral zone. Ideally, defensemen force teams to dump the puck past them and give up possession on the rush rather than enter the zone with control.

Good gap control when accepting the rush starts in the offensive zone. Reading the play and staying closer to their forwards can often break up offensive rushes because the opposing team will not have the options they want with the puck. Several skating options contribute to good gap control, including forward skating, backward skating, transition skating (both heels first and toes first), edges (both one-foot and two-foot edges), and more. Most young players do not practice with the gap control they need in a game. They need to push the gap, challenge the attacking player, and understand their spacing. If the defenseman can cause the player with the puck to make a decision before reaching the attacking blue line, their gap is likely pretty good. The defender is in a position to possibly force an offside or make the offensive player give up possession of the puck before the blue line.

If the defensive player is backing up inside the blue line and allowing the offensive player to skate, depending on their puck support, the gap could be a little too large. A defenseman's gap control should be roughly one stick length. Being that tight to players is challenging, but any good offensive player wants space. They want space to work in, they want space to make plays in, and they want space to score in. The defensive player's job is to take space away from the offensive players. Therefore, starting in the offensive zone, with the help of tracking forwards, the gap should be tight to the attacking forwards.

Developing this ability begins in practice. When I work with defensive players in practice, I tell them to push their gap so far that they get beat. By learning what the gap looks like when they get beat, they start to understand how tight they need to play. Learning to adjust their gap to make it tighter is much better than just sitting back in every practice and every game. Players should work on their skating in practice and get comfortable playing tighter to the attacking forwards. Coaches sometimes yell or get upset if a player gets beat in practice. This type of correction will make the player not want to get beat. Consequently, they will sit back (so they do not get yelled at). If a player gets beat, the coach should encourage them and help them develop.

SURFING THE NEUTRAL ZONE

An area that has started to come up more frequently is the idea of "surfing" in the neutral zone. Surfing means that a defensive player is essentially angling the attacking forward by skating forward toward them. Some NHL teams want their defensemen skating forward in the neutral zone to put pressure on the attacking forwards quicker. This can happen in one of two ways. First, the weakside defender comes across the ice in the neutral zone to start their checking angle. When this happens, the strongside defenseman falls underneath the weakside defenseman and covers back inside the dots to allow the weakside defenseman to angle across the ice. Second, with a tracking forward coming back in the neutral zone, the strongside defenseman angles to the wall and works to force the puck carrier to give up possession with a chip. In both cases of surfing, support is tracking back and the defenseman can move their feet into a good angle and steer the attacking player where the defender wants them to go.

In either case, the idea of surfing in the neutral zone essentially starts players checking rather than defending. Checking is putting pressure on the puck. The defender skates forward and takes time and space away from the attacking team. The defender is in the attacker's face and initiating the battle. Defending is accepting the rush and skating backward. The offensive team has more space to attack and potentially more space to make plays. Defensive players need to read plays and make good decisions. Each game has situations when checking is better than defending and other situations when defending is better than checking. Ideally, players can make their decisions quickly and correctly. If they make an incorrect decision, coaches need to help correct it. They can correct it right away on the bench or show video to the player later (or possibly both).

DEFENSIVE PLAYS FOR ACCEPTING THE RUSH

A defensive player can accept the rush in several ways, depending on where they are on the ice, where their partner is, and where the forwards tracking back are. Defenders have to counteract various attacking plays to prevent the attacking forwards from getting scoring chances.

1 vs 1

In this scenario only one defenseman is back to counter an attacking forward coming down on them. The defenseman works to keep their body in a good position with the knee bent, shoulders back, and head (eyes) up. Their stick should be in front of them and working to go stick to puck. Several problems can occur as the defender skates backward versus the attacking forward coming at them.

1. *The defender gets off balance and leans and reaches for the puck.* The attacking forward then has options about where to put the puck. The way to counter this problem is to maintain balance, keep the stick in front, and not reach for the puck. The attacking forward will then have to work around the defender to get to the net. The defender must not give the attacking player any opportunities to beat them.
2. *The defending player looks down at the puck.* The defender's glance to the puck is a green light for the attacking forward to work around the defender's stick and around their body. Some offensive players can do remarkable things with the puck. If the defender is watching the puck on a 1 vs 1, they may soon be facing off at center ice after a goal. To counter this, the defensive

player should work to keep their eyes up on the offensive player, perhaps watching the logo on their jersey or their chest.

3. *The defending player swings at the puck with their stick.* The attacking player can often predict that a swing of the stick is coming. This gives them a chance to put the defender off balance and work around their stick to get a shot on net. Normally, defensive players should not take a chance on getting the puck because of the risk of getting beat. Stick position is important. The defensive player should keep their stick to the puck and work to take away the offensive player's options.

The biggest point to think about with 1 vs 1 play when accepting the rush is to maintain defensive-side positioning against whatever move the forward tries to use. The defender always keeps their body between the forward and the net.

One thing that the defensive player must avoid is backing in so far that the forward can use them as a screen. The attacking player will try to shoot the puck past them from a spot where the goalie will have difficulty picking it up. Forwards learn how to move the defender over just enough to create a lane to the net. They can also cause the defender to open up their feet and then shoot the puck through their legs. The skill of the forward with this option is something to watch for. The defenseman must be aware of their gap against the forward and the consequences if they give the attacking player more space.

2 vs 2

A 1 vs 1 situation may turn into a 2 vs 2 scenario, which is a defender and their partner versus two attacking forwards. If that happens, a couple of things can change the defenders' positioning. First, where is the puck entering against them, and what are the forwards trying to do? The forwards will most likely try to turn a 2 vs 2 into a 2 vs 1 and work to attack against one of the defensemen. Often, the supporting player (player without the puck) will attack the inside shoulder of the defenseman off the puck and work to attack against the strongside defender. If this happens, the weakside defender can slide over and put pressure on the supporting player in the event they get the puck to deny them any time and space.

Communication between the defending partners is important. Young players often have trouble with 2 vs 2 plays because they try to stay with one player and end up crossing or getting lost. The easiest way to play a 2 vs 2 is to stay in a lane and clearly call out switches. Anyone coming into a defender's lane is theirs, and anyone leaving their lane is their partner's. If two players are in a lane (as explained earlier), the partner can slide over to be a little closer than normal to keep the gap tight. Teams can work on this in practice using a simple 2 vs 2 rush and having attacking players crossing. The defensive players call out switches and recognize options as the attack unfolds.

The biggest thing on a 2 vs 2 play is to hold defensive-side positioning. The defender always keeps their body between the attacking forwards and the net. If they want to score, the attackers must go through the defender's body to get to the net.

3 vs 2

A 2 vs 2 rush that turns into a 3 vs 2 rush becomes more difficult for the defending team. The forward has more space to work with, and the additional player on the attack gives the puck handler another option to create offensive chances. The first challenge when defending against a 3 vs 2 is to get the puck to the outside in the neutral zone and out of the middle of the ice. The defensemen may be able to break up a play by having a good gap and good sticks. The attacking forward may try a pass to the outside (which can be deflected) or a saucer pass (which can be knocked down) to move the puck into available space. With a big gap, this pass can be easy to support in available space. With a tight gap, the defensemen can challenge the forward to make a difficult pass to get the puck to available space or potentially force an offside on the rush.

Puck on the Outside

When the puck is on the outside (assuming it gets there), the defensive player must read the options as to what is coming at them. Through communication with their partner, the defensive player must identify what is coming at them and work to slow down the offensive rush to give their backcheckers time to get back in the play. If the puck carrier shoots the puck, the strongside defender is responsible for the shooter and the weakside defender is responsible for the net-driving player. Because only two defenders are up against three attacking forwards, they must give up something. The goalie tries to control the shot and rebound to avoid putting the puck into a space where the third forward can get it.

Area Pass Behind

If the puck carrier throws an area pass behind the strongside defender as they are entering the zone, the partner can slide in behind the strongside defender to take the net-driving player and put pressure on the puck carrier as quickly as possible. This scenario often allows an offensive chance if the weakside defender gives the net-driving forward too much time and space. The net-driving forward who feels pressure from the backside defender may pass the puck to the third forward in the slot. This pass can be flat across the ice because the third forward is typically a half step behind the net driver. But if that pass is too close to the goalie, the goalie may be able to break up the play or freeze the puck. A flat pass across the slot allows the third forward to get possession of the puck with space between them and the goalie. Defenders must quickly get close to the area pass to take away space. They can do this by skating and by having a good stick to make it harder to receive the pass.

Kick-Out Pass

The attacking forward may choose to kick the puck out to a player who is not moving as fast as the other two net-driving players, which can also confuse the defense. This scenario is tough for the defense. They must communicate about what is happening and work to keep defensive-side positioning on the two players going to the net. The puck carrier coming down the middle of the ice passes the puck to a player who is not skating. The player who passed the puck continues to the net, and another attacker is heading to the net as well. The backchecking forwards need to take the kick-out pass to the wide forward, and the defensemen must back up and keep defensive-side positioning against the two forwards driving to the net. If the backchecker arrives in time, the play can be broken up quickly. If the backchecker doesn't get there, the wide forward may get a shot. The defenders box out in front as early as possible. The goal is to keep the attacking forward in a spot that minimizes the goalie's movement across the slot and keeps the shot as clear as possible.

2 vs 1

Perhaps the most dangerous rush that a defensive player must accept is a 2 vs 1 rush. Two offensive players are against one defender on the way back into the defensive zone. The goal for the defender is prevent anything from going through them that will force the goalie to move across the crease. One of the hardest things to play against is an early pass that right away forces the goalie to adjust their feet and move. The early pass is also tough for the defenseman because they must slide or adjust their skating pattern to avoid giving up a breakaway.

The defender in a 2 vs 1 should take in as much information as possible as the other team is attacking. Knowing who has the puck is the first thing to be aware of. Is the puck carrier one of the other team's more dangerous players? If so, is that player a shooter or a passer? If the player with the puck is a great player who shoots a lot, that can affect how the defender is going to play the rush. The puck carrier might be a player who does not shoot as much but is a great passer. The defender might then force the puck carrier into making a play they do not want to make, which is shooting. Knowing the skills of the player who has the puck is important in defending against the rush.

Puck Position on Ice

The next thing that players should be aware of is what side of the ice the puck is on and what the opponent's passing option is. Is the puck carrier right- or left-handed? Is the player off the puck right- or left-handed? This information is important in predicting what plays could happen. If the player on the left side of the ice is left-handed and the other player is left-handed as well, the puck carrier has the puck on their forehand and the player off the puck is a one-time option. If the player off the puck is right-handed, they are not a one-time option unless they get close to the net where they can "short one time" (shoot a one timer with no backswing) the puck. The defender should be aware of that as the attacker starts to increase their speed to get to the net.

A debatable topic on 2 vs 1 concerns using a slide to take away a passing option. This play can be an effective way to shut down a 2 vs 1. Some NHL teams are on "auto slide," meaning that on every 2 vs 1 their defenseman hits the ice and slides. If that is part of the scouting report, it likely works against the defensive team. My thought on this is that when the player is on their backhand or the defender can influence the attacking player to put the puck on their backhand, that is when the defender can slide. The feet should turn a little so that they are aimed to the corner of the ice, and the belly should be flat to the ice. As the player slides, their stick can work either to come at the puck (a right-handed defenseman sliding to the right) or swing the other way to extend the feet (a right-handed defenseman sliding to the left or vice versa). If the defender can deny the passing option to the middle of the ice, the goalie has the opportunity to focus on the save. The slide is a read. The defender believes it to be a good option based on who is coming down at them. The offensive player may not be the leading scorer on the opposing team, or they could be a player who is known to panic with the puck. If the defender thinks that they can take away space by sliding and having an active stick, they should do it with authority. If they hesitate or put themselves in an awkward position, the slide will not work.

One thing to consider on the slide is the depth of the puck. The player sliding should know where the puck is relative to their body. If the player with the puck can stop and allow the defender to slide pas them, they are back in a good position with no one in front of them. If they can make a play over only the defender's stick, they have an advantage. When sliding, the defender should try to position their body in line with the puck. The player with the puck will then have to make a pass over the defender's body (which is higher than just their stick) and will have to work around the slide at their feet. If the defender can put their body in a good position relative to the puck, they can have more success on a 2 vs 1.

Forwards on 2 vs 1 plays usually try to work into available space. If the defender is up close to the blue line and their gap is tight, there is more space behind them than in front of them. The player off the puck will work to get into that space, and the player with the puck will try to create a good passing angle into that space. If the defender is back farther (closer to their net), there is space in front of them and not behind them. The player off the puck needs to be in the available lane at the right time to accept a pass. The defender should recognize that their gap may be a little too big and see that the attackers are going to move the puck. Having a good stick to knock down a pass or break it up is a good thing, but defensemen also need the skating ability to adjust their route should the pass work out.

Another tactic that could work would be a bluff to the puck carrier. The defenseman makes it look as if they are pressuring the puck with their stick and feet, but they are not actually moving. This motion may change what the puck carrier is looking to do with the puck, either passing or shooting. This play can be effective against players as they approach the net because it gets them to react to the defender, rather than the other way around.

The main goal for the defender on a 2 vs 1 rush is to prevent a puck from getting through them to a high-percentage scoring chance. The defenseman must work to stay between the puck carrier and the player off the puck. They keep their stick active and know what is happening around them. The defender tries

COMMON ERROR

An error that players often make is sliding straight back with their feet toward the net. Pucks can bank off them and in. Players can also fail to get flat and leave gaps for the puck to go under them. The goal when sliding is to slide toward or closer to the puck carrier to reduce space and to do it quickly. The quick slide can catch the puck carrier off guard and force them to throw the puck rather than pass it.

to force the puck carrier into their second or third option rather than their first option, using their positioning, their stick, and their feet.

Giving the Goalie Chances to Save

Goalies may have some information that allows the defenseman's job to be easier on a 2 vs 1. Defenders always want to give their goalie a chance to make a save. If the attacking forward can saucer pass a puck over the defender's stick to the back side to an attacking teammate who has an empty net, the defender has not allowed their goalie a chance. Defensemen should work to give their goalie the best chance to make a save on a 2 vs 1. Success comes from communication and understanding what the goalie wants to give up. What shot do they want to face? What are their odds of making a save?

In practice, coaches should have their players work on 2 vs 1 from various positions. Rarely do 2 vs 1 plays happen all the way down the ice. Players can practice from the far blue line, from the red line, from the close blue line, and from the corner or below the goal line. Several variations of 2 vs 1 opportunities occur in games. A 2 vs 1 may come from the boards (on either side) or from the middle. Coaches can help their defensive players prepare for games by working on different attack angles for the 2 vs 1.

READING THE CONDITIONS

The options for the forwards on the rush will be similar from game to game as they try to create scoring chances. As discussed in the previous chapter, Joining the Rush, offensive forwards try to create three things on the rush. Defenders should be aware of what the attacking forwards are working to do.

1. Speed
2. Width
3. Depth

When attacking forwards create these three things on the 3 vs 2 rush, the job of the defensive team becomes much harder.

Speed

The attacking forwards are looking to attack quickly. Speed on the rush can come from either the player carrying the puck or the net-driving player (or both). This speed opens up the net-drive option for the forwards or the area pass to the net driver. Some plays may also have the wide player with the puck putting it to the net, looking for a rebound or a deflection from the net driver. The intention of speed on the rush is to push the defenders back to open up lanes.

Width

The width aspect comes up as players get a little older and can pass the puck harder. The intention of creating width is to have the net driver push the defense back on the rush and open up a seam pass across the middle. The seam pass makes the goalie move laterally across the crease and opens up scoring chances for the team on the rush.

On this play, forwards often try to shoot the puck quickly. This shot can be a one timer (if the player is skillful enough and on the correct side of the ice) or a quick release without any additional stickhandling. Offensive players who know where they are shooting before they get the puck can release the puck faster. The passer must put this pass on the tape across the seam to allow the rush to get to the net. Players have two options on the shot:

1. They can shoot to the area that the goalie has not yet reached. If the pass is hard and on the tape, the shooter can beat the goalie to that area because they will not have a chance to set their feet.
2. They can shoot to the area that the goalie came from. If the pass is slower or a saucer pass, the shooter can look to come back across to where the goalie came from. The slower pass means the goalie will have time to get over to the new angle and will be set to the shooter.

Depth

Depth on the attack comes from the net driver, who is typically the second player across the blue line. Most teams look to have their net driver drive between the defenders so that they are available for an area pass. In some scenarios the net driver may be away from the puck and come from the outside lane on the opposite side of the ice. In that case, the third player is high and in the middle of the ice or on the strongside dot line. Some teams call this option a wide drive or potentially a double drive if they send both the normal net driver and the wide driver to the net. If the puck carrier has no option, the puck can go low to the strongside post where the forward has a chance to be the first player on the puck.

This play calls to mind something I learned from coach Dave Struch when we worked with Team Canada U17. He said, "Protect your drivers." What he meant by that was that a player who drives the net and watches a teammate shoot and miss the net now must backcheck. On the next rush, they may not be as excited to drive the net. Struch talked about giving net drivers a reason to drive the net by giving them a puck or a play that allows them to play offensively. Against this type of rush, defensive players have to be aware of what is coming at them to the net and where they can place rebounds that come to them. In most cases, defensive players should put rebounds to the corners, not out to the blue line where the opposing team's defenseman will get the puck and look to shoot it back at the net again.

ANTICIPATING THE OFFENSE TO PLAN YOUR STRATEGY

Teams that can create speed, depth, and width on the rush will make the job of the defensive team much harder. The defense will have to think and react rather than control what happens next. Against a 3 vs 2, the defense is continually trying to influence what the puck carrier does with the puck. If the defense can influence where the puck goes, they are back in control and can minimize the damage against them.

Forwards on the rush try to identify three things:

1. Where are as the opposing defensemen?
2. Where is their support? Who can they move the puck to?
3. Where is the backchecker?

While offensive forwards scan for these three things as they skate the puck through the neutral zone, defensive players are looking for the same things. Defensive players should be scanning for what options they have and where their backchecker is to determine how they play out the scenario on that rush. If the gap is tight, and the attacker chips it past the defender, the defensive partner can close. If the gap is larger and the tracker is close, the tracker can pressure the puck and the defenseman can take the net-driving player. If they have close support and there is no tracker, the defender can play up and work to prevent the puck from getting through to the net driver. The defender must have an active stick and feet to block (or redirect) a pass that the puck carrier is trying to get through them.

Anticipation

Anytime a player is on the ice against the rush, they must be able to recognize what the offense wants to do. The quicker that defensive players can see what is developing, the more prepared they can be to stop it. During their shift downtime, players should scan the ice and recognize where everyone is all the time. By careful observation, they can start to see what the opponent is looking to do as the offensive team. The defensive player's goal is to force the opponent to make either a more difficult play or a play they do not want to make. If by accepting the rush, the defensive player forces the offense to give up possession and put the puck in the corner, they have done a good job and sealed off the rush. If by accepting the rush, the defensive player has delayed the attack long enough to allow a tracker or backchecker to get back into the play and be a problem, they have done a good job as well.

Tracking and Communicating

If the defense can pressure the offensive team to make a decision at the blue line with either a chip or a pass, they have made the play harder because the offense must worry about the play going offside. If the defense can slow down the net driver at the blue line by forcing the puck carrier to slow down, they have done a good job. Whenever the defense can change what the offensive team is looking to do, they gain a little bit of advantage for their team. To do that, they need help. They need communication from their defensive partner, and they need a forward, or possibly all forwards, tracking the puck back. Good tracking by the forwards allows a defenseman to stand up in the neutral zone or keep their gap tighter because they know that help is coming. Without a tracking forward, they must give up more space to prevent a 3 vs 2 from becoming a 2 vs 1. Forwards must track the puck back so that the defensemen can stay up with the play in the neutral zone and keep the gap tighter against the attacking forwards.

Accepting the rush is a challenging aspect of playing defense. The defenseman's goal in skating is to skate just as fast backward as the attacking forwards can skate forward. The defenseman with this ability can more easily accept the rush against them. They can control their gap, and by scanning, they can recognize threats. Players who can accept the rush properly and minimize the offensive attack can be extremely effective in the defensive zone. With support coming back in the form of tracking so that five are players back, defensive players can put their team in position for a great success.

1 VS 1 NEUTRAL-ZONE CIRCLE

Level of Difficulty

Easy

Players

Full team required

Objectives

To work on accepting the 1 vs 1 rush coming down the ice

Setup

Forwards are placed at opposite tops of the circle on each side of the ice. Defensive players are in the middle circle with the pucks.

Procedure

The drill starts on the whistle with a hard pass from the defender to a forward. The forward must let the puck cross the top of the circle (ringette line if the rink has it) before they take off down the ice. After passing the puck, the defensive player skates backwards around the circle and picks up the other player as they attack down the ice. The defender should remain inside the dot line. If they get beat, they should get beat wide.

Coaching Tips

- Players will try to cheat in the drill, either to get a better offensive chance as a forward or to have a better chance to stop the forward as a defenseman.
- The forwards will cheat by leaving early before the puck crosses the top of the circle. The defensemen will cheat by giving either a slow pass or a bad pass off the boards or in the forward's feet.
- If a player cheats, the coach should stop the group and make them start again.

Variation

- As the forward is attacking, the coach can blow their whistle to have the forward either continue around the neutral-zone circle and attack the other end or loop back to the blue line they already went over and attack again. Either way, the defender will have to stop, get their feet up the ice, and work to get back again. This option is tough on the defender as they will really have to move.

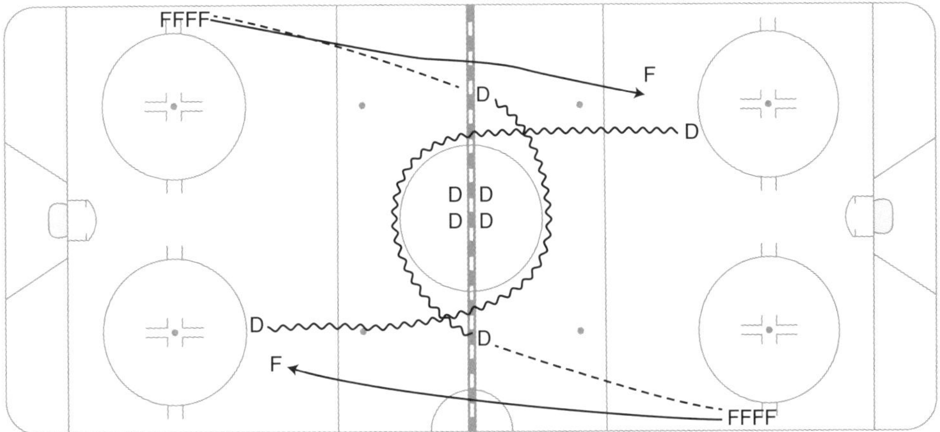

2 VS 2 HALF ICE

Level of Difficulty

Moderate

Players

Full team required

Objectives

To work on accepting the rush

Setup

Pucks are placed at the red line with a forward on each side. Two defensemen start just inside the blue line on each side.

Procedure

This 2 vs 2 drill starts when the players are ready. No whistle is needed because when the forward sees that things are good, they can start. F1 passes to D1, who passes to D2. F1 opens up and receives a seam pass from D2. F1 now has the puck and passes it back to the line where they started, and F2 attacks with F1 swinging. D1 and D2 gap up and pivot backward to accept the rush, staying in their lanes and communicating. F1-D1-D2-F1-F2.

Coaching Tips

- The defensemen can surf in the neutral zone to eliminate space, or they can accept the rush as the forwards attack.
- The defensemen must communicate and hold their ice.

Variations

- Offensive players can pressure with direct pressure and try to make it a 2 vs 1 rather than a 2 vs 2.
- Offensive players can cross and drop and force the defenders to react.
- The coach can add a second puck as a point shot with a box out for the defensive players and rebound control. The forwards look to deflect the puck and track rebounds, and the defensive players look to allow their goalie to see the puck and clear rebounds.

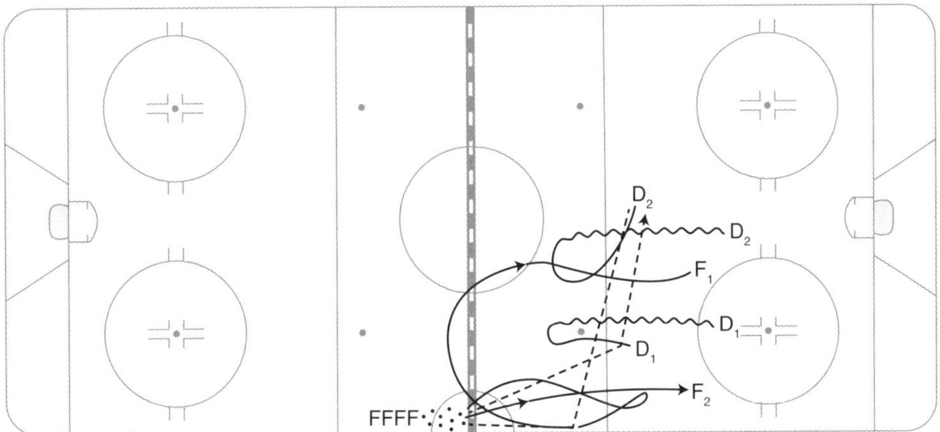

2 VS 2 × 2

Level of Difficulty

Moderate

Players

Full team required

Objectives

To work on accepting the rush and getting up ice with a good gap for the second 2 vs 2

Setup

The forwards are at both blue lines on each side with pucks. Defensive players line up near the red line in the middle of the ice. Two defenders start at the blue line with their stick on the line.

Procedure

On the whistle, one forward from each side leaves at the same side as the defensive players who are on the blue line (see 1 in diagram). One forward has a puck, and the other forward swings underneath them so that the drop pass is easier. F1 drops the puck to F2. When the drop pass happens, the defensemen can push off the blue line quickly and get ready to play the rush. With the defensive players waiting until the drop pass, it establishes a gap that is better for them to force the forwards to make a play in the neutral zone. After the first rush ends, the coach blows the whistle and two forwards from the other line skate around the neutral-zone circle, again exchanging the puck with a drop pass and attacking (see 2 in diagram). The two defensive players in the drill must get up and play the second 2 vs 2 with the forwards having a little more speed.

After they go past, two new defensive players move to the opposite blue line and the drill can start the other way.

Coaching Tips

- This drill emphasizes speed, and the defensive players might get blown away the first couple of times.
- They will have to trust their footwork and skating to keep them in good spots.

Variations

- The coach can let the 2 vs 2 play out if they want to work on other things with the drill, such as being harder on pucks, being first on pucks, or simulating a breakout with a coach as a winger.
- The coach can add a puck at the end that goes low to high for a point shot either directly from the waiting defensive player or after a defender-to-defender pass. This variation focuses the defense on working on the box-out portion of their defensive-zone coverage.

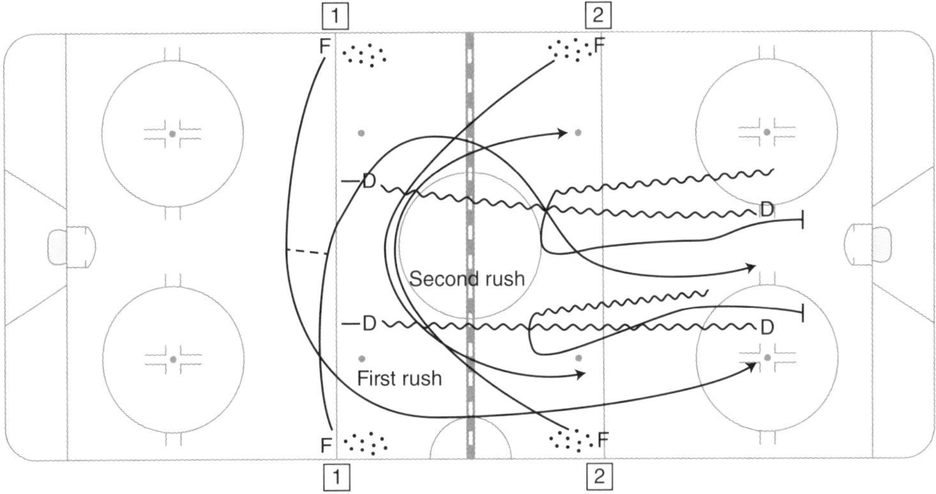

3 VS 2 AROUND THE PILE

Level of Difficulty
Hard

Players
Full team required

Objectives

To work on down low 3 vs 2 and on the rush 3 vs 2

Setup

Three offensive players set up in the offensive zone with two defensive players. Everybody else sets up in the center-ice circle. A coach has pucks in the middle circle.

Procedure

The coach spots a puck into the offensive zone where the offensive players play it. The two defensemen work to break up the play without allowing a dangerous shot to the net. Whenever the first puck is done, the coach blows the whistle and one of the forwards comes around the pile of players in the middle of the ice and grabs a spotted puck. The other two forwards support the puck, while the defensive players establish a good gap. The offensive forwards attack 3 vs 2 against the two defenders. As soon as they go past, the other side can have players move in and get ready to go.

Coaching Tips

- Defensive players should be communicating and trying to force offensive players to make their second or third decision with the puck.
- If defensive players can take away the easy option and force the attackers into making a tougher decision, they will have more success in shutting down the rush.

Variation

- The coach can emphasize the offensive attack options with net drives, dot-lane options, and speed. Shots should come to the net or pucks should go below the goal line each time three forwards attack, so there are no turnovers.

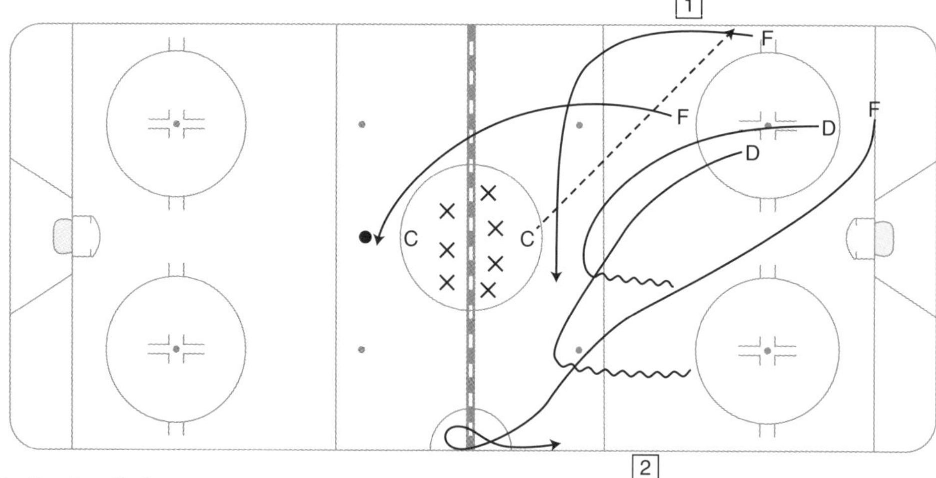

DIAMOND 2 VS 1

Level of Difficulty

Moderate

Players

Full team required

Objectives

To work on passing and puck support in a 2 vs 1 drill

Setup

Offensive forwards set up at the red line on each side. The defensive players are at opposite blue lines. Pucks can be on one side with the forwards.

Procedure

A whistle can start the drill, but it is not needed again for the drill as it continues. F1 passes to D1, and F2 moves into the neutral-zone circle and opens up. D1 hits F2, while F1 moves into the neutral-zone circle. F2 hits D2, who slides with the puck and passes to F1. F1 and F2 attack against D1 down the ice. The drill then starts the other way against D2. F1-D1-F2-D2-F1—2 vs 1.

The drill can go back and forth a couple of times and then stop and start the other way so that the goalie faces pucks coming from the other wing.

Coaching Tips

- This is a great passing and support drill.
- Players should be patient to create good passing lanes, and they should make passes without doing a whole bunch of stickhandles.

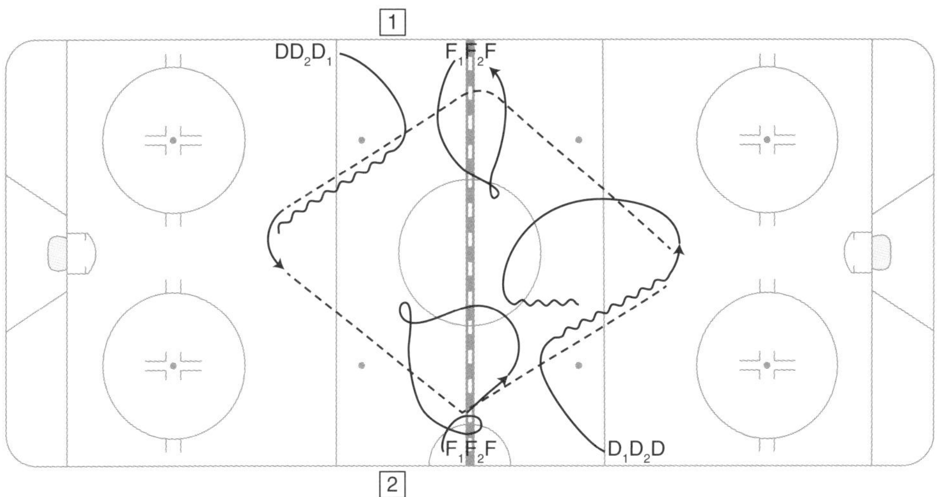

1 ON 1 × 2 SAME SIDE

Level of Difficulty

Easy

Players

Full team required

Objectives

This 1-on-1 drill focuses on keeping good defensive-side positioning while accepting the rush.

Setup

Defensive players with pucks set up at opposite blue lines, and the forwards are at the red line on each side facing the defensive players.

Procedure

On the whistle, a defensive player passes a puck to a forward (see 1 in diagram). The forward must allow the puck to cross the red line and can then take off down the wall. The defender moves after they pass around the neutral-zone dot and pivot backward to accept the rush. After the first rush ends, the coach at the back of the line of defensive players spots a second puck to the forward (see 2 in diagram). They pick it up and work to score, and the defensive player works to angle and check without skating backward. When the work with that puck ends, the drill can restart. Players should switch sides in this drill after a couple of minutes.

Coaching Tips

- On the initial rush, the defensive player should keep their outside shoulder lined up with the inside shoulder of the attacking forward. If the defender forces an outside shot, they have done their job because the goalie should make that angle save.
- On the second puck, checking becomes an important part of the drill because the defender must close off the space quickly. Players should check rather than defend by pivoting backward and moving closer to the net inside their own zone. They should be moving forward to take away time and space.

Variation

- The coach can throw a third puck to the net for a deflection from the forward and a box out from the defensive player.

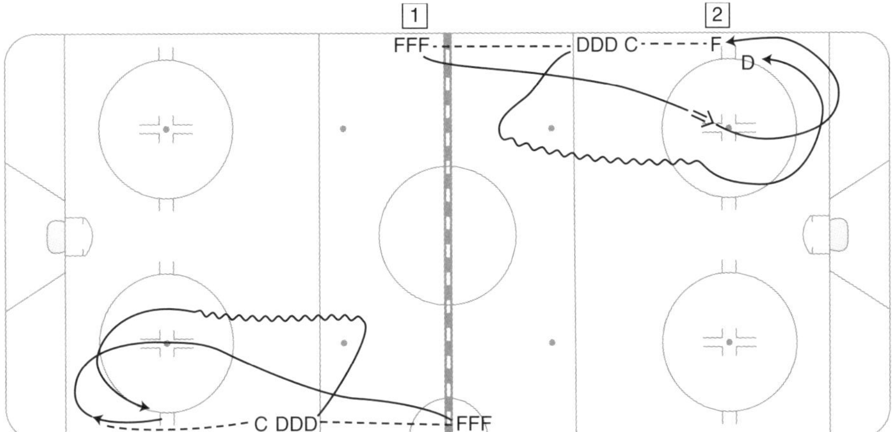

CHAPTER 8

Communication and Scanning

Communication is a key component among all high-level teams because it allows players to assist their teammates and rely on them in game situations. Learning to communicate with teammates is crucial to consistent play and play at higher levels. Defensive partners who play well together communicate well together. They talk on the ice, they talk off the ice, and they likely spend time sorting out what to do and when to do it.

Those who have witnessed an NHL team practice will readily remember how loud players communicate, even for something as simple as calling for a pass. Players call for an "over" in the defensive zone as their partner goes back for a puck in the corner. Whatever the option is, a teammate can help make decisions because they can see the play develop as the opponent brings pressure. Communication is a sought-after skill for any player. Consider a defensive player going to the corner to retrieve a puck and having a partner calling out to them. The partner is the player's eyes and can help them move the puck past pressure. They can see the pressure and where ice is available to move into. The retrieval play is much easier for those willing to listen to their partner.

OVERCOMING SHYNESS

Effective communication makes the game much easier for everyone on the ice. This concept seems so simple that we might expect players to do it without ever being reminded. But many players do not talk in practice and then, not surprisingly, do not talk in games. This lack of communication causes teams to have problems with breakouts and puck retrievals, to struggle coming back on the

Coaching Tip

A couple of years ago I was having trouble with communication in practice with a high school team. The players were not calling for passes or helping each other in lines for drills. Offering constant reminders and engaging them with extensive discussions about the importance of communication had no effect. I had had enough. I blew the whistle and called them all to the board for an explanation of the next drill. I started the presentation but did not talk. All I did was draw. I drew the routes for the players. I marked the passes. But the players had no idea what was going on. I knew what would happen when the players tried the drill, but I was prepared to sacrifice the time to see them fail miserably. When I was done drawing up the drill, I made a motion like, "OK, let's go" without saying anything. The players lined up in confusion. They did not know who started with the puck or where they passed it. They did not know which players went where and how they should move around the ice. I gave them three reps of the drill before I blew it down and asked them how important communication was. They got the message and started to communicate much better after that.

backcheck, and to flounder offensively with the available options on the rush. I tell players that they can be shy

- at home,
- at school,
- around their friends,
- but not on the ice!

In practice, the importance of communication should be emphasized daily. Coaches should reach the point where they do not have to say anything in practice about communication. Early in the season, coaches should tell players to talk, to yell for passes, and to call out plays. The idea is to build a team that communicates. The game becomes much easier when they talk.

UNDERSTANDING WHO YOU ARE PLAYING

An area that can be communicated long before the game starts concerns which players on the opposing team are dangerous. What are their tendencies? What should the team watch for when those players get on the ice? The easiest way to identify the most dangerous players on the other team is to look at the stat sheet. Who has the most goals and most points? A discussion with all of the defensive core can ensure that everyone is aware come game time. The defensive players should know who the opponent's shooters are and who their passers are. Again, the stat sheet is gold. A player who has a lot of goals but not many assists is a shooter. The opposite is true for pass-first players. Knowledge of the opponent can lead to success come game time.

DEFENSIVE PLAYERS WORKING TOGETHER

When on the ice, defensive partners need to work on their communication. One of the most important ways that players can communicate is helping their defensive partner retrieve a puck out of the corner. The defender going back into the corner needs to be spatially aware of two things:

1. They need to know where their partner is.
2. They need to know where the pressure is coming from.

This information comes from an effective shoulder check. Some coaches talk about taking two shoulder checks, one over each shoulder. But I think that players can do more than this, although not by doing more shoulder checks. Instead, they should do more scanning before they turn to become aware of where players are. This scanning starts when the player is looking up ice and accepting the rush. At this time, they should be identifying where and who the opponent's three forwards are. As the puck gets dumped past the defender, they can turn with an idea of where the other team's forwards are. They should know the same for their own team—where their defensive partner is as an option and where the closest forward is as a passing option for the retrieval. Having this in mind before the player turns is a good start to making a successful retrieval.

As the player starts to turn, their feet turn, their body turns, and finally their eyes turn. Keeping their eyes up ice allows the player to see the forecheckers for a half second longer. Now when the defender is into their first three or four steps to accelerate to the puck, their shoulder check is to confirm what they already know rather than to try to make a decision. Their decision results from a combination of what is coming at them, where their support is, and what their defensive partner is calling. This technique should allow a cleaner, more consistent exit, which is the goal for a defensive player going back into the corner for a puck that is dumped past them.

Scanning in the Neutral Zone

This idea can also be used in the neutral zone on pucks that get dumped past the defensive player. Ideally, their partner communicates the available options. The defenseman going back to get the puck has the quick-up option, the option to pass to their partner, the option to move the puck into the middle of the ice, and the option to move the puck across the ice to the weakside winger. This puck typically requires a pass to advance it. Rarely does a defender go back in the neutral zone and skate the puck back into the offensive zone. The best option should be communicated to the defenseman going back for the puck by their defensive partner, who can see everything happening from the middle of the ice or from a spot where they can get their eyes up the ice quickly.

Blue-Line Rule

One option that comes up when scanning the ice is a game situation that I call the blue-line rule. This rule takes effect when a player recognizes that they are under pressure as they retrieve the puck just inside their own blue line. Their defensive partner yells, "Blue line," which means that the retrieving player should simply chip the puck back off the wall into the neutral zone to trap the opposing player in the offensive zone. To start with this skill, players can push the puck off the wall. As they become stronger and more aware, they can look to elevate the puck to give them more time. When the puck gets chipped back into the neutral zone, rarely does an offensive player stop and get back on side quickly. More commonly, the attacking forward continues skating and loops back to the neutral zone. If the defenseman can get the puck back into the neutral zone, they buy themselves time to get back into position to accept the next rush. This play happens often because the game happens quickly and the defender-to-defender pass may not be there. At times the defenseman may not have time or space to work around the puck and get their eyes back up ice. This awareness of pressure is a next-level skill to knowing what options are available, even under pressure. As players start to understand the blue-line rule when going back for pucks, they will learn to spot the puck either harder or softer. They will look to put the puck into an area where a teammate can get it back or put pressure on the other team as they work to retrieve it. On this pressure-type play, the initial reaction is to move the puck out of the zone and get it to a safer spot on the ice.

OFFENSIVE-ZONE COMMUNICATION

When moving into the offensive zone, the communication that comes up regularly involves identifying plays with the team's forwards and the defensive partner. Telling a teammate to shoot, calling for a pass, or simply saying, "Reset" to tell the defensive partner to rim the puck back behind the net are all simple things that players can work on in practice. When the team starts to communicate in the offensive zone, they can extend their time in the offensive zone. As they do this, the other team gets tired. If the team can get a line change in while keeping possession of the puck, they have a serious chance to make something good happen. The defensive players can activate, they can dive down the middle, they can slide across the line, or they can activate down the backside to help create offensive-zone time with the puck. At times they will be used on offense, and at other times they won't. The ability to recognize the option that could work best is a high-level skill that can be introduced to defensive players at a young age. They can learn early how they can be effective in the offensive zone.

DEFENSIVE-ZONE COMMUNICATION

Communication in the defensive zone is probably the most important area where it can occur. The more that a team can communicate from goalie to defenseman and defenseman to partner, the quicker they can get the puck out of their zone. The less time they spend in their own zone, the more time they are spending in attacking with the puck and giving their team a better chance to win.

Problems with communication in the defensive zone usually result from players not reacting quickly enough to what is being said to them (or yelled at them) by their teammates. Teams should simplify the communication keys to make them easier to understand. For example, a phrase like "Turn it up" can be simplified to "Up," meaning to move the puck up the wall right away. One-word calls that are easy to understand will make the next play easier and more successful. Words that can used include the following:

- Over—move the puck to the partner.
- Up—move the puck up the wall right away.
- Net—move the puck in behind the net.
- Rim—shoot the puck around the boards while under pressure.
- Flip—work to elevate the puck to relieve pressure.
- Wheel—skate the puck around behind the net
- Bump—make a short, 6- to 8-foot (2 to 2.5 m) pass, potentially off the wall, to support or into available ice.
- Reverse—when feeling pressure from behind, use the wall while skating behind the net.
- Middle—while skating with the puck, move it to the middle of the ice.
- Glass—elevate the puck off the glass to relieve pressure.
- Time—pressure is not coming, and space is available to work into.

CONSISTENCY WITH COMMUNICATION

A challenge that coaches may have with their teams is getting them to communicate with each other all the time. The game becomes easier when teammates help each other make decisions or tell each other where pressure.is coming

Shift Downtime

I learned the concept of shift downtime from Paul Boutilier. When Paul referred to this with defensive players, he meant the time that players were on the ice but not actively involved in the play. This was a time to scan the ice and count to three (to locate the opponent's three forwards). The players had time to understand what was happening around them. Players who use their shift downtime properly can set themselves up for a better shift overall. They should be looking to see what situation is developing, where the puck is going to go, where they can be a better option for their partner, and where they should be to keep gaps tighter. In their shift downtime, they should be always communicating with their defensive partner about the upcoming play. Is a dangerous forward on the ice or coming on the ice? Is someone behind them as the strongside defender? What else might be happening?

from. Coming up with what to call everything is a job for the coaches and the team together. Everyone needs to know where the puck is going when a call is made. If someone says, "Over" to a defensive player, they will probably move the puck over to their partner using the defender-to-defender option. This term is common among players as they get to a higher level. Some teams worry about opponents knowing their calls, so they change the terms. Other teams are not concerned about the opposing team knowing, and they keep the terms simple. But player should know that some teams make calls to confuse their opponents. If the opposing team calls, "Reverse," the defensemen must be aware that the call is from the other team, not theirs. Video clips of this type of play often appear on highlight shows.

Communication is a key foundation of any successful team. A team that communicates well plays the game with more awareness because they help each other make decisions. Players who talk to teammates make the game easier for everyone. Communication starts in practice, and even before practice in the dressing room as players talk. Coaches can move players around in the room so that they sit beside other players and talk to different teammates each day. Building a culture in which players know each other and talk to each other is goal for every coach. Teams that communicate clearly and frequently will be teams that have successful seasons.

STICKHANDLING COMMUNICATION

Level of Difficulty

Easy

Players

A team of players

Objectives

To work on communicating at the start of practice for the first drill

Setup

The players split up into two groups. The first group has pucks and starts on the boards at the red line. The second group is spread out in the neutral zone and into the end zones.

Procedure

The group with the pucks starts skating around and looks to pass the puck to a player without a puck. The player who receives the pass then looks to get it back to the player who passed it to them when they call for the puck. This action continues with players calling for passes and moving the puck. After the first group goes for roughly 30 seconds, the groups switch. The second option in this drill is to have the pass receiver pass it back to a different player. Players cannot give the puck back to the player who passed it to them. This option really gets players communicating and calling for passes.

Coaching Tips

- This drill becomes interesting after the switch from option 1 to option 2. Passes may not be very good because lots of stuff will be going in with players moving in the neutral zone.
- This drill is a good way to wake up players at the start of practice.

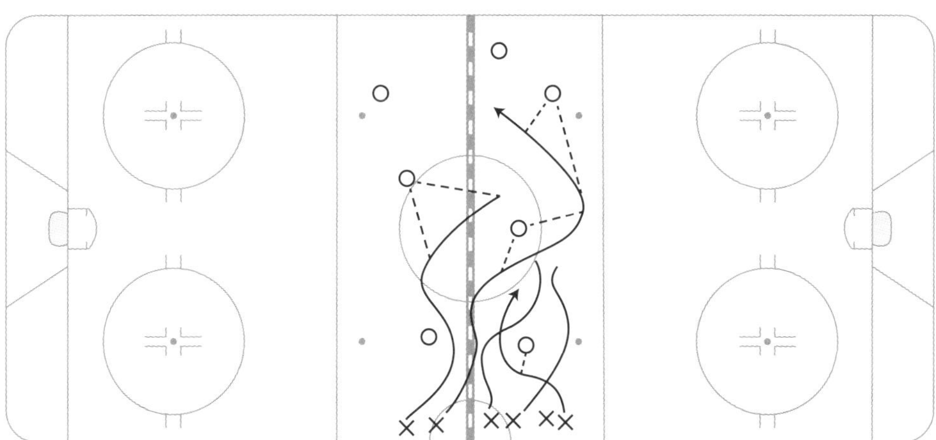

LISTEN TO YOUR PARTNER

Level of Difficulty

Easy

Players

Four or more defensemen or forwards

Objectives

To work reacting to calls from partners

Setup

One line of players starts at the blue line with a coach, who spots a puck.

Procedure

The line of players has three players going in the drill. The first player retrieves the puck, the second player is a forechecker, and the third player is a partner or first forward back. The coach spots the puck. The first player retrieves it, and the second player pressures one way or the other, either from the middle to the wall or from the wall to the middle. The third player moves to support the puck and makes a call that works for puck movement. They can move to the weak side of the ice for a defender-to-defender pass or move in behind their partner for a reverse or wall bump. They can also stay on the close post, and the player who retrieves the puck can absorb contact and bump it for the short pass. If another group of three is ready to go, they can start right after the first group finishes. If the same group goes again, they should rotate positions.

Coaching Tips

- Players may initially call the wrong thing based on the pressure coming at their partner. As players improve at the drill, their calls will become clearer.
- At the start of the season, players should work on defender-to-defender overs. As the season progresses, players can try other options.
- Giving players options in the drill throughout the season will help them improve.

Variation

- The drill can start with two players retrieving the puck, two forecheckers, and a low forward coming back to support the puck. The low forward must call what they see to the defensive players, who are now under pressure. The forecheckers can either come on the same side of the ice (representing a 1-2-2) or come to the two defensive players (representing a 2-1-2). The other players must react.

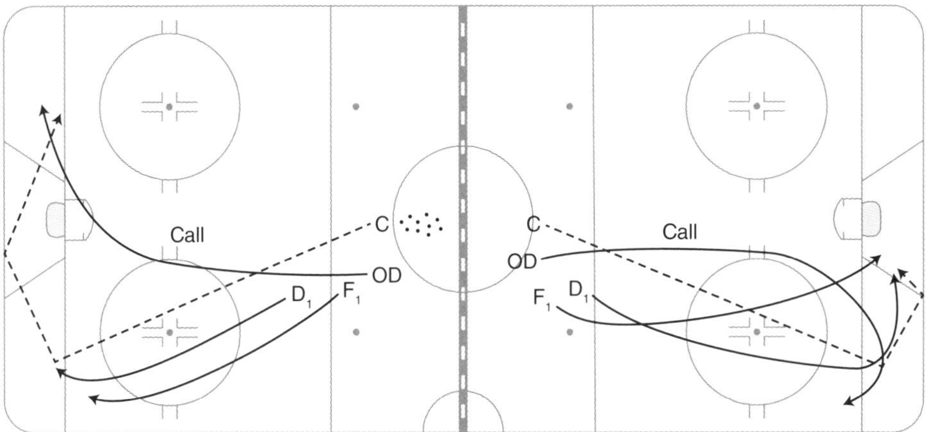

CALL OUT WHAT YOU SEE

Level of Difficulty
Easy

Players
Any number of players

Objectives
To have players call out numbers as they see them

Setup
The coach holds up any number of fingers between none and five.

Procedure
The drill has a coach in the middle, who will be showing numbers to players as they move through the drill. A player starts skating and grabs a puck on one side of the circle. As they grab a puck, they look over their shoulder and call out the number that the coach is holding up. After calling out the number, the player turns tightly, cuts back the other way, and does the same thing as the coach holds up another number. After the coach calls out the second number, the player turns tightly again, leaves their puck, and heads to grab the next one. The player is done after performing the action three times.

Coaching Tips
- Players must make eye contact with the coach to see the numbers.
- The coach can wait until players are a little past them so that they must look back over their shoulder to find the number.
- This simple drill gets players to start calling out what they see.

Variation
- Players can work in the opposite direction, which ends up having them turn the other way first. Ultimately, however, the pattern is a figure eight at each puck, so it ends up being the same thing.

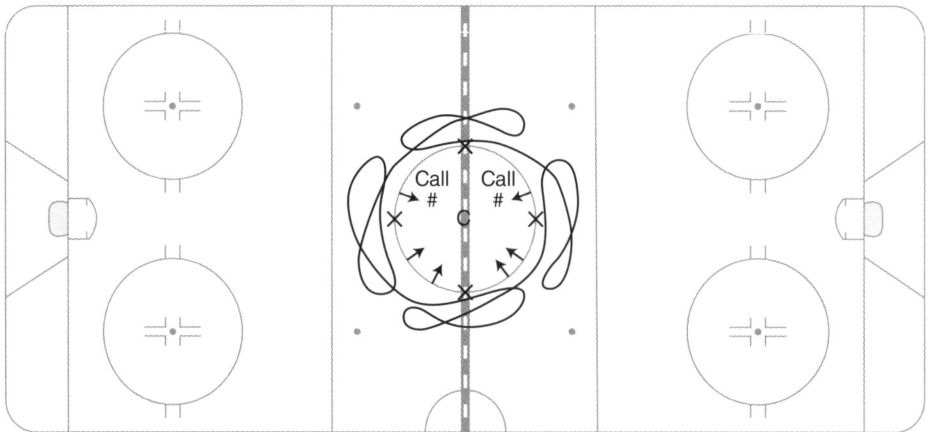

BLUE-LINE RULE

Level of Difficulty

Easy

Players

Any number of players

Objectives

To work on execution of the blue-line rule

Setup

A line of players with pucks and a coach are at the red line.

Procedure

The coach spots a puck just inside the blue line, and a player goes back for it. As they skate into the puck, they move the puck to the wall side of them and chip it back to the coach (1 in diagram). When the coach gets the puck back, the next player goes.

Coaching Tip

- Players should switch sides in this drill so that they can work on their symmetry skills (forehand and backhand).

Variations

- The player who just completed the drill can be a partner coming back in the middle of the ice. They call, “Blue” to their partner so that the partner knows they are getting the puck back over the blue line (2 in diagram).
- Pressure can be added on the puck-retrieving player so that they know what pressure on their hips feels like in a game.

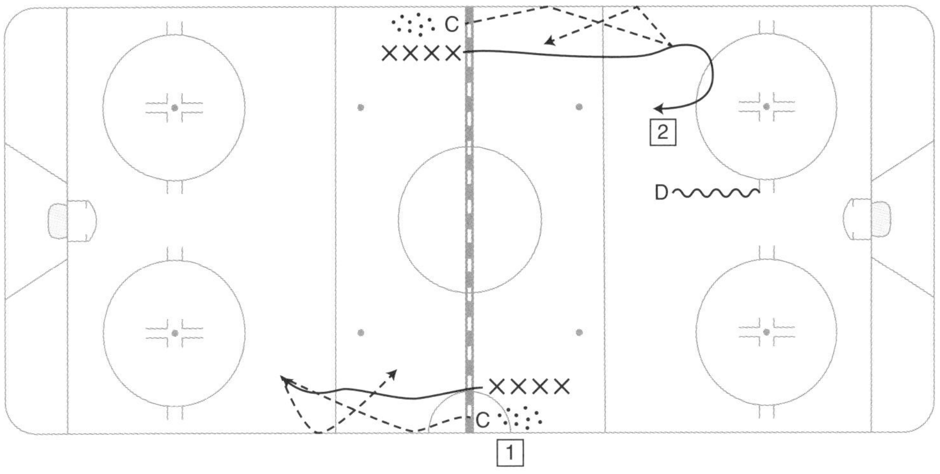

CHAPTER 9

Defensive-Zone Coverage

Defensive-zone coverage should be a focus for any team in practice early in the season. This emphasis will help reduce the number of goals that are scored against the team and will cut down on high-percentage chances in their defensive zone. Higher-level teams are always looking for defensive players who are responsible in the defensive zone because the first job of a defenseman is to play defense. The offensive side of a defenseman is the secondary item as the puck comes out of the zone.

Each team that a defenseman plays on will likely have a coach with a different philosophy about what should happen in the defensive zone. Some teams are man to man, some use more of a zone, and some play what is called five on a dice. More teams are using hybrids at the NHL and AHL level where players are asked to make reads based on what is happening in the game. In saying that, the basic concepts are similar in what players are asked to do in the defensive zone. Teams that have coverage in layers and teams that protect the house (the slot area around the net) typically have success over the course of the season.

DEFENSIVE-ZONE COVERAGE

The two main goals in the defensive zone are to take away space quickly and to break up clean possession. The ability to close quickly will set up a player for success in the defensive zone. Ideally, a team always starts with one defenseman in the corner on the puck. That way, if the team can keep defensive-side positioning, they should be able to close quickly and eliminate players. If the defensive team doesn't hold position, however, they do not close quickly and give away time and space. With the defense closing quickly on forwards in the corner, they can then work to break up possession. Defensive players want to force the forward to make a play they do not want to make—perhaps to put a puck back on the wall or make a low-to-high pass that is under pressure. The next defender can then close quickly. Whatever structure the team is playing in the defensive zone, the goal is to eliminate time and space quickly and then break up possession.

D1 and D2

When working with young defensive players, the idea of D1 and D2 can be useful. D1 can be a player in the corner, and D2 can be the net-front player. The placements of D1 and D2 are simple concepts whereby coaches can show the correct locations on a coach's board or in video. Coaches can then make sure that defensive players understand their responsibilities—working in the corner to deny options and working to control the front of the net. These key responsibilities cannot be overlooked. Understanding how to get to the corner quickly through skating and angles is a key to playing the position. An important aspect of strongside defensive positioning is not getting beat out of the corner and back to the front of the net. Keeping defensive-side positioning and making sure that their body is always between the offensive player and the net is a key for both young defensive players and older established pros.

D1 (Corner)

The D1 player's job is to initiate contact with the puck carrier by keeping defensive-side positioning, meaning that their body is always between the offensive player and the net. D1 should be on the puck quickly, working to take away the puck carrier and influence where they move the puck. D1's checking angle will allow their teammates to anticipate where the puck is going and take away that option. D1 can work to have their stick to the puck and their hips to the puck carrier's hips. Doing this will help to control where the offensive player is going. Should the offense try to cut back, D1 can finish them to the wall. Should the offensive player keep going, D1 can also finish them to the wall. Most likely the offense will try to skate away from pressure, so if D1 can make contact with the puck and disrupt possession, they have done a good job.

D2 (Net Front)

D2's job is to work to seal the net by standing on the close post if the puck is in the corner. They should remain net front until they are needed for help or support, or they can release out to be a passing option. If D2 is standing on the back post, a decent amount of space is available to a player moving into that area. The defense is working to shut down available space, so the net-front D2 should stand on the close post to be closer to the puck in the corner. At higher levels, this positioning will also allow the net-front D2 to help outnumber the offensive team in the corner by getting involved in the corner battle. With F1 (low forward), the team is strong in the corner, and the net-front winger (weakside winger F2) slides down into a position where they cover the front of the net. If a forward from the opposing team is net front, D2 is responsible for them. This net-front defensive player should be in a position so that their stick takes away a passing lane and their body takes away a shooting lane. If D2 thinks that a pass could come to their player, they can get closer and deny the passing option.

Forward Roles

Working with the defensemen, the forwards have important roles in defensive-zone coverage. Whichever structure the team is playing, the forwards' play is crucial. When the forwards close quickly on the half wall or on the defensive blue line, they take away the time and space that the offensive team has to make decisions.

F1 (Low Forward)

F1 (low forward) used to be the centerman more frequently. The game has changed a bit in that F1 can now be any of the three forwards. Forwards must learn about playing in the defensive zone and understand the roles of the three forwards. F1 low can work off D1 to help cover specific areas of the ice. Typically, this will happen in the defensive-zone corners and around the net. The easiest way to think about this is to regard F1 as a secondary layer to the coverage on a puck in the corner. They can be behind D1, who is on the puck in the corner. F1 is in a position where they are on the defensive side of the second player into the battle. Many younger teams use F1 as their centerman, but at the higher levels this position can be any forward who is the first forward back into the zone. This forward can communicate with the defensemen to let them know that they have support down low behind them. In a structure like five on a dice, the role of F1 is to play behind D1 and pick up that next forward or be in support for a loose puck.

F2 and F3 Wingers

F2 and F3 are the second and third forwards coming back into the defensive zone. These players could be the low players in the opposite end who are late on the backcheck compared with F1, who is ahead of them. These players are generally the wingers with young teams but could be any of the three forwards. F2 and F3 have important roles in defensive-zone coverage. They work to take away the offensive team's defensemen at the blue line and are responsible to cover the slot on the weakside of the ice. Players can use landmarks—markings on the ice that do not change from ice surface to ice surface—to know where they should be standing and reading the play from. Landmarks that are useful for the F2 and F3 are the hashmarks in front of the net and the top of the circle in line with the dot line. Wingers commonly stand in these areas as a starting point in the defensive zone. The strongside winger can be positioned near the top of the circle with one hand on their stick and their toes facing the wall. This positioning will deny pucks to the top and protect the lane to the net, keeping defensive-side positioning. The net-front winger can be near the hashmarks with one hand on their stick.

The F3 player who is net front helping cover the slot has a couple jobs. One job is to help cover anyone in the slot as well as to be aware of the offensive defensemen. The job of sliding to help cover a forward from the opposing team is a shared job between F3 and D2. Communication among defensemen and forwards is crucial in defensive-zone coverage. For example, the net-front defenseman must make sure that the team does not give up scoring chances from the soft area between all the defenders.

F2 (Slot Winger)

F2, the slot winger, is located somewhere between the hash marks and the top of the circle. They have the option to move a little to help cover an offensive slot forward. Their stick should be on the ice to take away space and block passing lanes. Ideally, their stick is in the middle of the ice, and their feet are facing the battle. They should be able to see both the puck and the opponent they are responsible for.

F3 (Side Winger)

F3, the strongside winger, is responsible for covering the strongside defenseman. F3 can start standing roughly at the top of the circle in line with the dot and with their toes pointed out toward the wall. They can see the battle for the puck, as well as the offensive defenseman they are responsible for. One key with this positioning is that F3 is always between their man and the net should the offensive defenseman try to activate. F3 may be able to shut down the wall in the defensive zone on pucks that are tightly contested, as long as the puck does not get past them. F3 can move to the wall as a passing option if that is needed, or they can move to close a passing option from the opposing team if needed.

Switching Positions

Players should understand that they may need to switch positions when in the defensive zone. If a free puck ends up between the hash marks and the goal line and F3 can get there first, they can go get it. F1 will simply take F3's position. F3 now becomes F1, and F1 becomes F3. This switch should happen quickly in defensive-zone coverage to make sure that there is always coverage and that the puck carrier has passing options.

Defensive players can also work on switches in the defensive zone. Suppose that the defenders push an offensive player up the wall and that player drops the puck to an offensive defenseman who is activating down the wall. With good communication, F3 and D1 can talk in the defensive zone and switch assignments. That way D1 does not end up chasing the puck out to the blue line. Having the defenseman closer to the net is more desirable in defensive-zone coverage for most teams. Players can switch if the defensemen and forwards communicate well.

Stickhandling in the Defensive Zone

Defensemen often ask whether they should have one hand or two hands on their stick in the defensive zone. The answer is that it depends on the situation. If a player is in shift downtime and can scan the ice, they can have one hand on the stick to take away passing lanes and fill space. If they are moving and closing on an opponent, players should have one hand on the stick to appear bigger than they actually are. They cover more ice with their stick extended than with their stick in the air and across their hips. The stick is important in the defensive zone because the goal is to take away passing options and fill space. Forwards should have their sticks on the ice as well while they are playing in the slot (weakside winger) or closer to the wall (strongside winger).

If the defenseman is battling in the corner, they may need to go to two hands to be stronger on their stick and be able to push a little harder on the offensive player. The defenseman who has two hands on the stick becomes stronger and more physical when lifting sticks or working to take away space when checking. The other place where players should use two hands is when they are boxing out in front of the goalie.

DEFENSIVE-SIDE POSITIONING

Another area that every player playing in their own zone should work on is keeping defensive-side positioning. If a forward is in the corner with the puck, the defender who is closing and attacking keeps their body between the offensive player and the net. This point has been mentioned in this chapter a few times, but doing it becomes harder as the offensive team creates movement in the offensive zone. As switches happen between wingers and forwards, defensive-side positioning needs to be kept. As battles occur on the boards, defensive-side positioning must be kept. In a few circumstances this rule does not apply, but if defenders are not in defensive-side positioning when the other team has possession of the puck, there is a good chance that something is coming to the net, either a player who gets behind the defender or the puck, but hopefully not both. By keeping their head on a swivel and being able to see everything happening in the defensive zone, players are better prepared to keep defensive-side positioning. At a young age, I was taught three rules to follow in the defensive zone:

1. Always be between your man and the net.
2. Always be able to see the puck and your player.
3. Never get beat back to the net.

Starting with those three rules, players can work on whatever system their coach puts in play. Whether playing man on man like some NHL teams do, or a zone, or five on a dice, players can adjust to what is happening in the game.

CLOSING, CONTROLLING, AND CREATING SPACE

The goal for the defensive team and defensive players is to take away space from the offensive team. One of the first things that defensemen at any age can work on is closing off space quickly and pushing the opponent away from the net. The faster that defensive players can take away time and space from an offensive player, the better. Any good offensive player is more effective if they have time and space to make a play. Defenders can close the space by working with their stick to go stick to puck, and they can work to close space quickly by moving their feet. First, we need to define what it means when the defense closes, controls, and creates space.

Closing space means reducing the space available to the opponent. If the offensive player has their back turned to the defensive player or is planning on controlling a rimmed puck, the defensive player works to close quickly. Their first two or three steps are hard to make the offensive player know that an opponent is coming at them. The defender leads with their stick and works to go hip to hip with the offensive player. One caution about closing quickly is to avoid exposing the chest or the logo on the jersey. If the offensive player sees the defensive player's chest square on, they have an opportunity to apply a reverse hit (or "sting"). They can plant their shoulder right in the defender's chest and push them back off the puck and off balance.

Controlling space means preventing the opponent from doing what they want to do. If the offensive player is facing the defensive player and already has possession of the puck, this is not the time to sprint at them because they can move the puck and jump past the defender. The defensive player must work to control the space and not allow their opponent to do what they want to do. The defensive player works to take away the offensive player's primary option. This can start with using a good angle and steering the opponent where the defender wants them to go.

Creating space means opening up space to work in for themselves or a teammate. A player can do this by pushing an opponent off the puck or by sealing the wall with their body to allow a half a second to make a play. Players can also create space by skating into an opponent's space as they are attacking. The opponent must then move around the player, which can create space for a teammate.

Now, in defining those concepts, situations occur where closing space, controlling space, and creating space differ.

50-50 Puck Advantage

If the defense can close space quickly, they make it a little harder for the offense to maintain the puck in the offensive zone. Ideally, the defense can create 50-50 pucks in which they can use their position to create an advantage. A 50-50 puck is a battle scenario in which either player can win possession of the puck. Body position and location on the ice can give one player a better chance to get possession of the puck.

Suppose that a puck is in the corner and you and I are standing net front. We are going to race to get the puck, but I do not have to win the race to the corner. All I must do is win the first few steps and move my body in front of yours. Rather than skating beside you for 35 or 40 feet (10 or 12 m) to the corner, if I can win the first 6 to 8 feet (2 to 2.5 m) and move in front of you, I will win the race to the corner. This idea can work for any player all over the ice. What players are working to do with 50-50 puck battles is finding a way to turn the odds in their favor. By using their body, their skating, their stick, and their awareness, they can create a better chance to win more battles. When they can win more battles, they become more of an asset on the ice as a defensive player.

Offensive-Zone Cutback

The concepts of closing, controlling, and creating space can also be viewed from an offensive perspective. The offensive player does not want to be pinned or forced to work in tight spaces. For that reason, forwards work to create space by spinning, turning, and faking.

A situation that comes up in games is the offensive-zone cutback. If the forward is climbing in the zone and pushes off the wall, they are trying to do two things. First, they are trying to get to the net. Second, they are working to create space if they do not get to the net. If they spin or cut back toward the boards, the defenseman must does not turn away from them and allow them to create space. The defensive player who is on the puck carrier must stop, face them, and work to get their stick back into position.

The idea of taking away space and keeping defensive-side positioning is something to think about on the offensive-zone cutback. The offensive-zone cutback is a strong move for forwards because it challenges the defensive team. The move

COMMON ERROR

Some players fail to move their feet as they watch plays develop. Therefore, the offensive player has time and space to make a play. By closing the distance between themselves and the puck, the defensive player can force the offensive player to throw the puck away.

COMMON ERROR

An error I often see from forwards in the slot is having two hands on the stick with the stick in the air. The player lifts their stick above their head to bring it over the top and back around, but the result allows pucks to get through. The F3 is not taking up as much space. By having one hand on their stick and their stick on the ice, the F2 and F3 take up more space and are harder to work around. If players think about keeping their stick on the ice and simply pull their stick back and reengage, they can cover space quicker.

can cause a defenseman to overcommit. The attacking player can bring another defender down to them as they are climbing, opening a passing lane to a teammate. As the forward climbs in the zone, an offensive defenseman can activate down the wall as well to create space. By forcing players to react to what they are doing, a forward gains confidence. All forwards want to have the puck on their stick, and they should want to challenge the net to score. The job of the defensive players (and teams) is to prevent the offensive team from creating space.

BOXING OUT

One area that defensive players need to work on is their ability to box out players at the front of the net to deny them access to deflections, high tips, rebounds, and second-chance opportunities for puck possession. Boxing out is made possible by good defensive-zone coverage and keeping gaps tight. Defensive players should initiate contact early and not allow the offensive players to get closer to the net.

The offensive defenseman at the blue line is looking to get pucks through to sticks or traffic. When the goalie has no sticks or traffic to worry about, their job becomes much easier. Keeping the front of the net clear and making it the hardest area for the opposing team to play in is a key part of winning games. Few teams that give up their slot area repeatedly see a lot of success. Coaches should always emphasize this point when teaching defensive players how to defend.

A situation shown to me recently is the idea of using the net to box out a player. The situation plays out as follows. The puck is in the corner, and it goes from below the goal line to the point. The offensive players are now working to get to the net. If the offensive player is starting below the goal line, the defensive player can overcommit to the board side. The offensive player then thinks they have space to get back to the front of the net. As soon as they go on the net side of the defender, the defender simply backs up or skates the offensive player into the post, quickly eliminating their space and not allowing them to get to the net front. This play can be effective for smaller or undersized defensemen who need to gain an advantage over bigger forwards. This idea of using positioning to box out is an important one.

Tie Up Offense's Sticks

Players can work on tying up the stick of the offensive player as the offensive player is working to get to the net. The defensive player has the choice to go over the top and push the opponent's stick down or come underneath their stick and lift it up. If the player is lifting, they must be aware that the opponent may try to spin back around them to get back to the net front. This move can be controlled with body position. As the offensive player spins, the defensive player readjusts their feet to be able to slide so that the opponent has trouble getting all the way around them. If the opponent spins, they are just spinning farther from the net, which plays into the defender's positioning. If the defensive player pushes down on the offensive player's stick, they may become a screen for their goalie. The defensive player must be aware of the shooting lane and their opponent's ability to pull their stick out and again work to spin. The offensive player can be kept on the outside if the defender is able to move their feet into a position where the opponent is not able to spin around them. The defender should try not to cross over their feet, which could force them off balance. They should keep their weight over their skates by not leaning or reaching. The defender should keep their body's posture in a position where they feel strong and are able to push opponents away from the net.

The net front must be the toughest area on the ice for the offensive team to go. They should not want to go there because they know they are in for a battle. Defensive players should stay within the rules and be prepared to challenge opponents working to get to available space.

Shut Down the Route

When working to box out opponents in front, defensive players need to keep lanes to the net clear for the goalie, or with as little traffic as possible. Defensive players should box out as early as possible to make it easier for the goalie as shots are coming to the net. If the puck moves low to high from the corner to the blue line, the defensive player should contact the forward and work to push them away from the net. The defender tries to make the forward change the route that they wanted to take to the net and then works to shut down that route as they spin off. As the defender is boxing out, they work to control the offensive player's stick to prevent them from getting access to the puck as they try to deflect point shots. A good box out means that the defensive player is physical and is denying the offensive player a clear line to the net. This skill can be worked on in practice. Defensive players box out early and try to keep sight lines clear as a point shot is coming to the net. A defensive player and a forward battle in front, each working to gain body position.

Knock Off Balance

To be successful at boxing out, defenders must be able to knock the offensive player off balance as they attack the net without taking penalties. They must win the battle for space by keeping defensive-side positioning and being stronger and smarter than the attacking forward. In this situation, players have two hands on the stick because they will be pushing opponents and battling for space and pucks. By pushing on the hips, the defender can turn the offensive player as the puck is coming so that they cannot be set for the puck, making their job much harder. A push in the back lets the offensive player facing the puck know that a defender is close to them and that they do not have time to stop the puck. Defensive players need to do this in a way that their pushes do not get called as cross-checks to a player's back in front of the net. Having control of their own hips, shoulders, and skates helps the defender maintain control of the other player. If the defensive player tries to push when off balance, they will have trouble boxing out. Players should work on this skill in the defensive zone with isolated box-out drills and pucks coming to the net from various angles.

Players who can use their skating effectively will often be successful in the defensive zone. Players who skate fast can close down space or win races to the puck so that they can advance it to a teammate. Players needs to be able to keep defensive-side positioning when battling in the corner or in front of their net. They should be able to use their stick to start checking angles, to go stick to puck against an offensive player, to deflect pucks, to and deny passing lanes. Players need to be able to communicate to partners to help them advance the puck smoothly out of their own zone. When defensive players understand and play with defensive-side positioning, the team will minimize the time they play in the defensive zone. Of course, players will make mistakes. The coach's job is to correct mistakes and to prevent the same mistakes from happening repeatedly. After one mistake is corrected, the defensive player will likely make another error, perhaps with the puck or with their position, and it will need to be corrected as well. Coaches should keep working to improve their players' performance in their own zone. When they become proficient in their defensive zone, they will spend less time there. Ultimately, that will lead to spending more time in the offensive zone, where it is much more fun to play.

DEFENSIVE-ZONE (DZ) BOX-OUT DRILL

Level of Difficulty

Easy

Players

Full team or six defensive players

Objectives

To work on controlling the front of the net against offensive players

Setup

A pad or rebounder is placed in front of the net, and a coach has a puck in the slot. Two sets of one offensive player and one defensive player are at the hash marks ready to go.

Procedure

The coach passes a puck off the pad at net front, and the offensive player tries to get the rebound. The defensive player works either to box out or to poke the puck away. The coach spots another puck for the second group, and they do the same thing. The coach spots a third puck into the corner where the group plays 2 vs 2.

Coaching Tips

- If a defensive player can get to the third puck first, they should do that and shut down the play.
- If the defensive player is second to the puck in the corner, they should react and stay defensive side but work to take away time and space quickly.

Variation

- A goalie in a butterfly stance can react to the rebound for the first two shots.

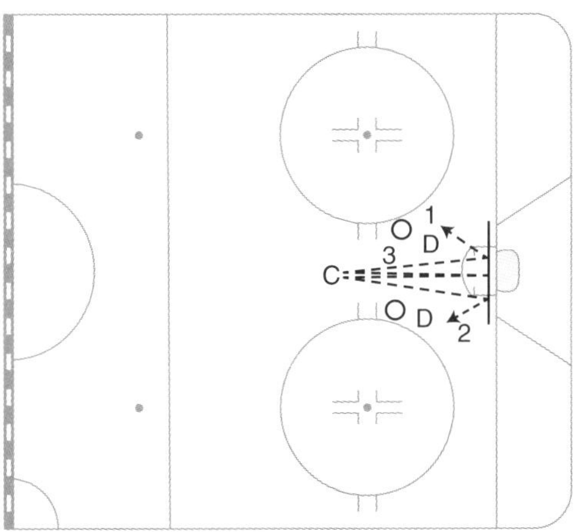

1 ON 1 × 2

Level of Difficulty

Easy

Players

Full team or six defensive players

Objectives

To work on defensive-side positioning against offensive players trying to score

Setup

Two offensive players set up on the wall—one on the hash marks and one in the corner. One defender lines up at the bottom of the circle. A coach has pucks in the high slot.

Procedure

The coach passes to the player in the corner, and the offensive player attacks to the net. The defensive player tries to shut down the play by keeping good stick and body position and by closing space quickly. When that play ends, the coach spots a puck to the second offensive player, who again is looking to score. The defensive player tries to close down that play as well, working to keep defensive-side positioning.

Coaching Tip

- This drill requires the defensive player to react to what they see and move their feet to close off space.

Variations

- The second offensive player can move to the opposite side of the net and start on the goal line.
- To push their players, the coach can make the drill longer by having four separate 1 vs 1 battles lined up on both sides. The defensive player must react to where the coach passes the puck.

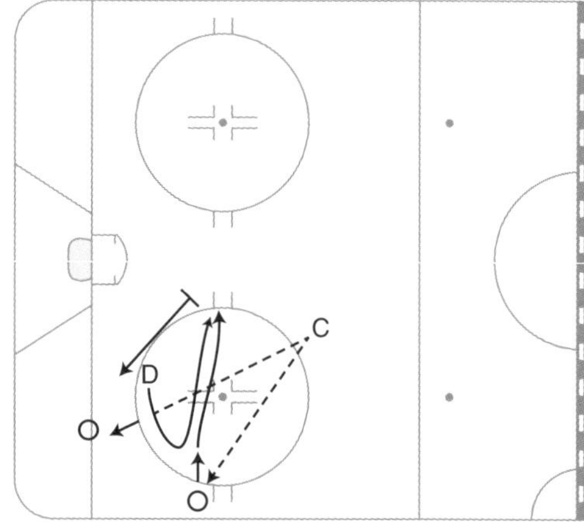

1 ON 2

Level of Difficulty

Easy

Players

Full team required

Objectives

To work on 1 on 1 with support in the defensive zone

Setup

A coach has pucks in the middle of the ice. An offensive player is on the half wall. A defensive player is close to the offensive player, and a defensive forward is behind them.

Procedure

The coach passes a puck to the offensive player, and the defensive player tries to close off space. The supporting forward moves with them and is ready to pick up any loose pucks. The supporting forward should not get too close because if their teammate gets beat, they must pick up the offensive player. Multiple pucks can be passed in during one rep to ensure that players get the hang of pressure and support.

Coaching Tips

- This drill is useful if the defensive-zone coverage looks like this.
- The supporting forward needs to learn to play in the defensive zone, so this drill works well with the forward and defenseman working against an offensive forward.

Variation

- This drill can be done 2 vs 3 as well.

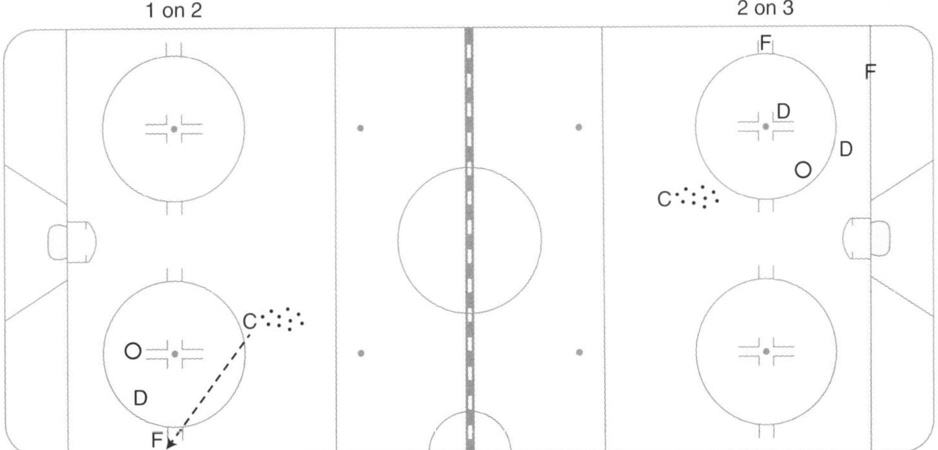

READ PRESSURE

Level of Difficulty

Easy

Players

Two to six defensive players

Objectives

To work on reading where pressure is coming from

Setup

One defensive player starts on the dot, and one starts on the bottom of the circle. A cone (or tire) can be placed at the top of the circle. A coach or waiting players have pucks on the half wall.

Procedure

On the whistle, the player on the bottom of the circle comes up to the dot, stops, and then heads back to the corner. The player who starts on the dot goes around the cone one way or the other and pressures the player in the corner. The coach spots the puck into the corner for them to play. The player at the top can either come from the wall into the middle or come from the middle toward the wall. The player going back for the puck must recognize which way the other player is coming and work to get around them. Players should switch between pressure and puck retriever and switch sides as well. The drill ends when the puck carrier skates the puck across the hash marks.

Coaching Tips

- The shoulder check is important in this drill, but if the player who starts at the bottom has their eyes up at the start of the drill, they should have an idea where the pressure will be coming from. The player pressuring must follow one path to get the puck and cannot change routes. The scenario on the right side of the diagram shows two possible paths to get around player D.
- This drill can be done on both sides with one side going at a time.

Variation

- One player can start on the hash marks on the wall with a forward on the bottom of the circle. This is now a defensive-zone coverage drill with a 1 vs 1 in the corner. The defensive player goes around the top of the circle and back into the corner to play 1 vs 1. The forward goes up to the dot and back into the corner to handle the puck spotted from the coach.

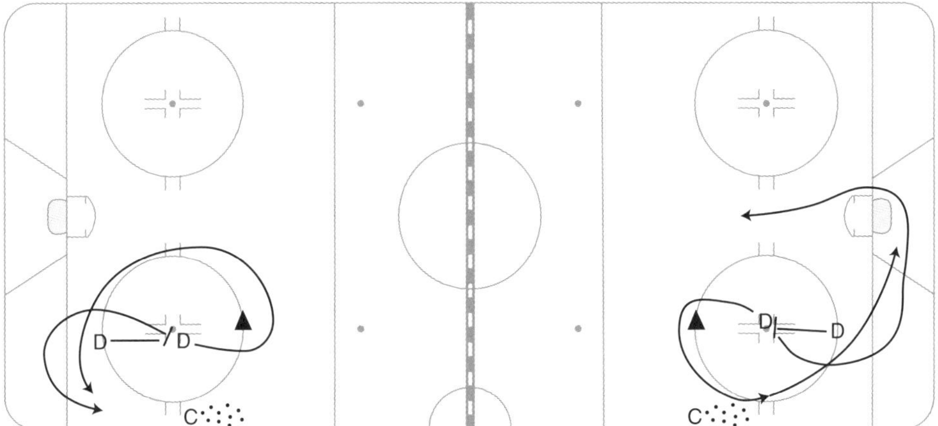

5 VS 5 OFF FACEOFF

Level of Difficulty
Easy

Players
Full team

Objectives

To work on various faceoff alignments and understanding each player's role on won faceoffs and lost faceoffs

Setup

Five offensive players line up in the offensive zone, and five defensive players line up in the defensive zone. The centers (C in diagram) take the faceoff and wingers (W in diagram) are on each side of the hash marks. There are two wingers and one center on each side of the draw. The coach drops the puck.

Procedure

The faceoff is live for the offensive team and the defensive team. The defensive team can adjust what they are doing if their team wins the draw. They can go strongside up the wall, over behind the net, weakside rim, or any other option they think will work. The offensive team can do the same thing with options off the draw if they win it. The defensive team adjusts and covers players off the faceoff loss.

Coaching Tips

- This drill is a useful simulation of what happens in games.
- Coaches can use this teaching drill to help players understand where they are going and why.

Variations

- Coaches can use this drill to prepare players for any scenario or alignment that may come up at higher levels.
- Coaches can run options that create a little bit of space to move the puck or potentially a chance out of the zone.

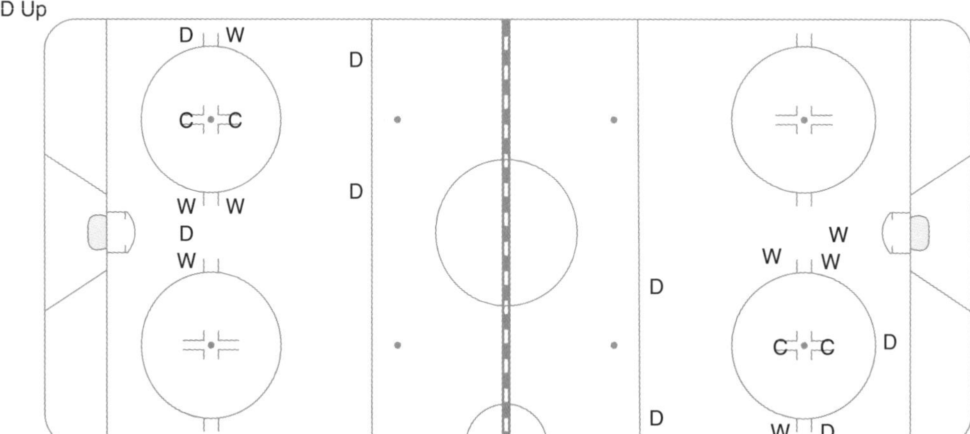

CHAPTER 10

Strategies in the Offensive Zone

As we move up the ice from the defensive zone into the offensive zone, we can look at several ways to create offensive chances by using the defensemen's offensive skill set. When coaches work with defensive players in the offensive zone, topics to focus on are keeping pucks alive, not getting shots blocked, and not turning the puck over. Having players learn to shoot with their eyes up is a good start to working on movement at the blue line. With their eyes up, players can see what is in front of them and which lanes are available. As they cross the blue line, they can also move defending players and recognize other options that may be available. Every defenseman should work on developing their ability to shoot with their eyes up so that they can see where the shooting lane is. If the player preparing to shoot can cause the opponent to move, their shot is less likely to be blocked. I encourage players to "use the lane they create" to get shots through from the point. This means that if a right-handed player is moving to the right, they should shoot to that side of the net. That way, the shot blocker does not get an opportunity to get back into the shooting lane.

SHOOTING FROM THE BLUE LINE

Shooting the puck from the blue line is a simple concept that becomes harder as players get older. Getting shots through from the blue line is a tough task because the opposing team will be working to block every shot. If the offensive forwards and offensive defenseman are on the same page, the forwards may be able to anticipate where the puck is going and work to deflect the puck on the net. If the offensive defenseman is sliding to the left, they can shoot to the left of the shot blocker so that the offensive forward has an idea of where the puck is coming to. This simple strategy in the offensive zone can work to get more shots through from the blue line.

Puck on Half Wall

Defensemen can work on activating from the blue line when the puck is on the half wall, meaning that it is close to the hash marks on the boards in the offensive zone. Players can do this in different ways depending on the area of possession and level of possession from the forward. The offensive defenseman has three options:

1. *Jump down the wall:* The offensive defenseman moves forward off the blue line and activates down the boards into the offensive zone.
2. *Jump down the middle:* The offensive defenseman sees that a lane to the net is available and moves down the dot line or inside the dot line to the net.
3. *Slide to the middle:* No ice is available in front of the offensive defenseman, so they slide laterally across the blue line into the middle of the ice.

Jump Down the Wall

When the offensive defenseman jumps down the wall, the best way to eliminate confusion is to have the offensive forward roll up the wall and work to get to the inside, essentially pushing into the dot line. This movement allows the offensive defenseman room on the wall to move down off the blue line and into the zone. The offensive forward should look to see what hand the offensive defenseman is and place the puck in a spot where they can do something with it. This can be in a protected position closer to the wall or on their forehand depending on the situation. The offensive defenseman often gets some space because they can catch the defensive team on a switch. If the reaction does not happen quickly, time and space can become available. A common error with this activation occurs when the offensive forward tries to pass the puck to the offensive defenseman rather than simply leaves it. When they leave the puck, the offensive defenseman knows exactly where the puck will be as they jump down the wall. If the offensive defenseman is expecting the offensive forward to leave the puck and the forward tries to pass it, the puck may end up going past the defenseman into the neutral zone. To make the play easier, the player who drops the puck to the defenseman as they activate simply stays closer to the blue line and covers for the defenseman as they enter the offensive zone down the wall.

Jump Down the Middle

If the wall is not an option, the offensive defenseman can jump to the middle of the ice. This play is effective in a situation when the defending team is taking away the wall in the offensive zone and there is now the threat of a low-to-high pass. The offensive defenseman who moves down the middle of the ice is in a dangerous spot where they have an opportunity to score if they get a clean pass. If they do not get a clean pass, they can continue through the slot and the other offensive defenseman can slide closer to the puck. This creates a problem for the defensive team because they must worry about switching or knowing where players are as they move. As the defensemen switch, the defenseman who started the play by jumping into the zone can slide into a space that is available for a one timer if a passing lane is available. This way of creating offense in the offensive zone enables the defensemen to activate, read, and move.

Slide to the Middle

When there is no space in front of the offensive defenseman to activate into, either down the wall or into the middle of the ice, they could have an option to slide without the puck. This happens when the offensive forward with the puck climbs the zone up the wall and has clean possession of the puck. Having the defenseman slide can get the team into a three-high attack that forces the defensive team to react to a new look. The three-high attack means that a forward is moving up higher in the zone and working to create space. This play can be effective in zone as players move around working to create space and shots. Moving a forward into a higher position can make it harder for the defending team to cover them as the defenseman slides into the middle of the ice. Essentially, they must react and move a player into a spot where they may not want to be. A defensive player may have to follow a forward up the wall and play above the top of the circle, or a defensive player and a forward may have to switch to cover the forward moving up the zone. Either way, the offensive team is making the defending team adjust to what they are doing.

Attacking Dots Below the Goal Line

Another way that defensive players can get involved in the offensive zone is by attacking the dots when the puck is below the goal line. This movement is effective if the defensive team is overcommitted to one side. As the puck changes sides in the offensive zone, space can open up. This can be done off cycles with passes to the weak side and then to the dot or by a player skating behind the net and making a pass to the defensemen and the player activating down the dot line.

Strong Side

If the forward is down low in the offensive zone and coming around the net, the offensive defenseman could have a chance to activate into the strongside dot where they can work to get a quick shot. The strongside dot is a good place to move into the puck. The strong side is the side of the ice where the puck is. This passing lane is a good one because the offensive defenseman can often catch the defending team sleeping if they can jump into the zone quickly. If the pass is a good one, they may be able to one time the puck as they move forward. This shot creates a lot of problems for the goalie because they must move quickly from their post to react to the shot. If the pass is not perfect, the defenseman can stop the puck and release it all in one motion. The objective with this type of play is to get the shot to the net before the goalie sets their feet and pushes out for the shot.

Back Side

The same idea can be used when activating to the backside dot. The backside dot is the area of the ice on the side opposite from where the puck is. As a forward moves down low or passing lanes are created, the backside-dot lane may be a good one for the offensive defenseman to find. This can happen in several scenarios (even strength, power play, 3 vs 3). Regardless of which one it is, the shot must come to the net quickly.

The timing of this backside play is important because the player needs to be in the passing lane at the correct time to create a shooting lane to the net. The seam can open up, and if the player is in it at the right time, they can create an excellent scoring chance. The pass will be hard, so the player must be prepared with their bottom hand to receive it. The shot must go to the net quickly because the shooter is racing the goalie to see who can get to the back post faster. If the player can elevate the puck, they can increase their chances to score. When I teach this backside play to young defensemen, I tell them that their stick should be on an imaginary line between the dot and the post. A common error is coming down too much to the middle of the ice, thus shortening the goalie's route to make a save. If the player can stay on the back side and force the goalie to come all the way across the crease, they can increase their chances to score.

Shooting From the Dot

Whether the player is on the strong side or the back side, one of the most important shots to work on is the shot from the dot. They should work on shooting when stationary and when moving. They should work on receiving passes and on any scenario that could come up in a game. Stationary shots are useful for working on puck placement. Shooting off flat passes helps players learn to release the puck quicker. Shooting from passes from the goal line is useful because these passes often occur in games. In addition, players need to understand how to move their eyes from pass reception to the net for the shot and recognize what options they have.

In NHL games, many pucks go to the net from the dot angle—the angle from the dot to the net. The dot angle is difficult for goalies because they know that the shooter has options. If the goalie pushes out too far, they leave space behind them for a deflection. If they do not push out far enough, they leave space over their shoulders. The goalie must recognize the options quickly and decide how much net they need to cover. The shooter has a couple of areas that they can work on to build confidence for taking that shot in games. They can work on elevating the puck to the short side over the goalie's shoulder or shooting low and hard to the far side of the net. These two areas are consistently available with or without goalies in practice.

Considering the movement on the line and the skills required to shoot effectively, building offensive defensemen takes time and practice. Players need to work through a variety of skills and a variety of scenarios that could come up in games. When working through those scenarios, players need to understand why they are working through them and how doing that work can help them maximize time in the offensive zone.

RESETTING THE PUCK

Defensive players can maximize their time on offense by resetting pucks in the offensive zone. First, they can keep pucks alive at the blue line, and second, they can rim the puck back behind the net to get it to a spot where their forwards have a chance to get there first.

Keeping the Puck Alive

One of the more important areas that young defensemen can work on is keeping pucks alive at the blue line. Whether it's called holding the puck in or being strong at the blue line, a defenseman who can keep pucks alive will extend offensive-zone time for their team. To do this, they must use good positioning without the puck and good scanning to be aware of what is happening around them and where there is time and space. Pucks can be rimmed around the wall, flipped over them, shot at them, banked past them, and more. The strongside defenseman must be prepared to handle pucks coming at them. Not every puck will be perfect, so they must work to practice situations that are not perfect—pucks that are bouncing, in the air, on the wall, on their backhand, and more—to be prepared for game situations.

Rimming the Puck

After stopping the puck, the player needs to be ready to make the next play. At times, they will have no option with the puck—no option to shoot the puck, no option to move the puck to their partner, and no available forward to move the puck to. In that case, resetting the puck is the only option. Defensemen must learn how hard they need to rim the puck to get it down below the goal line so that the forwards have a chance to regain possession. Working to extend offensive-zone time is a group effort that comes from support by players without the puck, communication from players without the puck, and passing ability of the player with the puck.

Keep Pucks Alive

Keeping the puck in is the priority. Players must be strong on their skates and their stick during every shift. If the puck comes at them in the air, players should catch it with their bottom hand on their stick. Right-handed defensemen catch with their right hand, and left-handed defenseman catch with their left hand. Using this technique helps players get the puck back to the ice quickly and then get back to two hands to make a play. As they place the puck down, their bottom hand is closer to their stick. If players catch the puck with their top hand, they have to go down to the ice and then back up to their stick.

WITHOUT THE PUCK

When the team does not have the puck, defensive responsibilities can come up in the offensive zone. By understanding their positioning and where the other team is trying to go, players can make better reads and plays.

Pinching

One of the first situations that comes up in the offensive zone when a team does not have the puck is the potential to pinch. Pinching means that the offensive defenseman comes down the boards to put pressure on the defensive winger or move into an available puck. The read on when to pinch is a tough one, but when players learn when to go and when not to go, they can extend their team's offensive-zone time and break up the other team's breakouts. Here are some things that defensemen should do when pinching:

1. Scan for support (their F3).
2. Accelerate quickly with the first three or four steps.
3. Scan the ice for their options.
4. Hug the wall tight so that no pucks can get past them with their stick to the inside of the ice.
5. Be prepared for physical play on the wall.

Assess When to Pinch

The first rule for pinching is knowing when to go. If a defenseman at the offensive blue line sees a free puck and thinks that they can get there, they should go and get the puck. If any thought creeps into their head that maybe they cannot get there, they should not go. Second guessing is not helpful, so if they think they can get the puck, then should go and get it. Even if they poke the puck into the offensive-zone corner, it is not coming down the other way, so they have done their job. When deciding whether to pinch or not, their first look should be to find their team's F3. If they do not have the F3 in a support position, they cannot go into the offensive zone. If the F3 is in a good spot, they can pinch because they have support behind them. As discussed in chapter 9, F3 must be responsible in the offensive zone and work to cover behind the defenseman if they pinch. A team that plays with structure makes the play appear seamless as the F3 covers for the pinching defenseman.

The next part of this is off a pass from the opposing team's defense to their winger. If the pass is tape to tape and direct and the player receives it, this is not a time for the defenseman to pinch. If the opponent has the puck and time to look, they can move it past the defenseman or chip it past them. The offensive defenseman is then in a tough spot. If the play is direct, the defenseman should back out, keep their gap tight, and allow their backchecker to track the puck through the neutral zone. If the back pressure is there, the gap can be a little tighter to force the offensive team to give up possession of the puck. If back pressure is not present, the gap will have to be a little looser so that the defenseman can accept the rush and see what is coming at them.

Act Quickly During the Pinch

If the pass is light or not clean and the defenseman thinks they can arrive at the opponent at the same time as the puck, that is a time to pinch. If the pass is thrown around the boards as a rim, that is a time to pinch because the player receiving the rim will not have time to receive the pass with no pressure. Putting pressure on the receiving player will make their play to receive the puck much harder. When the player decides that they are going to pinch, they should get moving down the wall. They should hug the wall with their body and get their stick to the puck on the inside of the ice. They hug the wall to prevent the player with the puck from chipping the puck past them. Ultimately, the goal of pinching is to reduce the options for the player with the puck to either turning it over or throwing it back into their defensive zone.

Be Prepared to Get Physical

If the defensemen are old enough to play with body checking, the physical aspect can quickly come into play. In this situation the offensive defenseman going down the wall must make sure to get the player or the puck as they pinch. If they miss the puck and it gets past them, they cannot let the opposing player also get past them and beat them up the ice. If the defenseman can finish their check along the wall, the opposing player cannot beat them back to their zone. This play does not have to be a big hit on the wall, but the defensive player pinching down the wall may need to contact the opposing forward. Defensive players need to get to the point where they feel they can pinch down the wall on either side of the offensive zone.

Stopping the Puck

Defensive players should work on starting off the wall and moving to the wall to keep a puck alive. They should try to stop the puck and get possession where they can make a play with it. If they have time and space, they can shoot the puck or pass it to their defensive partner. They can rim the puck to reset it in behind the defensive team's net so that their forward can get possession of it. Whatever they decide to do with the puck, they must first stop it. They can do this by using good body position and good stick position. As often as possible, they should use their stick to stop the puck. This is the best way to keep pucks in front of them with possession.

Using Skates to Stop the Puck

At time, players must use their skates to stop the puck. One position that players should stay out of is having their back against the wall when using their skates to stop the puck. If the puck bounces off their skate into the middle of the ice when they are on the boards, the other team may get a breakaway from their own blue line or a 2 vs 1 all the way down the ice. If the defenseman is moving to the right boards, they can use their right skate to stop the puck with their shoulders pointed forward. That way, they can protect the puck, take a hit (if hitting is permitted), and not lose possession or give up a chance going the other way. Likewise, the left foot can be used on the left wall to keep pucks alive.

Partner Positioning

When a defenseman is working to be strong at the line or hold the zone by keeping the puck alive, their defensive partner can fall off the line into the middle of the ice and a little behind them to provide support. The positioning of the defensive partner is important because they are covering

COMMON ERROR

Players often make errors in positioning as they prepare to handle the puck, which makes the task more difficult. Players should anticipate the puck coming around the boards so that they are in position with enough time to get their stick ready to handle the puck. Being comfortable handling the puck on both their forehand and their backhand enables them to make plays in games. Players may be put in tough spots, and they need to be able to handle the puck smoothly and make quick decisions to keep the play alive.

in the event a puck gets past the first player. This positioning along with F3 in the offensive zone creates a defensive posture in the offensive zone that basically eliminates odd-man rushes by the other team.

The idea of playing without the puck revolves around working to keep good positioning all the time. Players accomplish this during their shift downtime by scanning the ice, as discussed in chapter 9. Players never know when the defensemen can be an option and how fast the offensive game can roll to create a chance. On the flipside, players must be ready to defend against a turnover coming back the other way. Good offensive teams have input from their backend. Those players are always a threat to be included in the offensive attack. Defensive players may not be scoring during every shift, but they are involved in low-to-high plays or are activating into the zone to help increase time in the offensive zone. But defensemen are also responsible for defending through the neutral zone with good gaps if the puck comes back the other way. When players build confidence in practice, they can achieve more success in games.

Identifying skills that players are good at as well as skills that they are not as strong at can be a great start for a coach when planning practice and building options into their team's structure. Working on specific areas in practice with the defensemen and forwards can create more confidence as they work together in the offensive zone. Considering the previous chapters on skating, stickhandling, passing, shooting, joining the rush, and more, players can work to use their skills to spend more time in the offensive zone. Decision making is a key skill for the offensive defensemen. They are not expected to score on every shift or in every game. But the defenseman who can contribute to the offensive side helps their team spend more time and create more chances in the offensive zone.

DOT-LINE ATTACKS

Level of Difficulty

Easy

Players

Six defensive players

Objectives

To work on moving into the play and getting shots from the dots

Setup

Players line up at the blue line, and a coach has pucks on the opposite half wall. One player starts in the corner opposite where the players are lined up.

Procedure

The coach spots a puck for the player in the corner, who carries it around behind the net (see 1 in diagram). A player from the blue line starts to move in down the dot line as the first player comes around behind the net. The player with the puck passes to the player moving forward into the pass. The player shoots and then grabs the next puck from the coach in the corner. The drill continues.

Coaching Tips

- The timing of this play is important so that the activating player does not have to wait for the puck. The player moving down the dot line should skate into the pass so that they can shoot the puck harder.
- If the player who is shooting can one time the pass, that is preferred.

Variation

- This drill can also be done as a backside dot-line pass (see 2 in diagram). The player coming around behind the net must move a little farther to the goal line and then slip the pass on top of the crease to the player who is now on the backside dot line.

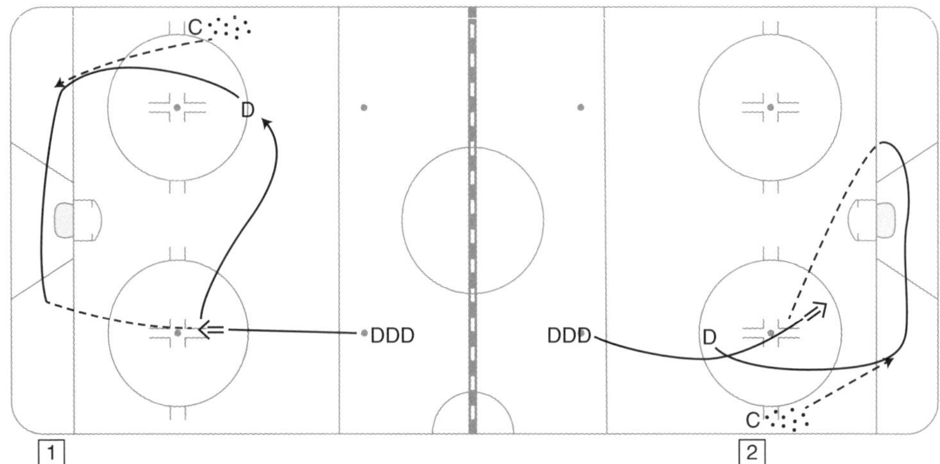

BACKSIDE DOT OFF PASS

Level of Difficulty

Moderate

Players

Six defensive players

Objectives

To work on passes that come on the power play from the goal line to the backside dot line

Setup

A line of players is on the half wall, one player is on the goal line, one player is on the backside blue line, and one player is on the hashmark near the net.

Procedure

The player on the hash mark starts the drill by getting a pass from the line and passing it back to the line as they skate in a circle. The player from the line passes down to the goal line, and the pass then goes out to the player now moving back to the net. The drill is repeated with a pass from the line to the player in the middle of the ice and then down to the goal line. This time, on the second pass down low, the player from the opposite side moves forward and the pass goes to them as they move into the zone. The player who skated in the circle replaces the player who moved forward into the zone. A new player starts down low, and the player who was down low is now between the hash marks ready to go.

Coaching Tips

- This drill simulates a passing sequence that happens in games. The puck should move quickly, and shots should come quickly to the net.
- This drill can be done without a goalie because they will get extremely tired moving repeatedly across the crease.

Variation

- The player down low on the goal line can skate the puck around behind the net and make this a strongside dot pass rather than a backside dot pass.

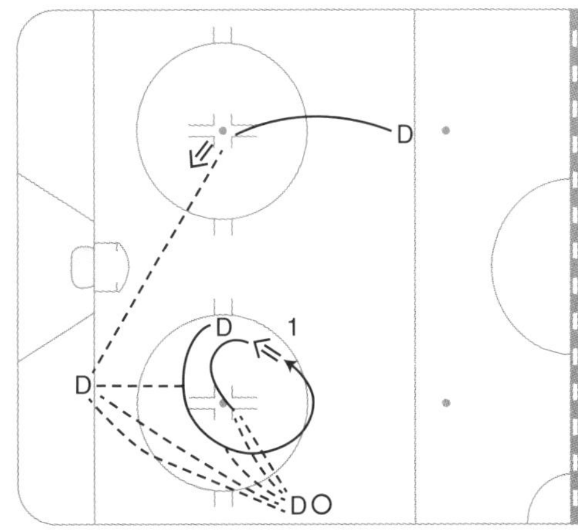

RESETTING PUCKS

Level of Difficulty

Easy

Players

Six defensive players

Objectives

To work on resetting pucks in the offensive zone behind the offensive net

Setup

A coach has pucks at the top of the circle on one side. A player is at the blue line, a player is net front and handles the rim, and a player is on the opposite half wall.

Procedure

The coach gives a puck to the player at the blue line. They do not have an option to shoot or to pass to their partner, so their best option is to put the puck back into the corner behind the net. The net-front player handles the rimmed puck, skates behind the net, and passes it to the player on the wall, who is acting as a winger. This sequence can happen three or four times per rep so that the player at the blue line knows how hard they can rim the puck to keep possession for their forwards.

Coaching Tips

- This set play can include verbal or nonverbal communication.
- The player must know their options and see things before they get the puck.
- The forward can anticipate the puck coming around the boards and prepare to handle the rim in a game.

Variations

- Many options can be used off this drill, such as a 1 vs 1 down low off a reset puck.
- Another defensive player and forward could be added net front to make it a 2 vs 2 with high support from the defenseman. If the forwards are in trouble, the defenseman can activate down the wall, dive down the middle, or hold the blue line as an option.

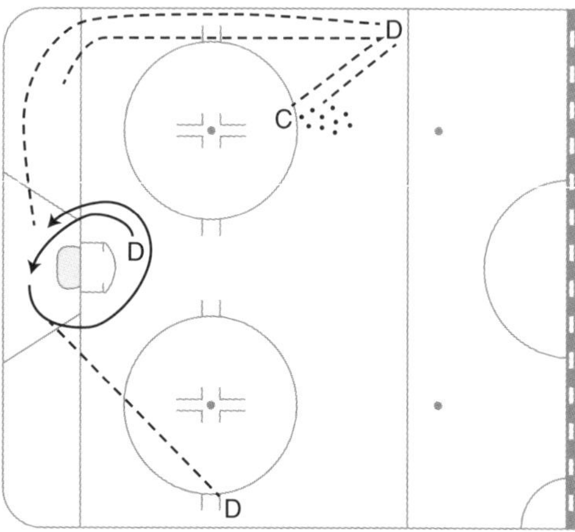

PINCHING DOWN THE WALL

Level of Difficulty

Easy

Players

Six defensive players or full team

Objectives

To work on pinching down the wall against another player

Setup

A coach has pucks in the corner, a player is on the wall, and a defensive player is at the blue line.

Procedure

The coach rims a puck around the wall, and the player on the wall must handle the rim. As soon as the coach rims the puck, the defensive player pinches down to keep the puck in the offensive zone. The player who starts at the hash marks tries to chip the puck past the defensive player, who tries to keep it alive.

Coaching Tips

- The defenseman who is pinching works on sealing the wall with their body and being prepared to battle.
- Pinching can extend time in the offensive zone if the player can make the right read and keep pucks alive.

Variations

- A support player can be added to the drill to give the player who starts on the wall a passing option. They can call middle or chip to the player who handles the rim.
- A high forward (F3) can be added to the drill to make this a 2 vs 2 battle with the F3 covering for the defensive player.

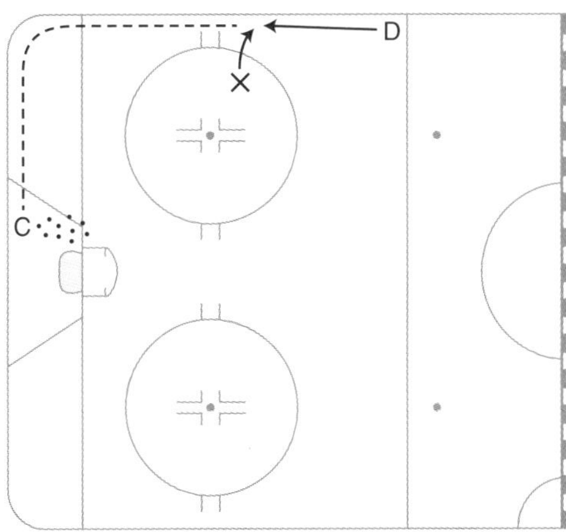

DIVING AND SLIDING

Level of Difficulty

Hard

Players

Two to six derisive players

Objectives

To work on diving on the inside of the winger, who is watching the defender on the strong side of the wall; to work on the one timer in the offensive zone

Setup

A coach has pucks at the half wall. Two players are at the blue line.

Procedure

The strongside defenseman (D1) moves off the wall and dives down the middle of the ice. They receive a pass from the coach for a shot. After taking their shot, they slide through the offensive slot and out the other side. The player who started on the far side (D2) slides over to the middle to cover for D1, who dove down. The coach hits D2, who quickly moves the puck to D1. D1 is in a shooting position and works to shoot it quickly with either a one timer or a quick release. D2 now becomes D1, and a new player starts in the middle of the ice as D2.

Coaching Tips

- This drill uses higher-level defensive movement in the offensive zone.
- Having defensemen involved and active in the play can create offensive chances.

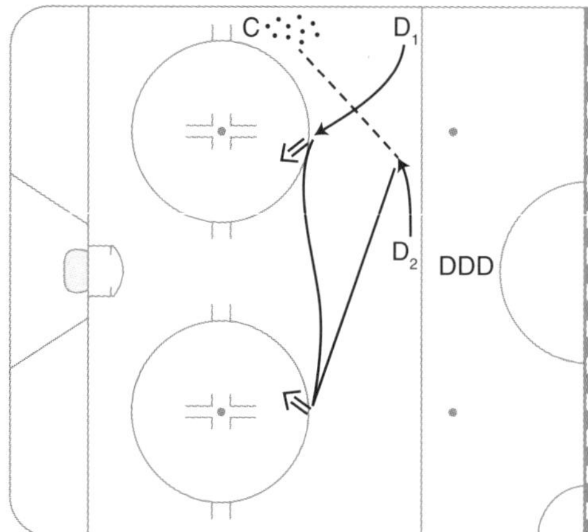

PUCK IN CORNER

Level of Difficulty

Moderate

Players

Six defensive player or the full team

Objectives

To work on activating a defenseman down the wall in the offensive zone

Setup

Pucks and players are at the blue lines with one player in each corner.

Procedure

A player (X1) comes forward toward the blue line, receives a pass from the player in line (X2), and gives it back to the line. The player from the line (X2) soft dumps the puck in the corner, and the player in the drill (X1) goes to get it. X1 retrieves the puck in the corner and brings it up the wall. As X1 gets between the hash marks and top of the circle, X2 starts down the wall. X1 leaves the puck for X2, and X2 carries the puck down the wall. X1 rolls into the middle of the ice and receives a pass from X2. X2 now becomes the player who starts the drill again.

Coaching Tip

- This drill can be done in one corner, in two corners when running stations (same side of the ice so that players work on both sides), or in all four corners as a full drill with opposite sides going.

Variations

- X1 can pick up the puck in the corner, bring it up the wall, and cut back. X2 from the blue line can dive into the middle of the ice and receive a pass from X1.
- X1 can pick up the puck, come up the wall, and cut back down low. Recognizing that they have no option, they can cut back again and pass the puck low to high to the defensive player (D), who slides and shoots. X1 comes to the net for a deflection.

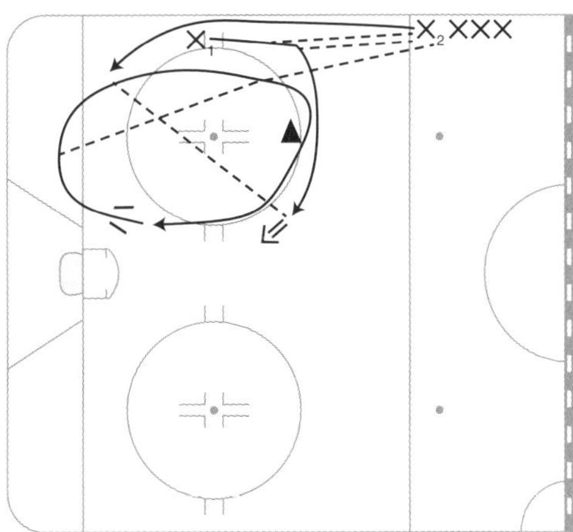

DOUBLE UP

Level of Difficulty

Hard

Players

Six defensive players

Objectives

To work on communication and awareness while moving through the drill

Setup

Two defensive players start on the dots in the zone, and one defensive player is on each side at the wall. Two cones (or tires) are placed in the high slot, one just outside the top of the circle and one inside the blue line.

Procedure

The players communicate about when to start. Both players leave at the same time from the dots, come forward to the top of the circle, and pivot backward. Turning from backward to forward to head to the corner, they pick up a puck in the corner spotted by the player from the line. They both then head to the cones. One cone is low, and one is high, so the players must call out which one they are going around to avoid a collision. They then retrieve a puck (spotted by the player in line) in the corner opposite from where they started and pass it back to the line. After their second puck retrieval, they head up to the blue line and must read whether they are the first or second one there. If they are first, they get a pass and shoot. If they are second, they get a pass, give it back, and get a second pass to slide and shoot.

Coaching Tips

- This communication and awareness drill forces players to scan the ice around them from the offensive blue line. They must listen and take in information being yelled at them.

Variations

- The coach can add a shot pass from the D as the player who passes to them heads to the net after giving the pass to the player at the blue line.
- The coach can add multiple shots with D1 (first D to get to the blue line) shooting first, then D2, then D1 sliding, and then D2 sliding.

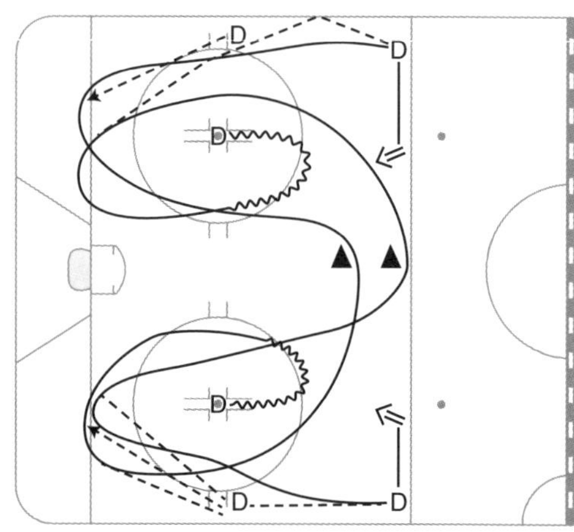

CHAPTER 11

Neutral-Zone Play

This chapter covers plays that take place between the blue lines, an area known as the neutral zone. This important zone in the game allows transition plays to happen, from defensive plays to offensive plays from the defense. It can also lead to space and offensive chances from the opposing team if the defensive players do not do their job. Situations come up in games when offensive forwards do not get pucks in deep or, on the other side, when a defensemen turn the puck over in the neutral zone. When forwards are driving and the puck turns over, they are then going the wrong way. The lanes that open up create chances going the other way. Turnovers result from good gap control and good tracking from the forwards. Tracking means that the forwards are putting back pressure on the puck and forcing the player carrying the puck into trying to do something they do not want to do. On these types of plays, quick transitions can catch the other team out of position because they are expecting something else to happen. Neutral-zone strategy revolves around two ideas:

1. Defensive options without the puck
2. Offensive options with the puck

Both areas are important in the overall outcome of a game.

DEFENSIVE OPTIONS WITHOUT THE PUCK

This play starts when defensive players push off the blue line with their footwork and skating. When pushing back into the neutral zone from the offensive blue line, player should think about getting into the middle of the ice. To do that, they turn, face the boards, and push into the middle. The opposite of that is turning to face the middle and pushing to the wall, which creates a lot of open space in the middle of the ice. Many young defensemen make this mistake as they enter the neutral zone, which puts them in a poor position outside the dots. The offensive team can exploit this mistake of failing to protect the middle of the ice.

Inside the Dots

The dots are a useful landmark for defensive players in the neutral zone. By using the dots, players can set their positioning to work together and deny opponents easy access to the net. As a rule, players should play inside the dots. If a player moves outside the dots, their partner should be in the middle of the ice or even a little closer to them (compared with farther away). When defensive players are inside the dots with good gap control, they force the offensive attack wide where they can be controlled or angled. Having defenseman in the middle of the ice allows the forwards to track the puck on the outside or push it to the outside, again taking danger out of the attack.

The attack becomes more dangerous as the numbers grow for the offensive team and they beat the defensive team back through the neutral zone. A 1 vs 2 is not that scary. Likewise, a 2 vs 2 is not that difficult for the defense because they can manage an attack by two offensive players. But if the forwards are not back and the offensive team adds a player, a 2 vs 2 becomes a 3 vs 2. This totally changes the passing options for the puck carrier. As the defenders are accepting the rush, their forwards must be working to get back through the neutral zone so that they can turn the rush the other way. A 2 vs 2 against the defending team can turn into a 2 vs 3 if the forwards get back into the neutral zone first. The goal is to get the puck out of the middle of the ice and into the outside lane where it can be controlled. The defensive players' gap can be much tighter when they have tracking support coming back to help them. The key is having back pressure from the forwards to enable the defensive players to have a tighter gap. The tracking by the forwards gives their defense a better chance through the neutral zone. If the team's forwards do not backcheck or are late on the backcheck, the opposing team will have lots of opportunity in odd-number situations.

Gap Control

Gap control is an area that defensive players need to work on constantly. This work can include forwards, who must skate backward through the neutral zone on the penalty kill and try to interrupt a power-play entry. When young defensive players skate backward in the neutral zone, many want to continue to back up to avoid getting beat. They think that backing up protects the net, and they are partially correct. What they do not realize is that by giving up the zone, they are allowing entry or options inside the blue line. This happens when players are not the strongest skaters and do not trust their transitions to move from forward to backward quickly enough. Or they simply cannot skate backward quickly enough to manage a rush. They think that backing up allows them to keep the play in front of them and work back to their own zone.

I want players to think differently. I want players to test their skating in practice as they try to maintain their gap control. If they get beat that is OK because they will learn how fast they need to skate or where they need to be. Coaches who get upset at players who get beat for trying should reexamine what they are trying to get out of practice. Practice is for players to learn about themselves as players and learn about situations that will come up in games. Gap control is a tough situation for players to think about. They need to trust themselves enough to do it regularly in games.

With gap control, players can think about being one stick length away from an attacking player coming down on them. With this one-stick length, the defensive player is taking away space. A good offensive player wants space through the neutral zone, and a good defensive player takes space away.

Slide Laterally

With good gap control, the defensive player has an option to slide laterally should they need to shut down the wall if the attacking forward is trying to get past them. Players should do this quickly and move from the dot line to the wall by simply turning their gliding leg and pushing off the leg on the inside of the ice. This allows them to move over laterally and stay in front of the offensive player or potentially finish a check against them. They can do this with their hips facing forward and moving at a 45-degree angle, not directly sideways. If they move over at a 90-degree angle, they get one shot at the player coming down on them. Sometimes that works out, but more often it does not. By sliding back with the opponent, the defensive player can maintain defensive-side positioning, keeping their body closer to the net coming off the wall.

Surfing

The idea of sliding leads into another form of taking away time and space called surfing, which is essentially skating forward at the attacking forward and angling them into a space where the defender wants them to go. This can be done by the weakside defenseman coming across the ice and angling through the neutral zone, or it can be done by the strongside defenseman if they are inside enough to move with a good angle. If the weakside defenseman is coming across the ice, the strongside defenseman can fall underneath them to protect the middle of the ice. Players must trust their skating and work to angle to break up the offensive player's possession of the puck. Ultimately, the defense is looking for the attacking player to chip the puck into an area where they have a player to get it back.

With good positioning inside the dots in the neutral zone and good gap control, the defender can force the attacking forward to give up possession and chip the puck past them. If that happens, the defensive player has done their job. Their defensive partner must go to get the puck in behind the first defender and work on breaking out the puck. If that happens, the first defender gets back into a support position and communicates to their partner about which option to use.

COMMON ERROR

A common error that occurs with surfing is the failure of the strongside defenseman to fall underneath to protect the weakside defenseman angling across the ice. The middle of the ice is therefore available to another attacking player who can streak into the space to receive a pass. The defending team does not want to give up this kind of opportunity. Surfing works best when gap control is tight and players can close off available space quickly to shut down the offensive attack.

Breaking Up Attacking Passes

As the defenseman is accepting the rush through the neutral zone, they may be up against two offensive attacking players coming at them. This can be a 2 vs 1 or a 3 vs 2 with one player on the inside and one player on the outside. The offensive team may work to try to get the puck from the inside of the ice to the outside of the ice. If the defenseman is in a good position with good gap control, the passing lane may not be there, so the offensive player may try to saucer pass the puck over the defender's stick. The defenseman has a great opportunity to break up the play if they can use their eye-hand coordination effectively. The easiest way to do this is to go quickly from one hand to two hands and bring the stick off the ice. The motion then is simply to move the stick down toward the puck and knock it out of the air. This happens extremely quickly, and players must be confident in their abilities to break up plays consistently. The best players in the NHL feel comfortable knocking down the puck and getting it going quickly the other way. The harder way to break up the attacking pass is to do it with one hand on the stick. The player has less control of their stick, which makes reacting to the saucer pass more difficult. For either method, one-handed or two-handed, defensive players need to work on the skill because they can use it in the defensive zone (passes to the slot), neutral zone (passes from the inside of the ice to the outside), or potentially in the offensive zone around the net to score.

1 on 1 in the Neutral Zone

The basics of playing defense in the neutral zone are about playing 1 on 1 with good gap control. The assignment is to line up the outside shoulder with the inside shoulder of the attacking forward. If the player can maintain inside position on the forward, they will force the attacker to go around them on the outside. This position enables the defensive player to push the forward away

Making Changing Easier

In any shift when a player is on the ice as well as during their time on the bench, they should be scanning so that they are aware of what is happening in the game. If they are on the ice, they know who is on against them and what they are trying to do. If they are on the bench, they are aware of who is coming next and where the puck is. When players focus on what is occurring on the ice, their team can make good line changes as the game is going on. When making line changes, players look to fill the wide side of the ice first. The first defensive player out heads to the far side of the ice. This concept is important for the second period when line changes are a little harder. If one defensive player changes, they can head to the far side of the ice, allowing the other defensive player to move closer to the bench. This rotation on the ice when not in possession of the puck is a key to changing effectively in games.

from the net and maintain good position when doing it. If the defender needs to turn from backward to forward, they can. Alternatively, they can continue to maneuver backward. In any case, holding inside position is a key part of playing defense. From this position, the defender can recognize what is coming at them and minimize offensive threats. With a good gap, they can make it harder for the offensive team to enter at the blue line, and they can see where the other offensive players are. Are they looking to net drive and get behind the defense? Or are they looking to push the defender back and clear a lane to move the puck across the available seam to their width player? Being inside the attacker gives the defensive player an opportunity to break up plays with their stick or force the attacking team to work around them.

OFFENSIVE OPTIONS WITH THE PUCK

The first part of retrieving the puck in the neutral zone is getting to it quickly. Players skate rapidly back to the puck so that they have more time or can move the puck faster. I have seen coaches teach players various ways to get to the puck. Some have players skate forward and turn around the puck, whereas others have players skate backward and look over their shoulder to grab the puck. I am not a big fan of skating backward to the puck because doing so makes it harder to gain control of the puck and make a play back up the ice. I prefer to have players skate forward to retrieve the puck and get it loaded in a spot where they can pass it quickly.

Common Types of Passes

If a player has lots of time, they are looking to turn pucks to the middle of the ice so that they have more passing options. A player turns the puck up the wall for one of two reasons. First, pressure is on them, and they are working to escape because the pressure has taken away the middle of the ice. The player might be using deceptive skating or trying to shake off an opponent, so they turn it back up the wall. Second, the player may want to pass the puck up the boards quickly and turning it up the wall is faster than going to the middle of the ice. Typically, when a player has the puck in the neutral zone, they will have the same options to move the puck.

Defender-to-Defender Pass

This situation occurs when the partner is slightly behind the player on a hinge, or is staggered, and the player can move the puck to their partner on their forehand. When the defensive partner is a little bit behind the player, the passing angle should be easier. The goal with the defender-to-defender pass is to move the puck away from pressure into available space so that the partner can move it up the ice. Little stickhandling should occur before the player passes the puck. Likewise, the partner should receive the puck and move it again without much stickhandling. Eliminating stickhandling helps to transition the puck and get it back into the offensive zone quicker.

Strongside Winger

The pass to the strongside winger can be referred to as a quick up or up. The intention is to get the puck moving right away toward the offensive zone. This happens when the other team is line changing or lots of space is available on the same side of the ice. The quick up can be a direct pass (tape to tape) or an indirect pass (off the wall) to the strongside winger. The strongside winger often pushes up and stretches the zone out either to deflect a pass into the offensive zone or bump it back underneath to a player skating into the zone. Depending on the pressure that a player feels, they must recognize their options and decide what to do next. If the next play is for them to change, the puck must get deep. In that case, tipping the puck into the zone is probably the best option to avoid turning the puck over at the blue line. If the player receiving the pass is fresh, they can look to make a play or chip it in and forecheck on the dumped puck.

Center

A pass to the center happens often when the other team takes away the strongside winger but leaves a gap in the middle of the ice. Typically, the opposing team's neutral-zone forecheck is spaced out with a bigger gap between their forward and the defensemen. If they are in a 1-2-2 forecheck, the middle of the ice could be available. This space is a good passing option if the center puts themself in the right spot. The centerman (or player in that lane) is looking to time the play with good spacing and a good angle. This pass should be hard and into a spot where the player can continue skating through the space.

Weakside Winger

The option to pass to the weakside winger has become more popular with teams as they work to transition the puck quicker. Rather than going from defenseman to defenseman to winger, teams are trying to transition the puck quickly across the ice directly to the winger. This pass spreads out the defending team to cover width when they are coming out of the zone on the puck side. The defense must readjust their angles and changes their gap based on where the weakside winger is. The center can support this pass and move that way across the ice to be either a net-driving player or a support option for a chip or direct pass from the winger. Teams should talk about this play before a game and work on it in practice. Defensive players who have this option in mind check across the ice as they turn the puck to the middle. Players must be able to snap the puck across the ice for this play to work. If players cannot pass the puck hard enough rink wide, they must work on that skill in practice before the team uses this passing outlet.

Defense Skating

Space may at times be available as the defenseman turns the puck up. They then have an opportunity to move up the ice with the puck and react to the available space. The defenseman's best option is usually to join the rush rather than lead it, but leading the rush may occasionally be the play. The defenseman with the puck can work to skate and attack with speed. If the defenseman gets across the midline of the ice, their partner can fall underneath them for a drop pass or as support as they move through the neutral zone.

NEUTRAL-ZONE TRANSITIONS

A topic that often comes with teams is the question about whether the defensemen should be active in the rush through the neutral zone on transitions. My answer to this is yes. If an opportunity arises for the defensive players to join the rush or support the puck, they should be active. They can join the rush late as a passing option or could potentially be in the rush with the forwards (leading with the puck or supporting as width or net drive) into the offensive zone. As long as the team has clear possession of the puck and someone from the other team is behind them, the defensive players can be active. But if they do not get a puck or think that the puck could be turned over, they should get out of the rush and back into position.

Faceoffs

Faceoffs in the neutral zone are a great way to create possession and start an offensive attack or get the puck in behind the opposing team's defense and start their forecheck. When the puck is won, having a set play on a faceoff helps. The play could be something as simple as making a defender-to-defender pass and hitting the red line to dump the puck in. There could be more to it with wingers switching lanes and looking to hit one of them as they swing away with speed. A question that often comes in discussions about neutral-zone faceoffs is what the defensive players do. My thought on this is that the defensemen have the wingers and need to stay in a spot where they can cover the wingers and stay above them. If their own team's wingers win the draw, they are putting pressure on the opposing team's defense. Whatever option is being run on the draw and depending on where the faceoff is (closer to their own net or closer to the other team's net in the neutral zone), the team should have a couple of plays drawn up to get the puck out of the neutral zone and quickly into the offensive zone.

Managing the Puck

Teams face a difficult challenge in the neutral zone when they turn over the puck and give the other team a transition opportunity. The team is thinking offense and suddenly they are now thinking defense. Players end up in the wrong spots. Lots of space is available, and passing lanes are not covered. The easiest way to guard against this is to manage the puck in the neutral zone. Passes are on the tape, and pucks are put in behind the opposing defense. Pucks are skated with protection into the zone, and players know their routes and passing options. Commentators on television talk regularly about this aspect of the game because it often the determines the outcome. Whoever controls the neutral zone, they say, wins the game. The team with the puck must manage it, and teams without the puck are working to turn it over. Whoever does it better has a better chance of winning.

Regroup Zones

This topic comes up as teams develop more structure. As players get older, layers can be added to their game so that more options are available when regrouping. Various options are available for the regroup depending on the depth of the puck. Players can concentrate their positions around three areas where the puck lands, defined as zones. These options are important as coaches build structure into their team's game in the neutral zone.

Rim Zone

Pucks that land between the offensive blue line and red line fall into the rim zone. In the rim zone, the puck is going back into the offensive zone hard around the boards. The forwards can anticipate that play and start to head to the opposite side of the ice. The defenseman's job is to push the puck hard around the wall so that it gets to the other side where the forwards are heading. One forward can come back below the puck to make sure that there is a re-rim option back down low.

Up Zone

Pucks that land between the red line and defensive blue line fall into the up zone. In the up zone, the idea is to move the puck quickly back up. The pass from the defensive player to the forwards can be either up the wall, into the middle, or across to the weakside winger. The intention is to get the puck moving quickly back up the ice without giving the defending team time to get into a structured forecheck or get a full change in. The offensive team works to get back to the puck quickly and get it moving back up ice again.

Over Zone

Pucks that land below the defensive blue line fall into the over zone. Devin Himpe, a skills coach with the Jets Hockey Development Program, calls this the build-it zone. The over zone is where the defensemen work together and support each other. The goal here is to move the puck from defenseman to defenseman and have a controlled regroup with structure and forwards filling three lanes. This idea of filling lanes gives the defensemen options with the puck. After the puck goes from one defenseman to the other, the player with the puck can go either to the strongside winger, into the middle lane, or across to the weakside winger. The other defenseman is also an option to build speed and put pressure back through the neutral zone. If the puck goes back to the first defenseman, they could gain speed and look to attack.

NEUTRAL-ZONE RETRIEVAL

Level of Difficulty
Moderate

Players
Full team

Objectives

To work on turning pucks up in the neutral zone and putting good passes on the tape for the forwards

Setup

Forwards start at opposite blue lines, and defensive players are in the middle circle on each side. Coaches have pucks at the blue lines opposite the forwards.

Procedure

On the whistle, the defenseman heads back for a puck spotted by the coach. They pass to a forward (F1), who comes down the wall to open up. F1 continues down the ice and shoots (see 1 in diagram). The defenseman comes up, pivots backward to get a second puck, and turns it to the middle. A second forward (F2) comes into the middle of the ice and times the play to receive a pass on the dot line. F2 receives a pass from the defenseman, continues down, and shoots (see 2 in diagram). The defenseman follows the play. The coach now rims a puck into the corner, where F1 handles the rim and passes to the defenseman for a point shot.

Coaching Tips

- The defenseman can be evasive and add some deception into their neutral-zone puck retrievals.
- The defenseman should go back as quickly as possible to get pucks.

Variation

- In the offensive zone, the defenseman can get a pass, slide, and pass back to F1, who supports the puck up the wall and then passes to the defenseman for a shot. If they can one time the puck, they should do so with control because F2 will be around the net looking for a rebound or deflection.

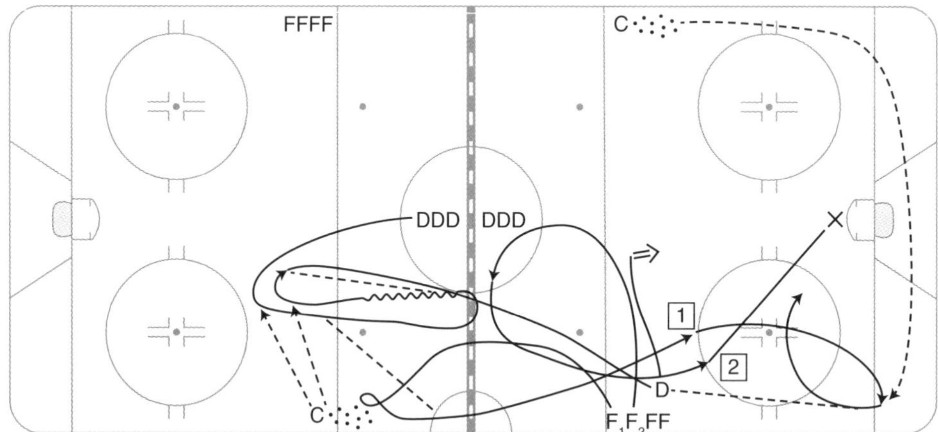

SHALLOW AND DEEP

Level of Difficulty

Easy

Players

Six defensive players

Objectives

To work on moving the puck from defenseman to defenseman in the neutral zone

Setup

A coach has pucks at the red line, and two defensemen start at the bottom of the circle.

Procedure

The coach spots a puck past the defenseman (D1) on one side, and the other defenseman (D2) supports the puck. D2 can be a little bit underneath D1 to hinge, or stagger, for the pass. D1 moves the puck to D2 and hinges underneath the puck. D2 passes back to the coach, who spots the puck on the other side for D2 to grab and pass to D1. D1 passes to the coach, and the coach spots the puck a little deeper on the third and fourth pucks.

Coaching Tips

- D1 hinges every time. The pass from defenseman to defenseman is then easier and comes at better angle.
- Players should work to eliminate unnecessary stickhandles so the that puck moves quicker.

Variations

- Different passing sequences can be added to the retrieval, such as seam passes across the ice or quick up passes up the wall.
- The sequence of defender-to-defender passes can include passes below the goal line so that players must retrieve passes deeper in the zone coming from the neutral zone.

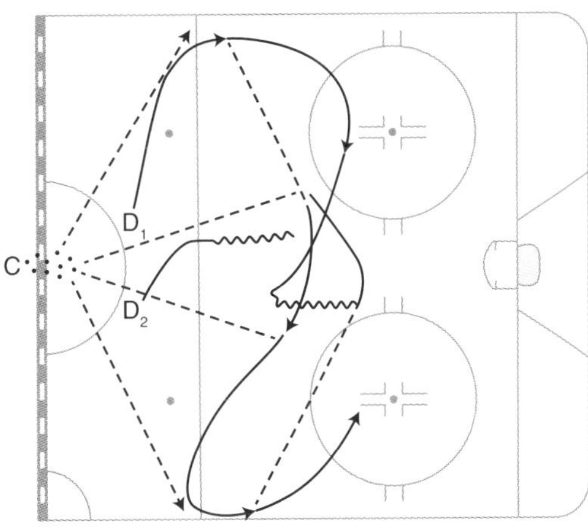

NEUTRAL-ZONE REGROUP × 2

Level of Difficulty

Hard

Players

Full team

Objectives

To work on retrievals and puck movement for defenders in the neutral zone

Setup

Forwards are at each end of both blue lines with pucks, and defensive players are in the middle circle. Pucks are placed in opposite corners. One defenseman starts on each side, and the two forwards they are facing are the players they regroup with.

Procedure

On the whistle, both sides start at the same time with opposite forwards leaving. F1 passes to the defenseman in front of them and opens up on the wall. The defenseman pushes to the middle and passes back to F1. F1 continues down to shoot. The defenseman continues around the circle and starts with F2 from the other side. F2 gives the defenseman a pass and opens up. The defenseman pushes to the middle and passes to F2. As this exchange is happening, F1 gets back on side and supports F2. F2 passes to F1, who enters wide and passes to F2 for a shot. F1 picks up a puck in the corner and passes to the defenseman, who follows up for a shot with traffic. The same thing is happening on the other side of the ice at the same time.

Coaching Tips

- This is a big drill with a lot going on. Players need to be watching and paying attention in line so that they know where they are going and what they are doing.
- Communication and passing are important to enable each rep to work.
- The forward who passes the puck from the corner can get above the screening forward as they are coming to the net to create another layer in rebound coverage.

Variations

- Passes can be added at the start of the drill from the forwards to the defenseman. The forward starts with a pass to the defenseman, who gives it back to the forward, who in turn passes it back to the defenseman as they are opening up. They continue down the ice to shoot or move it to the supporting forward.
- The defenseman can shoot either with the screen in front or for the forward coming from the corner for a high tip. The angle is important because this player must time the play and not get too tight to the net.

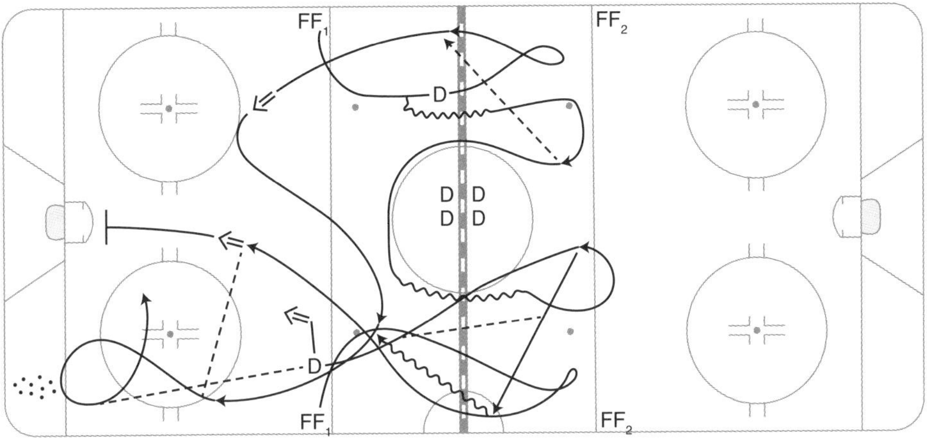

ROCKET REGROUP

Level of Difficulty

Moderate

Players

Full team

Objectives

To work on transitioning the puck quickly from the neutral zone into the offensive zone

Setup

Two forwards (F1 and F2) and two defensemen (D1 and D2) are positioned around one half of the circle, and the same setup is used on the other side of the circle. Pucks are all in the middle with the coaches.

Procedure

The coach spots a puck to the wall on one side (to the opposite wall from the other side of the circle), and the strongside defenseman (D1) goes to get it. The other defenseman (D2) supports D1 and receives a pass. The forwards support the puck, and D2 passes to F2 in the middle of the ice. F2 passes to F1 out wide. F1 enters the zone wide, F2 drives the net, and D1 and D2 follow up. F1 can shoot or pass to the net-driving forward for a deflection. The coach spots a second puck into the corner. F1 grabs it and passes to D2, who can pass to D1 for a shot with traffic.

Coaching Tips

- This big drill has eight players working (four players each way).
- Passes needs to be hard and accurate so that they can be received cleanly.

Variations

- Offensive-zone entries can change where players pass; sometimes they hit the net driver, and other times they hit the width defenseman who is active in the rush.
- The advanced option to this drill is to have the forwards go around twice in the neutral zone with a regroup defender-to-defender pass and then another defender-to-defender pass before entering down the ice and shooting.
- On the second puck in the corner, the forwards can change their option from making a direct pass to cycling the puck and then going low to high, switching sides behind the net, going low to high, and finally supporting the defenseman up the wall.

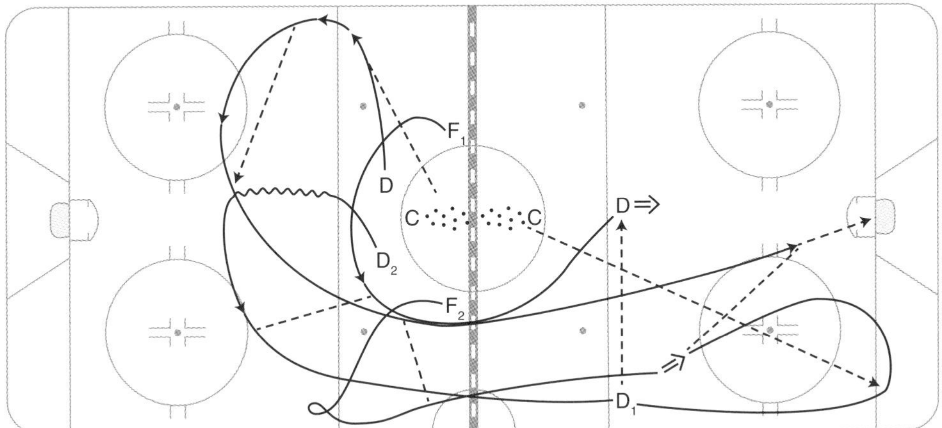

NEUTRAL-ZONE RETRIEVAL FOR DEFLECTION

Level of Difficulty

Moderate

Players

Full team or small group

Objectives

To work on retrievals by defensive players in the neutral zone

Setup

Forwards start in the corner, and defensemen start in a line at the blue line. Pucks are placed at the top of the circle on the side opposite the forwards.

Procedure

A forward starts the drill by passing up the wall to the defenseman. The defenseman slides and shoots the puck as the forward is heading to the net for a deflection. The defenseman then retreats into the neutral zone to grab a puck from the other end and pass to the supporting forward, who makes their way into the neutral zone after the deflection. The defenseman passes to the supporting forward, who enters wide and shoots again. The line passes to the defenseman for a third shot. The drill then starts again. This drill can be done from both sides at the same time.

Coaching Tips

- This drill trains players to shoulder check in the neutral zone.
- The defenseman can turn the puck either up the wall or into the middle of the ice to pass to the forward.

Variations

- The drill can change to have the defenseman join the rush to get a pass from the forward rather than take the second and third shots. The second shot now comes from the defenseman, who is active in the play. The forward must find the defenseman joining the rush.
- A second forward can be added for a layered round attack, a seam pass on the second puck for a shot, and a stack screen or high tip option.
- A second defenseman can go net front (with two forwards) to box out on the first shot, play a 2 vs 1 on the rush for the second puck, and box out on the third shot from the blue line.

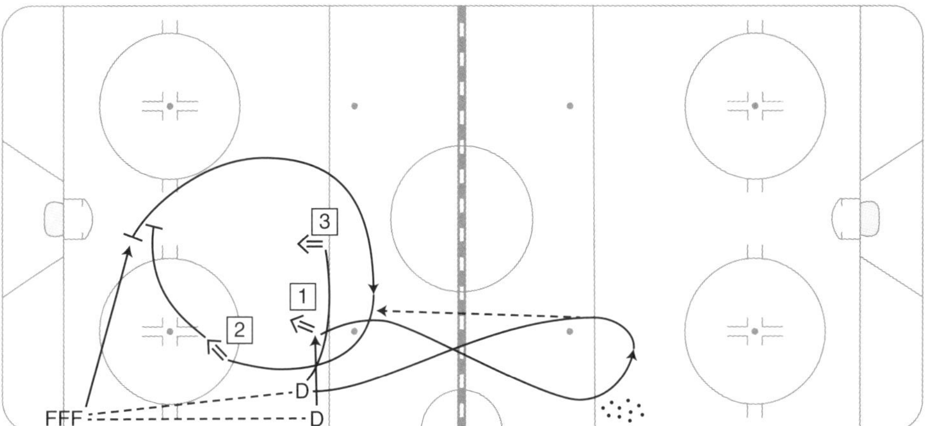

NEUTRAL-ZONE FIGURE EIGHT

Level of Difficulty

Moderate

Players

Full team or small group

Objectives

To work on retrievals by defensemen in the neutral zone

Setup

Forwards start at the top of all four circles against the boards. Defensive players are in the middle circle. Coaches with pucks start between the circles in each zone.

Procedure

When a coach blows the whistle, a defenseman (one from each side) comes back and grabs a puck. Forwards from opposite sides leave together. The defenseman passes up the wall to the forward, who is either swinging or opening up. The defenseman continues skating and comes back for a second puck from the coach, now on the other side. The second group of two forwards leaves from opposite sides (one from each side). The defenseman must be patient and keep their head up so that they do not run into the player from the opposite side coming down to shoot.

Coaching Tips

- This warm-up drill gives defensemen an opportunity to work on passing the puck hard and flat.
- With both sides going at the same time, many players are moving.
- Defensemen must move with their head up and be aware of their surroundings.

Variations

- The defenseman can make an indirect pass up the wall to the forwards.
- The opposite forward can leave with the defenseman so that the pass is a cross-ice pass rather than up the wall. This more advanced option is appropriate for players who can execute a cross-ice seam pass.

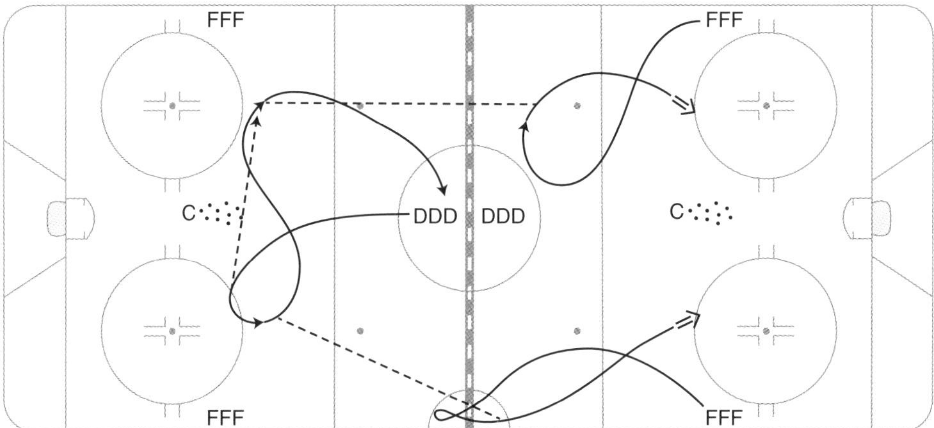

NEUTRAL-ZONE TRACKING

Level of Difficulty

Hard

Players

Full team

Objectives

To work on tracking by forwards and communication between forwards and defensive players

Setup

Two defensemen start at the red line. One forward starts at the top of the circle on the wall, one starts at the top of the circle in line with the dot, and one starts on the far side. The player on the boards starts with the puck. The setup is the same in the other end, and the drill can work with alternate sides going.

Procedure

When the coach blows the whistle, the player on the boards starts to skate at about half speed. The player on the dot line tracks the player down the wall, lifts their stick, and steals the puck to bump it to the defenseman (D1). D1 passes to D2, who moves the puck to the player backchecking on the far boards. The player who was tracking the puck turns and follows the puck to drive the middle of the ice and the net. The player who was tracked comes back and is the next player on the dot line for the next rep. The forwards in the rep of the drill grab a second puck and pass it low to high. The defenseman can either shoot or pass to their partner for a shot.

Coaching Tips

- This drill improves players' tracking and communication.
- The defenseman should be vocal and tell the forwards to keep coming.

Variations

- The defenseman can stay up, and the player on the wall can chip the puck past them. The tracking forward then picks up the puck and passes it to the defenseman, who moves it out the other side. The forward continues to support the puck.
- The second puck can be played with various options as directed by the coach. A cycle can be used in the corner and then low to high. Forwards can switch sides below the goal line and pass it low to high. They can roll up the boards with the defenseman activating down the wall. The defenseman can dive into the middle of the ice as the forward rolls up and more. The players can be creative on the second puck.

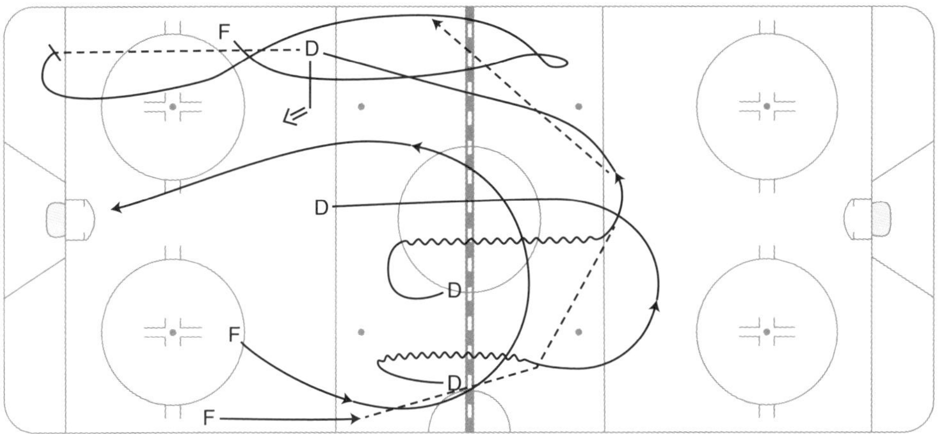

CHAPTER 12

Applying Concepts to Practice

When working with defensive players in practice, one of the first things to think about is developing individual skills and then working those individual skills into team ideas. If players have trouble with skating and coaches are asking them to do more difficult things, the success rate will be very low. Coaches need to be patient because development takes time. They should give players an opportunity to work on specific things before expecting them to play skillfully. Their game instincts will come as they improve their individual skills. If players struggle with the puck, they should work with a puck in practice. They should work on their hands and their passing. They should receive passes from a coach to get more reps at pass reception. Players improve when they understand what they are working on and can see how it relates to them and their play.

Every drill in practice should include something that players can work on to get better. Players should be thinking about how they can improve in each drill and in each practice over the course of the season. When players start to think that way, they can really start to develop. The problem is that many players miss this concept and just go through the motions when doing the drills. They take their turn in the drill and maybe miss a pass or miss the net on a shot without thinking much about it. They then wonder why they are not getting better.

A big part of a practice plan is a focus on something specific for player development. When coaches do not have a clear path, they waste an opportunity to improve their team. Players should come to practice with an open mind and be willing to take suggestions to improve. A practice that allows players to build on specific topics or run various options in drills helps them see how the topics relate to games. Coaches can build and develop practice plans to advance player development.

In practice, if the coach can get players to think about and focus on the details of what they are working on, they will progress. I had a team on the ice the other day, and one of the things I told them was, "I want you to play with pace, but I want the pace to come from puck movement, not from you skating faster." The drills we were doing included a ton of passing, but they were not done at full speed. All that I asked the players to do was to think about the timing and setting up good passing angles so that they could receive the passes as they came to them. This idea was different for the team because they were used to going as fast as they could. The problem with that was they missed a lot of passes and skated through lanes all the time. Ideally, this concept will improve their passing and teach them to adjust their skating speed to be in better spots. Players will be more effective in practice when they understand why they are doing drills in a specific way. Coaches should tell players why they are doing a drill, let them ask questions, answer their questions, and clarify any uncertainty.

BEGIN WITH BASICS

When I run a 10- to 11-week spring development program for defensemen, we do not do any shooting for the first 3 or 4 weeks. We want players to work on the skills that enable them to get the puck out of their own zone first. If players cannot get the puck up the ice and into the offensive zone, they will not get to shoot in games. Therefore, we start with the basics of skating, puckhandling, and passing. We work on how to retrieve the puck in the corner in the defensive zone, what their options are to move the puck by themselves and with their partner, where they should be to support their teammate, and more. The goal of this work is to help players realize the importance of their job on the ice and the value of getting the puck up the ice with control.

CHALLENGE EACH POSITION

In their practice planning, coaches should think about drills that will challenge each player to work on something. This can be skating, puck control, passing, or shooting, but with each drill, players need to be told what they are working on. This key part of practice helps players understand how the practice is advancing their development.

SET UP A PRACTICE PLAN

Most hockey coaches have a similar setup for practice:

- Some kind of warm-up skate
- Some kind of warm-up with shooting

- Some kind of drill to get more players involved
- Core part of practice focused on what players need to work on
- Second drill with key components (maybe with more players or game simulated)
- Challenge at the end of practice (small-area game, game, skate)

With this, if the coach can dedicate time to focus on specific things, they will see players progress through the season. Most teams, unless junior or professional, do not have additional time for skill work at the beginning or end of practice. Most teams get 50 to 90 minutes of practice time, and their practices focus on topics to work on. At the junior or pro level, players get additional time before and after practice because their team books ice time that is longer than the practice slot. For most minor hockey teams, the 60-minute slot is their 60-minute practice. Each day consists of a new opportunity for the players to work on different areas. My thought on this is to focus each day on a different topic with a different set of drills.

Order of Progression

On the development side, players need to work on things in an appropriate progression. When I teach something, I always start stationary. The time devoted to stationary work depends on the player and their level, but I always introduce new topics to players in a simple way. I work in this progression:

- *Start stationary.* This stage introduces the topic to the players.
- *Add motion.* This stage allows players to work on the skill while moving.
- *Add speed.* This stage gets players closer to game pace and challenges them to react properly.
- *Add game-simulated drills.* This stage adds decision making to the players' reps and gets them to understand how things will look in games.
- *Add pressure.* This stage is as close to game pace as possible using pressure and game scenarios.

This plan allows players to work on specific things and work in a progression to get them up to game speed. By showing them what they are working on and allowing them to focus on that topic, players can retain the information. If the expectation is that players will "just get it," coaches are missing out on a teachable movement. Players who are thrown into the game at a young age are missing out on development opportunities. Coaches should start players slowly with new skills (no matter their level) and have them work through hand position, puck movement, body position, eye position, puck position, and more. All are important for this type of progression. Players may develop faster in certain areas than others, depending on their age and level. The coach has the job of seeing how players are doing and moving them on to the next stage when they are ready.

Assess Skills

Coaches will be able to see where their team is strong and where they are weak. They need to determine how much time goes toward each area of strength and weakness. If players can show the coach that they understand a topic and it comes out in games at the right time, everyone is doing their job. If players need more help in specific areas, practice is the place to start. Sometimes players will not understand a topic in practice, so they will need to come back to it. Certain topics will take longer to sink in. The coach should plan to revisit the topic in the near future. Players should have another opportunity to work on it, possibly in a different way. Saying it one way or doing it one way may not produce the desired result, but coming back at it from a different angle could be a solution. One of the best parts of coaching is having the opportunity to figure that out.

TRY NEW THINGS

Some teams tend to use the same drills over and over, and players just go through the motions. Coaches may have a favorite drill to work on something specific, and that is fine. But they might gain something by changing the drill slightly to get players to work on doing something a little differently, such as making an extra pass the second time they do the drill. Coaches could drop the drill for a couple of practices and then come back to it. I like to return to drills that we do early in the season to see whether progress has occurred. If a coach runs the same practice with the same drills repeatedly, players will certainly get better at that drill, but they may not get better at applying that drill to games.

Seeing a young team have fun in practice can give the coach a great feeling. A lot of that feeling is based on how the coach plans practice. They can work to find ways to have more players involved in drills, challenge players to be passers so that they understand the importance of puck movement, and challenge other

Change It Up

I had a coach who had their team book in for 10 sessions a couple of years ago. His request to me was to run the same practice 10 times so that the team got better at that one practice. I answered, "Unfortunately, I can't do that." I told him, "What I can do is run similar topics in practice with drills progressing as we work through the day. I will challenge players to think and apply the topics I put forward in drills to figure out how they relate to each player and how they can help them in games." The team worked hard through the 10 sessions and really got a lot out of the skates. I hope that I changed the coach's mind about running the same practice all the time.

players to be shooters so that they work to get more shots on goal. The key to this is switching the players around so that they get to do both. The drills should challenge players to work on specific things that are age appropriate and match their skill level. With young players, working only on slapshots does not make sense. Coaches can teach them wrist shots and shooting off a pass to work on a quicker release and then later introduce slapshots. Players eyes will light up when the coach says for the first time that they are working on slapshots.

Make It Fun

A key part of the business of skill development is making it fun. Coaches should create an environment in practice that allows players to enjoy practice in a way that helps them continue to develop. I was reminded about this with my daughter, who plays volleyball and works with different coaches on different nights. I saw the joy in her on one night but not the next. The crazy thing was that her coaches ran almost the same practice, but they delivered it completely differently. Both worked on the same skills in practice—footwork, passing, setting, and hitting. One coach, however, had simple drills that allowed the players to see success. The team played games to work on positioning and passing. The other coach used more challenging drills that created confusion, had a strict attitude and applied punishment, and scheduled little game time. My daughter's experience really opened my eyes about the importance of how material is delivered to how a player might feel on the car ride home. When players leave the ice surface after practice, they should be smiling and wanting to come back for more.

Continually Provide Opportunities to Develop

Defensemen need to be able to see the benefits of practice, and coaches need to provide the development opportunities. If a coach is stressing good gap control in games, players need opportunities to work on gap control in practice. If a coach is talking about getting shots through from the top in games, they need to offer opportunities in practice for their players to shoot with their head up.

FIT PRACTICES AROUND THE TEAM'S NEEDS

The job of developing defensemen in practice can be done a several ways. Coaches can do full-ice drills that allow players to work on specific topics such as gap control, angling, passing, spacing, 1 vs 1, 2 vs 1, 2 vs 2, and more. They can do half-ice drills that address passing, breakouts, and regroups. They can split and work with just the defense on specific topics like puck retrievals, passing, shooting, net-front battles, corner work, and 1 vs 1. Whatever the practice is for the group, coaches need to have a plan in mind for what they want to see coming out of the day.

Players Need to Challenge Themselves, Too

I often get calls from older players who want to work on skating. They tell me, "I never really worked on it before." Coaches need to provide opportunities to develop every skill, but players need to do the work. As mentioned earlier, players should remember the basics. They should work on their skating first and as often as they can. Training can be done off the ice and in the gym with hip, core, balance, and leg work. Players can work on their flexibility to help prevent injuries and extend their range of motion. With strong skating mechanics, everything else becomes a little easier. As their puck skills get better, they can work to do things faster with their eyes up. Spatial awareness is a key part of decision making, so players should focus on scanning with their eyes as often as possible. They should work on their shot, every shot—wrist shots, snap shots, slapshots, one timers, quick releases, and backhands. They never know what type of shot they will need, so they must work on them all. Good shooting mechanics allow different options in the offensive zone to happen more frequently. Players need to understand options in the neutral zone and work on them in practice. A hard pass to a good spot gives the receiver a chance to do something with the puck.

After players have developed a strong skill set, they can start to work on using it in games. Plays in the defensive zone are part of a team's structure, so players should listen when the coach is explaining and asking questions to assess their understanding.

Full-Arena Practice

If the coach is using a full-ice practice to work with their players, they should make sure that some drills are focused on developing strategies for defensemen. A 2 vs 1 drill for the forwards should include teaching the defensemen to recognize who is coming at them—whether the attacking player is right-handed or left-handed, what the player off the puck is doing, whether the puck carrier is looking to pass or looking to shoot. The defensemen should be taught to stay between the attackers, to make the puck carrier pick their second option, and more.

If the coach is doing a retrieval drill that ends up with a shot in the other end, they can give the defensemen specific things to focus on in both the retrieval and shooting portions of the drill. Are they shooting from the wall or sliding and shooting? Are they taking a slapshot or a wrist shot? Is the shot in the air or on the ice for the deflection? These questions should all be answered in the explanation of the drill at the board. By giving players specific things to think about in bigger drills, the coach can dramatically change the execution of the drill in practice.

Half-Ice Practice

If the practice consists of half ice only, the coach must be creative in using the space to allow players to work on specific areas of their game. Stations can be set up to work on puck control, skating, and passing with players spending five to eight minutes at each station. Players can work on the specific topics, and then the coach can tie those topics back to the game. After the stations, a bigger drill can puts the topics into a game simulation. The coach should challenge the players to think about what they are doing and why they are doing it. With a half-ice practice, coaches must be creative in working on areas to help their team play at a higher level.

Practice Specific Positions and Players

If the players are split up by position, coaches should know how much time is available to work with the defensemen and then put together a couple of key concepts for practice. These topics could be footwork, puck control, passing, retrievals, supporting partners, or shooting. Whatever the topic is for that day, players should have dedicated time to work on the associated skills. If goalies are not needed, they can work with the forwards or with a goalie coach if one is available. My suggestion is to use drills that focus on specific topics at the start of the season. As the season goes on, other elements can be added to the drills as players improve. Topics to think about in practice for defensemen splits include the following:

- Skating (forward, backward, edge development, transition skating)
- Puck control
- Receiving passes
- Passing (defenseman to defenseman, defenseman to wing, defenseman to center)
- Receiving bad passes (in the feet, in unexpected areas)
- Retrievals by themselves
- Retrievals with a partner
- Inside defenseman retrievals (strongside defenseman is up, weakside defenseman gets pucks)
- 1 vs 1 corner work
- 1 vs 1 net-front work
- Boxing out
- Shooting from the wall
- Shooting from the middle
- Shooting off defenseman-to-defenseman passes

- Attacking the pass for shots
- Activating down the wall
- Jumping down the dot-line seam
- Backdoor shooting
- One timers
- Shooting off indirect passes
- Stick position
- Eye-hand coordination
- Shoulder checks
- 2 vs 1 awareness
- 2 vs 1 slides (for more advanced players)

My advice to coaches when they are planning a split is to give players the information they need so that they can see success happen in games. Players might not get it right away. They may need to work through the drills a couple of times, but if coaches give them the information and then let them try things, they will work closer to success.

KEEP GIVING FEEDBACK

With any style of practice (full ice, half ice, splits), coaches must give players information to think about in the drills. The players then need to use the information they receive. The players will probably not get everything on the first time working through a drill, so coaches will likely have to make corrections. One thing that frustrates team parents is watching their players continually execute a drill incorrectly without receiving input from the coach about how they can do it better. The coach who continually makes suggestions to the players and gives them things to think about as they do the drills will receive nothing but positives from the parents. Coach feedback and coach involvement in practice is the starting point for any team to have a successful season.

COMMON ERROR

I watch a lot of practices and often see teams split up their forwards and defensemen. Most teams go right into having their defensemen shoot from the blue line. Players have trouble with passing, with puck control, and with skating, but they are working on shooting because that is fun for the group. Players need to develop in a lot of areas, so they need to work on everything, including shooting.

SUCCESS DOESN'T ALWAYS MEAN WINNING

When evaluating whether a season was successful, the only teams that should be judged by winning are those at the professional (or very high) level. For younger players, a successful season means that they have improved. They have developed their game and are performing at a higher level. They are skating with more balance and are more aware of what is happening around them in games. They can recognize pressure and support and make decisions that allow their team to move the puck up the ice. When players see success in their hockey season, they will want to come back the following year. Players will not win every game, so they must learn to challenge themselves in practice to be as good as they can be. A player's attitude toward practice often dictates how much success they will see over the course of time.

One of my key philosophies in coaching is building good people as well as good players. This means teaching players to be respectful and hard working. I try to bring older players back into the program to coach and give back to the younger players. As a coach of a young team, I want to build good sportsmanship in my players. A team that treats each other right and works together will have an influence on the players long beyond their hockey days. When I coached a U18 team, I told them, "I do not expect you to be best friends, but I do expect you to respect each other." This meant that the group was to treat each other in a courteous way and learn to work together. Years later, I ran into a player who told me that he remembered that message and used it with the team that he was now coaching. That meant a lot to me.

CHALLENGE EACH PLAYER

When I worked with Hockey Canada, we had exit meetings with players after camp. We had some great players at camp, and many went on to be high NHL draft picks. When I met with one player and asked him how camp went, he told me it went great. My response surprised him. I told him for the first four days of camp (which were practices), I did not notice him. For the last three days of camp (which were games), he was the best player on the ice. I told him that if he wanted to be a high-level NHL player, he had to learn to work in practice because at the rate he was going, just playing in games would not be good enough. His reaction was interesting. He told me that I was the first person to tell him that he was not good enough. Everyone else told him all the time how good he was. He got used to being good, so he stopped working every day. But my vision for him was to be not just good but to be incredible. We will see how that plays out as he prepares to step into the NHL, and I am hoping that he has learned to practice with more effort and make practice a focus.

With practice now, I get to see a lot of players and work with a lot of teams. The common problem that I see is that players fail to see how drill work during practice relates to executing those skills in a game. If coaches can connect that piece for players, they will get more out of practice. When coaches and players work on areas that need to be improved, they will see better performance in games.

Every player, regardless of age and ability, should have the opportunity to develop. Through the drills that they use in practice, coaches give players that chance. They pick drills that they think their players can do at the start of the year and gradually build up the level of difficulty based on what the players need. Many coaches watch high-level teams and think that their team should be able to execute the same drills the same way. It will not happen that way because players need time to develop. Coaches need to challenge both themselves and their players to continue to develop.

As a final thought for this book, I encourage young defensemen to watch the game with a focus on the defensive players. They should concentrate on what the defensemen are doing and how they play. They can study their puck movement and their decision making. As players get older, they will notice differences in how defensemen play the game. Some are more offensive, and others are more defensive. Some are physical, and others are positionally sound without hitting opponents. From there, players can develop their own specific game. One of my favorite things about coaching is that each player is different and brings a different challenge. My job, and the job of every coach, is to figure out how to get through to them and challenge them to be their best!

ABOUT THE AUTHOR

DAVE CAMERON is the head coach and program director of Jets Hockey Development, a skating and skills coach for the Winnipeg Jets and Manitoba Moose, a development coach for Team Canada U17, and a Hockey Canada skills consultant. He has more than 20 years of experience coaching players of all levels: professional athletes (NHL, AHL, and ECHL), college athletes, and young athletes just learning to play the game. He has helped many players achieve their goals, including being selected in the WHL Bantam Draft, making the jump to the NCAA, being selected in the NHL Entry Draft, and winning the Stanley Cup. Cameron specializes in individual skill development such as power skating, shooting, stickhandling, passing, and position-specific skills. He believes that confidence is built from practice and players can continue to get better through detailed work in specific areas.

Cameron played minor hockey in the Winnipeg area before moving on to the WHL, where he was drafted by the Pittsburgh Penguins in 1998 (third round, 80th overall). He returned to Winnipeg to attend the University of Manitoba, where he obtained a degree in kinesiology before starting his coaching career.